Good Morning

Beautiful

People

Good Morning Beautiful People

Angel's Prayer of the Day

ANGEL L. MURCHISON

Trilogy Christian Publishers A Wholly Owned Subsidiary of Trinity Broadcasting Network 2442 Michelle Drive Tustin, CA 92780

Trilogy Christian Publishing/ TBN and colophon are trademarks of Trinity Broadcasting Network.

For information about special discounts for bulk purchases, please contact Trilogy Christian Publishing.

10 9 8 7 6 5 4 3 2 1

Library of Congress Cataloging-in-Publication Data is available.

ISBN: 978-1-64088- 3116

E-ISBN: 978-1-64088-315-8

To my family and the body of Christ.

To my brothers and sisters, you are amazing people. Although we had very little in material things, your kindness and unselfish ways was an example to me. I saw how you gave to everyone and helped as many as you could, denying yourselves. You all tried in your way to make life better for others. I love you all.

Although we never had expensive clothes to wear nor elegant meals to prepare, we were thankful for what we had. It was enough. Thank you for giving to me. As a child, you cared for me. As a teenager, I shook your world through many years of rebellion. As an adult, I am honored to be your sister and friend.

To my deceased sisters, Ethel (Hooky) and Jennye, your lives have taught me much. Through much pain and adversity, you pressed on each day until you entered into the loving arms of your Heavenly Father. You taught me more about life than I could ever read in a book about perseverance with your many challenges and handicaps. You have made it home now to your eternal home.

To every Sunday school teacher, pastor, prophetic voice, and every person that prayed for me or spoke into my life, thank you. It is so true, so very true. Jesus is the way, the truth, and the life. He has a plan for every life, and I am thankful to journey with him each and every day. Your reward awaits you.

To my deceased parents thank you for life. Although mom you died when I was eight years of age, the spiritual inheritance you imparted to me was great. I look forward to meeting you both again in our heavenly home.

Introduction

Good morning, God's beautiful people, good morning. It is my desire that you will journey with me every morning for the next 365 days. May the Holy Spirit guide you and may the scriptures come alive to you in a fresh new way. The Holy Bible tells us that God's word is life to our very being, it is health to even the driest bones. In order to discover the richness of journeying life every day with God, we must first know him through his Son, Jesus.

Once we know Jesus, we will desire the fullness of the Godhead. His Holy Spirit will lead us each and every day if we allow him. Journeying life with Jesus and learning to hear his voice is vital as we walk with him day by day. He speaks in so many different ways.

My prayer is that this book will be one that would cause you to hunger to know Jesus in a deeper way. May the Holy Scriptures come alive each day in a new way and change us all to be more like him.

I write from my heart, and I share my life experiences with you as I journey my days with Jesus. One thing for sure, life is exciting, even on our worst days. He has promised never to leave us nor forsake us, and he has proven that to be true to me in so many ways. I can promise you, Jesus will do the very same for you. He is no respecter of persons.

If you are hurting or broken, my prayer is that you discover Jesus as your healer. If you need a miracle, he is the miracle-making Jesus. Open your heart, listen for his voice, and have eyes to see him working every day on your behalf as we pray together.

It is also my desire that you will discover the love of the Father on this journey like you have never known his love before. It is just downright amazing. I promise through this journey you will experience him for yourself in new ways as you draw near to him. That's what he promised us—he would draw near to us.

As we pray and dwell in his presence every day, we will discover more of his heart, and he will fill the longings of our hearts. Oh, the love of our Father.

Enjoy the journey and let's believe God together!

The Father's Love

Oh, Father, your love for me is so hard to comprehend. You died for me when I was yet a sinner.

Love, you had no boundaries, you took my sin, and you made me whole again. Such love, the love of my Father.

When I chose the path of the evil one, you loved me and led me to your path again. Such love, the love of my Father.

When I cried because of all the pain, you healed my pain and removed my shame. Oh, such love, the love of my Father.

Where others wounded me, you bound up my wounds and filled me with joy. Such love, the love of my Father.

When I needed guidance, you left me your Word and your Holy Spirit. Such love, the love of my Father.

Whatever the future holds for me is in your hands, for your love has made me whole.

My Father you say in your Word that the footsteps of the righteous are ordered of the Lord. That's my future because of the love of my Father.

The love of my Father was the very first writing I penned. As I sat behind my desk at the Aroostook County Action Program in Caribou, Maine, during my lunch hour, I began the journey of asking God himself to teach me by the power of his Holy Spirit about his love. With my Bible on my desk and a bowed head before him, I picked up my pen and wrote, My Father's Love. I had no idea the journey ahead from the prayer I prayed that noon would forever change my life. My prayer is that it will change yours as well. There is nothing like experiencing the Father's love for yourself. No man can give you this, and no man can take it away. You just need to pray, believe, and receive the love of your Heavenly Father. He is waiting.

The Best Is Yet to Come, Believe!

Good morning, beautiful people, good morning. It's here, the New Year has arrived, and here in Maine, the winds are blowing, and the fresh snow has been fallen for hours. I love to look at the trees with the beautiful snow. The freshness of the white powdery snow reminds me how precious the blood of Jesus is and how it makes our lives clean.

Today, many people will make resolutions, and I will as well. However, I sense the time has come beautiful people to join the revolution. Ephesians 3:20–21 tells us, "Now to him who is able to do immeasurably more than all we ask or imagine, according to his power that is at work within us, to him be glory in the church and in Christ Jesus throughout all generations, for ever and ever!" Give a shout, beautiful people, the best is yet to come. Shout again, I am joining the Jesus revolution. One last shout, I believe the Word of the Lord. Let's pray.

Father, thank you for a new year, another new beginning. There is so much more to what we know and see. We want to experience every promise you have made to us. Numbers 23:19 tells us that "God is not a man, so he does not lie. He is not human, so he does not change his mind. Has he ever spoken and failed to act? Has he ever promised and not carried it through?" Father, we recognize you are the omnipotent (all-powerful), omniscient (all-knowing), and omnipresent (everywhere present) God. We recognize we can journey with you where the supernatural happens every day. You are our God, and we are your people.

Father, thank you that this is our best year yet. We release all of the previous year and step into the New Year with a shout, "I am part of a revolution. Amen!"

Have a blessed day, God's beautiful people. Enjoy every day this year, for your God reigns. He always has, he always will, and he will forever be. Rise up and believe.

Dive In and Chart the Course

Good morning, beautiful people, good morning. As I journal goals for this year, I sense the time has come to jump in with everything I have. I believe it is the same for you. We operate in one of two realms, fear or faith. As we walk by his spirit, trusting our master knows what's best and taking steps of faith, then we will fulfill our destiny. Let's dive right in at the beginning of this year. Remove all limitations, face every fear, and together discover what faith in our God will do. Let's pray.

Father, thank you that when we have faith in you, nothing is impossible. You take our lives, grant us favor and strength as we step out into the deep. Your Word tells us "Without faith it is impossible to please God, because anyone who comes to him must believe that he exists and that he rewards those who earnestly seek him" (Hebrews 11:6).

Father, strip away every fear that holds us back. May we come to realize that every experience in life, whether success or failure, is for your glory. May your glory shine in us every day as we journey deep into the unknown, knowing your love is never ending. "Deep calleth unto deep" (Psalm 42:7).

Father, steer our ship and chart our course today and every day throughout this year in the kingdom direction. May our faith and your grace be sufficient for the journey we are on. Amen.

Have a blessed day, God's beautiful people. Dive in and chart the course. He's got you! This is your year! Believe.

Did God Say Double Portion?

Good morning, beautiful people, good morning. Trust, trust, trust God for your double portion. He said it, not me.

Instead of your shame you will receive a double portion, and instead of disgrace you will rejoice in your inheritance. And so you will inherit a double portion in your land, and everlasting joy will be yours. For I, the Lord, love justice; I hate robbery and wrongdoing. In my faithfulness I will reward my people and make an everlasting covenant with them. Their descendants will be known among the nations and their offspring among the peoples. All who see them will acknowledge that they are a people the Lord has blessed. (Isaiah 61:7–9)

Father, thank you that You, O God, are a God of that gives back double. Thank you that You love justice. Today we continue to put our trust in You no matter what it looks like, no matter how wronged we have been. You tell us, oh God, that you are our vindicator (Psalm 26:1).

You are the God of payback according to Hebrews 10:30–31. We thank you for payback in our nation. We thank you for payback in every area of our individual lives. Thank you for being a God of justice. We continue to put our trust in You. Amen.

Have a blessed day, beautiful people. The battle belongs to the Lord. Trust Him. He returns double. He doesn't lie.

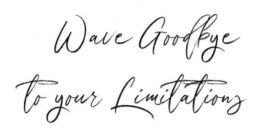

Wave Goodbye to your Limitations

Good morning, beautiful people, good morning. Are you wondering what your future looks like? Dream big, have faith, and wave goodbye to yesterday. You are on your way to destiny. In Matthew 17:20 to be exact, Jesus tells us to have faith. For truly, I say to you, if you have faith like a grain of mustard seed, you will say to this mountain, "Move from here to there," and it will move, and nothing will be impossible for you. Let's pray.

Father, thank you for being the God of impossibilities. Limitless Jesus, lead us this day. You have the keys, the divine appointments, the divine connections. You are the all sufficient one. We will not grow weary in doing well, for in due season, we will reap a harvest (if we faint not).

Today we take the limits off ourselves and you, O God. We believe Luke 1:37 that tells us with you, O God, nothing shall be impossible.

We pull down every hindrance, everything and anything that would hold us back. You are our God, and we are your people. In you, there are no limits and no boundaries. We walk with the highest authority on the earth, the authority of Jesus Christ. Even the wind must obey.

Together, all across this globe today, we declare our visions; our destinies are coming to pass. This is our season. This is our time with no limitations.

Limitless Jesus, the world shows us every day what they can do. Today, O God, show the world what you can do through us your people. Amen.

Have a blessed day, God's beautiful people. Never forget Jesus Words in Luke 18:27, "What is impossible with man is possible with God."

Let It Go and Be Amazed

Good morning, beautiful people, good morning. As we begin a new year, let's wipe the slate clean. Let's be real. We all have been done wrong. Maybe it was a coworker, a relative, or maybe it's the neighbor that made life so hard for you that you thought you would never recover. Well, guess what? If we forgive everyone that has hurt us or done us wrong, God himself will pay us back. Who would you rather pay you back? God or that person? Maybe that person doesn't even realize the extent you have been wounded. Well, let's start the new year with a clean slate for everything and everybody.

In 1 Samuel 30:18–19, we learn that David recovered all. We will recover all as well if we follow God's plan. What's the plan? Forgiveness.

In order to receive forgiveness for ourselves, we first need to forgive others. "For if you forgive other people when they sin against you, your Heavenly Father will also forgive you. But if you do not forgive others their sins, your Father will not forgive your sins" (Matthew 16:14–15). Let's pray.

Father, thank you that you give us the grace to forgive. Thank you that you are the God that restores all that was stolen. You made a public spectacle of our enemies; they were defeated at the cross (Colossians 2:15). As we offer up forgiveness to all that have hurt us or done us wrong, the blood of Jesus will wipe our slate clean.

Father, we look forward to journeying the year with a clean slate. Amen.

Have a blessed day, God's beautiful people. Declare today! All has been forgiven.

Children around the Globe

Good morning, beautiful people, good morning. Today let's pray for all the children around this globe.

He called a little child and had him stand among them. And he said: "I tell you the truth, unless you change and become like little children, you will never enter the kingdom of heaven. Therefore, whoever humbles himself like this child is the greatest in the kingdom of heaven "And whoever welcomes a little child like this in my name welcomes me. But if anyone causes one of these little ones who believe in me to sin, it would be better for him to have a large millstone hung around his neck and to be drowned in the depths of the sea. (Matthew 18:2–6)

Jesus said, Let the little children come to me, and do not hinder them, for the kingdom of heaven belongs to such as these. (Matthew 19:14)

And they brought young children to him, that he should touch them: and his disciples rebuked those that brought them. But when Jesus saw it, he was much displeased, and said unto them, Suffer the little children to come unto me, and forbid them not: for of such is the kingdom of God. Verily I say unto you, whosoever shall not receive the kingdom of God as a little child, he shall not enter therein. and he took them up in his arms, put his hands upon them, and blessed them. (Mark 10:13–16)

Father, thank you for children. Today we join our faith all across this globe and pray for safety, protection, and love to abound for children.

Today, God, we petition your throne room on behalf of children. Expose what needs to be exposed and bring truth to light we pray. May children know that they are loved first by their Creator. We pray parents today would teach their children about you Jesus. You said in your Word that if we train up a child in the way he should go, and when he is old, he will not depart from it (Proverbs 22:6). That is your promise to us, and we receive it. I thank you that you watch over your Word to perform it (Jeremiah 1:12).

Thank you that we are not called to perfection as there is no perfect parent. I thank you that you make every crooked way straight on our behalf.

Today we bring every child before you and ask you to bless them. Amen.

Have a beautiful day today. Bless a child today. You are his representative.

Dear God, Please Help Us Watch Our Words

Good morning, beautiful people. Proverbs 18:21 tells us that "death and life are in the power of the tongue, and they that love it shall eat the fruit thereof."

Today let's try to examine the words that we speak. Every word that comes out of our mouths, let's examine its fruit. If it doesn't build up, or it doesn't edify ourselves or others then let's not say those words. Sometimes, even in our joking, words stay with the individual as truth. Ephesians 4:29 tells us do not let any unwholesome talk come out of your mouths but only what is helpful for building others up according to their needs that it may benefit those who listen. Now that's good advice. Let's pray.

Father, thank you for the power of your Holy Spirit to show us when we are speaking words that are not edifying. Father, your word tells us in Proverbs 25:11 that a word fitly spoken is like apples of gold in pictures of silver.

Highlight our words today, O God, may we be sensitive to every word that comes out of our mouths. Father, since we will eat the fruit of what we say, empower us to speak blessings over our own lives. Thank you for the folks you entrust us with to speak blessings over their lives as well.

Oh, the power of your Word. Shape our lives according to your Word, we pray. We declare we are blessed according to your Word, O God. Amen.

Have a blessed day, beautiful people. Watch your words. Speak God's Word.

Declare your Anthem Today

Good morning, beautiful people. Today, let's pray together Colossians 3:1–17.

Since then, you have been raised with Christ, set your hearts on things above, where Christ is seated at the right hand of God. Set your minds on things above, not on earthly things. For you died, and your life is now hidden with Christ in God. When Christ, who is your life appears, then you also will appear with him in glory. Put to death, therefore, whatever belongs to your earthly nature: sexual immorality, impurity, lust, evil desires, and greed, which is idolatry. Because of these, the wrath of God is coming. You used to walk in these ways in the life you once lived. But now you must also rid yourselves of all such things as these: anger, rage, malice, slander, and filthy language from your lips. Do not lie to each other since you have taken off your old self with its practices and have put on the new self, which is being renewed in knowledge in the image of its Creator. Here there is no Gentile or Jew, circumcised or uncircumcised, barbarian, Scythian, slave or free, but Christ is all, and is in all. Therefore, as God's chosen people, holy and dearly loved, clothe yourselves with compassion, kindness, humility, gentleness, and patience. Bear with each other and forgive one another if any of you has a grievance against someone. Forgive as the Lord forgave you. And over all these virtues put on love, which binds them all together in perfect unity. Let the peace of Christ rule in your hearts, since as members of one body you were called to peace. And be thankful. Let the message of Christ dwell among you richly as you teach and admonish one another with all wisdom through psalms, hymns, and songs from the Spirit, singing to God with gratitude in your hearts. And whatever you do, whether in word or deed, do it all in the name of the Lord Jesus, giving thanks to God the Father through him.

Father, thank you for your word. Today, all across this globe, we declare this is our anthem. Every day is a new beginning, and we declare we will walk in the ways of our Lord. Yesterday, where we failed, we ask for forgiveness. Strengthen us to be the very best witnesses for you in a land that is desperate to know you, O God.

Your Word states in Psalm 133:1, "Wherever there is unity, you command a blessing."

Today we declare unity according to the written Word of God all across this globe. In families, marriages, work places, cities, and government hear and obey the word of the Lord and receive his blessing. Amen. Have a blessed day, beautiful people. Declare your anthem.

Decisions, Decisions, Decisions

Good morning, beautiful people. I went to see the movie God's Not Dead some time ago now. It's a great movie, and I was blessed. I received a couple of texts from friends who went to see the movie as well, that read God is not dead. I couldn't help but respond with a text, "He is alive and well, and his spirit lives within me. Jesus died, but he arose again."

I am always amazed when people say they don't believe in God. It makes my heart sink really, for I know they believe a lie. Life is a journey, it isn't always easy, doesn't always go in ways we think or plan, but I am thankful today that the creator of the universe knows every detail of our lives. His love for us is so hard to comprehend that he would lay down his life for us, but it's true—it really is.

I remember having a pastor that told us after he preached his well-prepared anointed sermon, "Don't take my word for this. Go home and look this up in your Bible for yourselves." That was excellent advice, and I did just that. I took my journal along with my Bible, and I began the most incredible journey I have ever been on. The Lord revealed himself in the mountaintop experiences, as well as in the deep valleys. In every place, Jesus met with me, and I can declare before the world today, Jesus is alive. The word of the God is true. It's alive, it's active, and it's sharper than any two-edged sword (Hebrews 4:12).

Today I say the same to you, "Don't take my word for it. Ask Jesus to reveal himself to you." I am certain you will soon discover he is alive; his word is true; and his Spirit desires to live within you. You will find yourself on an incredible journey, one that will change your life forever. Take time to read the book of John in your Bible. Let's pray.

Father, thank you for laying your life down for all mankind. Thank you today you are alive and well, and your spirit does live within all who will ask. No one will be denied if they ask and receive. Today we join our faith and pray and believe many will come to know you this season all across this globe.

We have not because we ask not. Today we join our faith with every reader that will dare to believe your word that they too will receive the greatest gift ever given—Jesus. We pray many will choose to believe today and begin the journey of knowing you, Lord, for there's nothing greater than journeying life with Jesus. We give you thanks. Amen.

Have a blessed day, beautiful people. Declare it, sing it, and, most of all, believe it. God's not dead!

Didn't God Say All Things?

Good morning, beautiful people, good morning. Life has so many twists and turns. I have been believing God for five years for something. Five years seems like a long time, but in the scope of a lifetime, it really isn't. It takes patience and perseverance in believing his promises. When I hear the number 5, it reminds me of God's grace. His grace has kept me thus far, and it will keep you as well. That is the meaning of the number of five—grace.

Today, let's thank him once again that he said all things. Let's thank him once again for his love and grace. His grace is sufficient. Amen? Amen!

Father, thank you that you said all things. Romans 8:28 tells us, "And we know that in all things, God works for the good of those who love him, who have been called according to his purpose."

Father, thank you that your grace is enough for every situation in our lives. Second Corinthians 12:9 tells us that your grace is sufficient for us; your power is made perfect in our weakness. Therefore, I will boast all the more gladly about my weaknesses so that Christ's power may rest on me.

Father, thank you for the grace in the waiting. May it deepen our trust in you and your timing and reassure us that all things are possible as we remain strong and meditate on your Word. Amen.

Have a blessed day, God's beautiful people. His grace is sufficient, and he said all things.

Do You Build Bridges or Burn Them Down?

Good morning, beautiful people, good morning. As I was driving across the bridge in town the other day, I remembered a conversation I had recently at a women's retreat I attended. Although this meeting was different than what I was used to, and although it was unfamiliar territory, something was drawing me. I had prayed about it and asked the Lord if it was his desire for me to go. Deep in my heart, I felt his approval. I knew two people that would be there, one the local sister in town (the only sister in town, and she sure is special) and the woman I had met at McDonald's on New Year's Eve. The other close to fifty women was total strangers.

The experience blessed my heart, and although there were things I didn't fully comprehend, I met women that knew the Lord and was on a journey with him. I saw the same joy, pain, sorrows, and regrets that women all across this globe have. I made friends, and I did things I never thought I would ever do. I was part of a skit (there were three of us in our group), and I helped the other two broken women stand tall again as they were lying wounded, hurt on the journey. They had taken some huge blows in life, and I prayed for them and spoke the word of the Lord to them. Then I continued down the path, and I started to fall. Hurt, pain, and disappointment had come my way. These two ladies ran to me one on each side, and they prayed for me and helped me stand strong once again. Then the two other ladies sang a song (I didn't dare to add my tune), and I ended with a prayer.

We joined our faith for every woman across this globe who was broken, wounded, hurt, or disappointed that God would use us or send someone to help to strengthen them. We prayed for strong and confident women in whom God created in his likeness to arise and touch the world for such a time as this. This was the very first skit in my whole life I ever remember being a part of (totally out of my comfort zone).

Mary, Esther, Deborah, and Hannah are examples of these extraordinary women in the Bible that did exploits. Today put your name here (Laurie, Candace, Judy, Janice, Christine, Launa, Mildred, Dee, Florence,

Vera, Mary, Joanne, Marilyn, Beth, Robin, Lisa, Debbie, Amy, Gail, Vicki, Teresa, etc.). You are gifted. You are loved greatly by the man that created you. There is no need to compare you to anyone just him. He fashioned you, uniquely designed you, created you, and desires you to build bridges with others all across this globe. The gift he has deposited in you the world needs it.

So today, just because someone may not look like you, pray like you, or even believe like you, it is still okay. He has a plan and if we will build bridges from church to church, home to home, business to business can you begin to imagine how it would impact our world. Since everything we do is for his glory and not our own, I pray we will take steps to build bridges. Ask him to help us be bridge builders and not to burn each other's bridges down. Let's pray.

Father, thank you for another day. Thank you for every reader, every person reading this post. Make us bridge builders, we pray. We ask you to forgive us when we spoke negative, didn't act kindly, or made a remark when we should have remained silent.

Father, we pray you will help us to be bridge builders. Help us not to tear down bridges' others built. God, perfect the cracks in us that we all may reflect you to this world. For every person who is sick, we pray health. Every person that needs a breakthrough, we intercede on their behalf today, and thank you for breakthrough. Thank you for open doors of opportunity. God of the universe, be God of us today. We pray for every church service, Lord, across this globe; may they speak truth, shine light, and may many come to know you as their Lord and personal Savior this day.

Father, thank you for pouring out your spirit. Reign, Jesus, reign. Fresh anointing fall fresh on us, we give you all the praise and all the glory in Jesus's name, we pray. Amen.

Now declare, God's beautiful people, I am a bridge builder.

"Two are better than one, because they have a good return for their labor. If either of them falls down, one can help the other up. But pity anyone who falls and has no one to help them up" (Ecclesiastes 4:9–10).

A Dark Night

Good morning, beautiful people. Today let's pray Romans 5:6–10.

You see, at just the right time, when we were still powerless, Christ died for the ungodly. Very rarely will anyone die for a righteous man, though for a good man someone might possibly dare to die. But God demonstrates his own love for us in this: While we were still sinners, Christ died for us. Since we have now been justified by his blood, how much more shall we be saved from God's wrath through him! For if, when we were God's enemies, we were reconciled to him through the death of his Son, how much more, having been reconciled, shall we be saved through his life!

Father, on Good Friday, you were crucified. It was a dark, dark day. Little did they know they did not have the power to keep you down. You know firsthand the pain of betrayal. You also paid a dear price for our salvation. How do we ever say thank you?

Today if you have invited Christ to be Lord of your life, you are righteous. Today declare, I am the righteousness of God through the blood of Jesus Christ. If you haven't invited him into your life, talk to him about it. He loves you and is waiting. Amen.

Have a blessed day, beautiful people. Praise him for your righteousness.

God Is Love...

Good morning, beautiful people. Today let's pray and believe his Word together.

You may not know me, but I know everything about you. (Psalm 139:1)

I know when you sit down and when you rise up. (Psalm 139:2)

I am familiar with all your ways. (Psalm 139:3)

Even the hairs on your head are numbered. (Matthew 10:29–31)

For you were made in my image. (Genesis 1:27)

In me, you live and move and have your being. (Acts 17:28)

For you are my offspring. (Acts 17:28)

I knew you even before you were conceived. (Jeremiah 1:4–5)

I chose you when I planned creation. (Ephesians 1:11–12)

You were not a mistake, for all your days are written in my book. (Psalm 139:15–16)

I determined the exact time of your birth and where you would live. (Acts 17:26)

You are fearfully and wonderfully made. (Psalm 139:14)

I knit you together in your mother's womb. (Psalm 139:13)

And brought you forth on the day you were born. (Psalm 71:6)

I have been misrepresented by those who don't know me. (John 8:41–44)

I am not distant and angry, but am the complete expression of love. (1 John 4:16)

And it is my desire to lavish my love on you simply because you are my child and I am your father. (John 3:1)

I offer you more than your earthly father ever could. (Matthew 7:11)

For I am the perfect father. (Matthew 5:48)

Every good gift that you receive comes from my hand. (James 1:17)

For I am your provider, and I meet all your needs. (Matthew 6:31–33)

My plan for your future has always been filled with hope. (Jeremiah 29:11)

Because I love you with an everlasting love. (Jeremiah 31:3)

My thoughts toward you are countless as the sand on the seashore. (Psalm 139:17–18)

And I rejoice over you with singing. (Zephaniah 3:17)

I will never stop doing good to you. (Jeremiah 32:40)

For you are my treasured possession. (Exodus 19:5)

I desire to establish you with all my heart and all my soul. (Jeremiah 32:41)

And I want to show you great and marvelous things. (Jeremiah 33:3)

If you seek me with all your heart, you will find me. (Deuteronomy 4:29)

Delight in me and I will give you the desires of your heart. (Psalm 37:4)

For it is I who gave you those desires. (Philippians 2:13)

I am able to do more for you than you could possibly imagine. (Ephesians 3:20)

For I am your greatest encounter. (2 Thessalonians 2:16–17)

I am also the Father who comforts you in all your troubles. (2 Corinthians 1:3–4)

When you are brokenhearted, I am close to you. (Psalm 34:18)

As a shepherd carries a lamb, I have carried you close to my heart. (Isaiah 40:11)

One day, I will wipe away every tear from your eyes and will take away all the pain you have suffered on this earth. (Revelation 21:3–4)

I am your Father, and I love you even as I love my son, Jesus. (John 17:23)

For in Jesus, my love for you is revealed. (John 17:26)

He is the exact representation of my being. (Hebrews 1:3)

He came to demonstrate that I am for you, not against you. (Romans 8:31)

And to tell you that I am not counting your sins. (2 Corinthians 5:18–19)

Jesus died so that you, and I could be reconciled. (2 Corinthians 5:18–19)

His death was the ultimate expression of my love for you. (1 John 4:10)

I gave up everything I loved that I might gain your love. (Romans 8:31–32)

If you receive the gift of my Son Jesus, you receive me. (1 John 2:23)

And nothing will ever separate you from my love again. (Romans 8:38–39)

Come home, and I'll throw the biggest party heaven has ever seen.

(Luke 15:7)

I have always been father, and will always be Father. (Ephesians 3:14–15)

My question is…Will you be my child? (John 1:12–13)

I am waiting for you. (Luke 15:11–32)

Father, thank you for your love for mankind. We join our faith today all across this globe that many will come to experience the greatest love, the greatest joy, and the greatest peace. Living their lives in the one who laid his down for us. Jesus, how do we ever say thank you? We just want to praise your name.

Our hearts are full of thanksgiving and gratitude for being our God. All across this globe today…receive him. If you know him, ask him to know him better. Amen.

Have a blessed day, beautiful people. God is love. Believe.

A Woman That Is Impacting the World

Good morning, beautiful people, good morning. Last week, I spent five days with seven of the most incredible people and an instructor who was so gifted it was almost beyond words, but I so want to share. I will try to give you a glimpse into a week of training that is so vital in the world today.

On Saturday, as she left our airport, I couldn't help myself from going to the airport to say goodbye to a woman who impacts regions of people all over the world. I am blessed to meet so many people, but I can honestly say this woman and her impact on the world and on people's lives leaves me almost speechless. It really is an honor to be in her presence, let alone sit under her instruction.

Colonel Gale J. Yandell, International Fellowship of Chaplains, Inc., thank you. Thank you for your deposit in our community. Our lives have forever changed, and I know our group will run with what you have imparted to us. May we be found faithful with the knowledge we have gained. To God himself be all the glory. Wow, what an honor we were given.

Steve, Blake, Sarah, Kristie, Ayo, and Nancy, good morning, beautiful people. I miss you already, and I pray this morning for our next step. Senior Chaplain Robin Beckwith, thanks for your continued persistence in bringing this training to our area. I see the world this morning in a fresh deeper way of God's amazing plan for all his creation. Life is so important and the destiny he has for all mankind. My life feels so full. I pray many, many others throughout our world will take this training. Let's pray together once again from Matthew 6:9–13, the Lord's Prayer.

Our Father in heaven, hallowed be your name, your kingdom come, your will be done, on earth as it is in heaven. Give us today our daily bread. And forgive us our debts, as we also have forgiven our debtors. And lead us not into temptation, but deliver us from the evil one. For thine is the kingdom, and the power, and the glory, for ever and ever, Amen.

Have a blessed day, beautiful people. Share some goodness today in God's kingdom!

Are You a Name Dropper?

Good morning, beautiful people, good morning. This is the most powerful name I know. I love when I can stamp his name on my life.

Father, thank you for loving us when we were yet sinners. Jesus, thank you for willingly laying down your life for mankind. We come before you this morning, praying in agreement. We thank you today for God assignments. Use us to be a witness to the world around us and show them, Father, that, yes, prayer is the key. Anyone can call on your name, and you do hear.

Thank you for being a man of your Word. Your Word states in Numbers 23:19, "God is not human, that he should lie, not a human being, that he should change his mind. Does he speak and then not act? Does he promise and not fulfill?" Thank you that we can believe your Word.

We join faith today and pray many will call on your name. The greatest name anyone can know. I am already looking for my red pen to put your heart on the answer to my request.

Today we receive the Word of the Lord. We believe, and yes, we declare prayer is the key. Amen.

Have a blessed day, beautiful people. Drop his name to someone today! He's the man with all the power.

Do You Feel the Winds Blowing?

Good morning, beautiful people, good morning. As I listened to the wind blowing during the night, I kept praying, Lord, let the winds of revival blow across our nation to the nations. As I looked out my window, all I could see was the beautiful white snow drifting across the fields and roads.

This morning, everything looks still, fresh, and clean. Today let's thank God for breathing fresh on our land, rebuilding our lives, and washing our sins as white as snow. When God breathes on something, everything changes—everything.

Father, thank you for the fresh fallen snow and the winds that are blowing. We embrace this new season as the winds sweep across our lives. Blow, spirit, blow as you renew us, refresh us, and bring change in our spiritual lives once again.

Father, continue to lead us and guide us according to your spirit. "For you said it is not by might nor by power, but by your spirit" (Zechariah 4:6). Open our hearts and our minds to the teaching of Jesus Christ.

Father, let the good news of the gospel spread throughout the land by every means possible. We believe revival winds are blowing, and the harvest is coming in. We give you all the glory. Amen.

Have a blessed day, God's beautiful people. Believe in the changing winds of revival. Let Jesus breathe on you fresh and anew today.

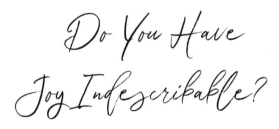

Do You Have Joy Indescribable?

Good morning, beautiful people, good morning. Today let's thank the Lord for joy.

Light in a messenger's eyes brings joy to the heart, and good news gives health to the bones. (Proverbs 15:30)

You make known to me the path of life; you will fill me with joy in your presence, with eternal pleasures at your right hand. (Psalm 16:11)

But let all who take refuge in you be glad; let them ever sing for joy. Spread your protection over them, that those who love your name may rejoice in you. (Psalm 5:11)

Rejoice in the Lord always and again I say, rejoice. (Philippians 4:4)

For the kingdom of God is not meat and drink but righteousness, and peace, and joy in the Holy Ghost. (Romans 14:17)

Rejoice always, pray continually, give thanks in all circumstances. for this is God's will for you in Christ Jesus. (1 Thessalonians 5:16)

Father, thank you for joy. Thank you that the joy of the Lord is our strength (Psalm 28:7). Today all across this globe, we join our faith for the God of all hope to fill us with joy and peace in believing, that we may abound in hope through the power of the Holy Ghost (Romans 15:13). Thank you that our joy is not dependent on our circumstances, for we put all our trust in you.

O God, you said, "Weeping may endure for a night but joy cometh in the morning" (Psalm 30:5). Thank you for that promise. Thank you for the joy of children. When the disciples argued who was the greatest, you took a little child and had him stand beside you. These were your words, O God, in Luke 9:46–50, "Then he said to them, 'Whoever welcomes this little child in my name welcomes me, and whoever welcomes me welcomes the one who sent me. For it is the one who is least among you all who is the greatest.'"

We speak to the nations today and pray Psalm 47:1–3, "Clap your hands, all you nations, shout to God with cries of joy. For the Lord Most High is awesome, the great King over all the earth. He subdued nations under us, peoples under our feet."

We declare joy, joy, joy indescribable today and full of mercy. May the joy of the Lord be deep down in our hearts today. Amen.

Be a Blessing

Good morning, beautiful people, good morning. Today let's pray Isaiah 58:7–8.

Is it not to share your food with the hungry and to provide the poor wanderer with shelter—when you see the naked, to clothe them, and not to turn away from your own flesh and blood? Then your light will break forth like the dawn, and your healing will quickly appear; then your righteousness will go before you, and the glory of the Lord will be your rear guard

Father, we believe in you. Today we join our faith together and desire to be doers of your word and not just hearers. You created us to be a blessing to others. Today there are some who have lost their way, and we pray you will use us to help them get back on the journey. God, you are the healer. We pray healing for the sick among us today. We pray for food, shelter, and every unmet need across this globe.

May the body of Christ take the gift they have been given (you are an important piece of the puzzle) and help another in need. Thank you for calling us to action this day. Amen.

Have a blessed day, God's beautiful people. Time for you to give an encouraging word, smile, and help someone in need.

Didn't God Say He Orders Our Footsteps?

Good morning, beautiful people, good morning. This morning, as I review some of the recent events happening in the world today, I rest assured God orders our footsteps. He tells us man makes their plans, but God orders our footsteps. It makes this quiet gal want to shout!

Father, thank you that you knew the end before the beginning (Isaiah 46:10). You have predestined our lives. "No weapon formed against us shall prosper, and every tongue which rises against us in judgment, you shall condemn. This is the heritage of the servants of the Lord, and our righteousness is from God, says the Lord" (Isaiah 54:17). Thank you for the rich heritage in Jesus Christ.

Every step we take is planned by you. Life was your idea, and you are the God that finishes everything before it started. We decide if we follow you or follow man. We choose to follow you.

Psalm 139 tells us, "For you created our inmost being, you knit us together in our mother's womb." We praise you because we are fearfully and wonderfully made; your works are wonderful. We know that full well. Our frame was not hidden from you when we were made in the secret place, when we were woven together in the depths of the earth. Your eyes saw our unformed body; all the days ordained for us were written in your book before one of them came to be. How precious to us are your thoughts, God! How vast is the sum of them! Were we to count them, they would outnumber the grains of sand. When we awake, we are still with you.

Father, thank you that the earth was formed by you, and you will always have the final say. The earth is the Lord's, and everything in it, the world, and all who live in it. For he founded it on the seas and established it on the waters (Psalm 24:1–2). To that, we say amen.

Have a blessed day, God's beautiful people. Delight yourselves in him, and he will give you the desires of your heart (Psalm 37:4).

You Got This

Good morning, beautiful people, good morning. Today, let's be challenged to go beyond ourselves and do something kind, generous for someone to show the love and compassion of Jesus Christ. The world is waiting to be touched by Jesus. You are his hands and feet extended. You got this!

Father, thank you that you laid down your life for us. You paid the ultimate sacrifice that we could live life. Today, there are so many needs in people's lives all around us. Forgive us, God, for not being the church you asked us to be. We are the church. The buildings are just that, made of wood and steel. What good are they if they have no people? You are all about people. You died for people. Your heart is for everyone. There is not one who is not worthy of your love.

Father, give us your heart, and, Holy Spirit, lead us to the person that needs a kind word, a hot meal, warm clothes, or whatever the need may be. Father, may we begin our journey today with great joy, knowing we are serving you.

Thank you for binding up the brokenhearted and setting captives free. At the end of the day, may we hear you say well done thy good and faithful servant. May we hear that every day until we go meet with you. Amen.

Have a blessed day, beautiful people. You got this!

"For even the Son of Man did not come to be served, but to serve, and to give his life a ransom for many" (Mark 10:45).

You Can't Buy This—It's Already Been Paid For

Good morning, beautiful people. Let's thank God for his grace today.

Father, thank you for grace. Thank you for your great love for us. There is nothing that we can do to earn this. You loved us enough to pay the price, the full price, and nothing can be added to it. You said it is finished.

After this, Jesus, knowing that all things were now accomplished, that the Scripture might be fulfilled, said, "I thirst!" Now a vessel full of sour wine was sitting there; and they filled a sponge with sour wine, put it on hyssop, and put it to his mouth. So, when Jesus had received the sour wine, he said, "It is finished!" And bowing his head, he gave up his spirit. (John 19:28–30)

Father, how do we ever say thank you? We want to worship you both day and night. Never forgetting our brokenness and how you turned our darkness into light. When you said the work was finished, the price has been paid; it's exactly what you meant. Today all across this globe, people can talk with you (pray) and receive forgiveness of their past, present, and future sins. They can experience life abundantly here on earth and eternal life in heaven. Amen? Amen!

Have a blessed day, God's most beautiful people. The price has been paid.

Don't Ever Stop Dreaming, Beautiful People

Good morning, beautiful people. I love to flip the pages through my old prayer journals and reflect on the prayer times I have had with God. Throughout the years, I have penned the journey and the many questions I asked him and the answers he gave to me. As years go by, these journaled prayer times have meant so much to me as I reflect back on how I cultivated a relationship with the Creator of the universe.

This morning, I smile big as I flip the pages of a prayer asking God how to help people dream again. Singer, Songwriter Annie Charles and I were preparing to go to the Los Angeles Dream Center for a two-week mission. I laughed, I cried as I sought the heart of God and why he directed us to go. A mission I will never forget.

In the years ahead, I would walk out the process in my own life and journey it with others as well. I have discovered there are many missions right here in my hometown. I didn't realize how difficult it is for people (including me) to step back out in areas of our lives after a difficult circumstance.

When we realize how much we are loved and cherished by our Creator, it changes everything. He tells us there is nothing that can separate us from his love. He tells us we were bought with a price. He tells us he will never leave us nor forsake us.

Some folk can always help us see past failures, mistakes, and help us stay stuck. Not Jesus! He's saying, "Get back up, step right up, step out again. Up, up, go, go. I love you. You're mine. I will never leave you nor forsake you. I got you covered." Can't you hear him, beautiful people? He is the good Father.

Dream as big as you want, my daughter, my son. I have your back. I will lead and guide you. I created mankind with great intelligence, and I have gifted you. Don't let fear of the unknown hold you back. Step out, step out, go, go.

Have a blessed day, beautiful people. Dust off your dreams, get back up, step out, and go, go! Hope to meet you on the journey.

"For I know the plans I have for you, declares the Lord, plans to prosper you and not to harm you, plans to give you hope and a future" (Jeremiah 29:11).

Did God Really Say No Matter What?

Good morning, beautiful people, good morning. This morning, as I listened to worships songs, I couldn't help but think of how much God loved mankind to sacrifice his Son for our sins. I never want to forget what it cost him for me to live free.

"For it is by grace you have been saved, through faith—and this is not from yourselves, it is the gift of God, not by works, so that no one can boast" (Ephesians 2:8–9).

Sometimes the longer we walk with God, and he changes us, it is easy to see the imperfections in others. We will never arrive in perfection until we go meet Jesus. Until then, he changes us from glory to glory (2 Corinthians 3:18). Aren't you thankful for his mercy and grace? Aren't you glad that he is a God of truth? Let's pray.

Father, thank you for mercy and grace. Thank you that we are all a work in progress. We didn't get saved one day and reach perfection that same day. Life is a journey, and you teach us daily through your Word, worship, fellowship, trials, etc. Our lives are in your hands. Nothing can separate us from the love of God (Romans 8:38–39). That is so reassuring.

As we pray for the next generation this morning, let us embrace them with love and understanding as they are growing up in a culture that has changed very quickly. Let's pray they will come to full understanding of who God created them to be at an early age.

Father, we pray for the next generation. Draw them to yourself, we pray. May they come to the knowledge of your saving grace. Father, your Word tells us it's not by might, nor by power, but by your spirit (Zechariah 4:6).

Thank you for pouring out your spirit on the next generation. May they walk in the knowledge of the love of their Heavenly Father. May we see them rise up to heights that we could only dream of. You are an amazing God, and nothing is too difficult for you. Amen.

Have a blessed day, beautiful people. Bless a youth today!

Dance with Me

Good morning, beautiful people. Isn't it good to be alive? We should celebrate life every day. Today I wanted to share a small portion from a Bible study I wrote from my own experience to women suffering in silence from the aftermath of an abortion. Journey with me today even if you haven't experienced such a trauma. Thank God himself that you haven't. I hope and pray it will build compassion in you for the many millions of women that have.

In the first part of this study, we admit we are hurt. We face head on the wrong decision that was made. In the second part of this study, we grieve the loss of a life that never made it past the womb. The third part of this study is a day of remembrance for our child.

I have had the opportunity to journey with many women from across this globe that are post-abortive. From our young women to our beloved elderly, many carry the same secret. The pain of an abortion is a pain they wish they never experienced and struggle to share.

I will post this study on my website this week, free of charge, so that Jesus can heal you right at your point of your need. He wants you to be free. Jesus paid the price so you don't have to carry the pain anymore. Jesus was free to me; he cost me nothing. That's why I like to do ministry Jesus style.

Most times, fear is the triggering emotion that brings a teen, a woman, and or their families to take steps they will someday come to regret.

At the first Healing Waters Women's Conference (2016), I journeyed my own study again and wrote another letter to my son, Jeremiah. This is what I penned on that special day.

Jeremiah…I told you so, my special child, I told you so. God would open doors for me to speak about the pain and trauma of abortion. Women will be set free. I miss you still. I miss you much. I know you are with Jesus, and I'll see you again someday. Oh, Jeremiah, how I love you (lots of hearts)! You are the only child I have that likes to hear. I told you so. Mom.

On our final day, we do a small remembrance for the life that was not born. On six white pedals in 2016, I wrote the following words with a heart underneath each word: loved, cherished, he loves his momma, I will embrace him someday, never forgotten, and healed.

At the Healing Waters Women's Conference (2017), I added one more white petal to my remembrance, precious. Precious, he is…

At the Healing Waters Women's Conference this year (2018), dancing…I feel like dancing as I wait on you. It is time to live free, beautiful people. Live life free in Jesus.

Life is a precious choice. Celebrate your day, beautiful people. You have a lot to be thankful for. Dance, dance, and dance.

"You turned my wailing into dancing; you removed my sackcloth and clothed me with joy, that my heart may sing your praises and not be silent. Lord my God, I will praise you forever" (Psalm 30:11–12).

Be Honest, Do You Really?

Good morning, beautiful people. Let's get honest this morning and answer this question together. Do you really believe in prayer? Do you really believe in the prayer of agreement? Let's get real with ourselves and get real before our Heavenly Father today. He knows already how we all will answer these questions.

If we all really believe in the power of prayer, let's look at some tough questions. When was the last time you prayed? Where were you sitting when our church called a prayer meeting? When was the last time you joined your faith with and on behalf of someone else?

If you have prayed, are you believing and receiving the answer? Are we filled with expectation? Have you closed off the voices of the naysayers and those with negative words contrary to the Word of God? Are you surrounding yourselves with people of likeminded faith?

Jesus says he hears and answers prayer. That is the bottom line, his final answer. Can you believe it? Can you receive it?

Let us join our faith together today for whatever your needs may be. I have some as well, so let's bring them all before our King.

Father, thank you for Jesus. We come before you this morning praying in agreement. Your word tells us in Matthew 18:19 that if two of you on earth agree about anything, they ask, for it will be done for them by my Father in heaven. We choose today to believe the holy scriptures.

We join faith together across this globe for every need. (Tell him what you have need of.) Healing for the sick, deliverance for the bound, food for the hungry, finances for the needy, and love on earth to abound.

We pray the prayer of agreement according to Matthew 18:19, "Again I say unto you, that if two of you shall agree on earth as touching anything that they shall ask, it shall be done for them of my Father which is in heaven." Amen.

Today we declare we believe; we declare we are receivers of the word of the Lord. Thank you for restoration. Thank you for grace. Thank you for mercy. Thank you for justice. Thank you for ordering our footsteps. Thank you for journeying the day with us. We receive.

Have a blessed day, God's beautiful people. Jesus has the final answer to everything that pertains to us. Believe.

Awaken the Treasure

Good morning, beautiful people. I wanted to share with you a treasured memory.

I laugh as I awoke this morning, remembering the day called yesterday. I was busy with the daily chores called housekeeping when I received a call from my daughter inquiring about a treasure hunt for my grandson. Somehow at that moment, laundry seemed unnecessary, dishes could wait, and the dust on the furniture could hold for another day. I quickly went to our favorite store, The Dollar Store, to find a few treasures for him to discover. Together, we hid the mini Frisbee, M&M's, and stickers. We took turns seeing the amazement of a child as he looked diligently to discover the hidden treasures.

It brings to the forefront of my mind this early morning the treasure each life brings to the universe uniquely created. Each person created with gifts and talents who is needed for each community to function. I ponder what the world would be like if everyone realized their value, their purpose. No one person is more important than the next; just uniquely created individuals all created in the image of our God. Wouldn't it be amazing if each person found their purpose in life, fulfilling the plan they were designed for? Everyone destined for the same greatness.

I pray each day that all human life would discover the truth about who they are on this journey. Somehow the ship becomes battered by the storms of life, and soon people begin to believe the lies planted only by the enemy of their soul.

Today, find the hidden treasure in yourself and then look for the treasure in the folks you will encounter this day. I realize sometimes those hard places in life have hardened the shell of the heart, and people become mean, scared, hurt, and bitter. Their journey has caused them to slip and lose that hope. Maybe you will be the one to help tear down that wall of pain and give them a renewed sense that they too are important.

Today, awaken the treasures in your world, your sphere of influence. Maybe you can help unlock the hidden treasure in someone else's life today. You may be the one to give them the courage to keep on the journey.

Be the very best you can be today. No need to compare yourself to anyone. You are great. Allow your greatness to spill over into the heart of the one that has lost it today.

May you discover many hidden treasures on this day. Let it be your day of amazement like the wonder of a child. Destiny awaits.

Oh, I hear the phone ringing. Have a great day. My treasure hunt has now begun.

Have a blessed day, beautiful people. You were created in the image of God himself. You are his treasure.

Father, thank you that we are your treasure. Your love for us is just downright amazing. Your love is unstoppable, full of mercy. It is true you would wage a war for your people. You gave your very life. Oh, the love of our Father.

Today, we join our faith together that the revelation of the love of Christ would be evident in the lives of your people. Together all across this globe, we pray the world would see the love of Christ in us and experience it through us and desire to journey life with you. Do a deeper work in us today, we pray.

Thank you for your love. Lead us to people today that have lost the value they have in life. Use us today that we may be instruments of hope to those without it, we pray. Amen.

Let your treasure hunt begin.

"May the God of hope fill you with all joy and peace as you trust in him so that you may overflow with hope by the power of the Holy Spirit" (Romans 15:13).

As We Pray

Good morning, beautiful people. Let's continue to pray and stay in faith, believing together.

Father, you are the best connection any person on this earth could possibly have. For everyone that feels like there is no hope, you are their hope. You send help every day. You send it right from on high.

To journey life with the Creator of the universe is just downright amazing. We love how your Holy Spirit guides us each and every day if we ask. You reveal yourself in the most amazing ways. Thank you for being our God and us your people. Your love is amazing.

We confess we don't always understand your ways, and your thoughts are so much higher than ours (Isaiah 55:8–9). Oh, but you have proven yourself so trustworthy. Faithful Father, teach us all things that we may know you the Godhead, love divine. When we don't get things just right, you, O God, look at us and say they are mine. "I love them with an everlasting love" (Jeremiah 31:3). "I paid the price" (1 Timothy 2:6). You cover us with your love. That alone makes our heart sing for joy every day.

Father, thank you for fulfilling the purpose you have for our lives that you predestined before the foundations of the earth. Thank you for leading us, directing us, and making every crooked path straight. Thank you for being our greatest connection. Holy Spirit, guide us and may we leave a trail of blessings wherever you lead us this day. Amen.

Have a blessed day, God's beautiful people, and if you don't know him, you are only a few words away from the greatest connection your life will ever know (pray). Tell him in your own words that you desire to journey life with him. He understands your language. You were created in his image (Genesis 1:27).

Jesus is your greatest connection in life. May the Christ in Christmas come alive in your heart and soul today as we pray.

"Therefore, I tell you, whatever you ask for in prayer, believe that you have received it, and it will be yours" (Mark 11:24).

Sprinkle Love Everywhere You Go

Good morning, beautiful people. Today let's pray and believe these scriptures together.

For God so loved the world, that he gave his only Son, that whoever believes in him should not perish but have eternal life. (John 3:16)

No, in all these things, we are more than conquerors through him who loved us. For I am sure that neither death nor life, nor angels nor rulers, nor things present nor things to come, nor powers, nor height nor depth, nor anything else in all creation, will be able to separate us from the love of God in Christ Jesus our Lord. (Romans 8:37–39)

But God, being rich in mercy, because of the great love with which he loved us, even when we were dead in our trespasses, made us alive together with Christ—by grace you have been saved. (Ephesians 2:4–5)

God shows his love for us in that while we were still sinners, Christ died for us. (Romans 5:8)

But you, O Lord, are a merciful and gracious God, slow to anger and abounding in steadfast love and faithfulness. (Psalm 86:15)

Father, thank you for your love. Today all across this globe, may love abound. We pray that people who struggle to receive your love would have a new revelation. You loved us while we were yet deep in our sin. Thank you for your Word and changing us more into your image each day. Oh, how you love us and, oh, how we love you. Amen.

Have a blessed Valentine's Day, God's most beautiful people. Sprinkle love everywhere you go.

Be Careful with your Giving

Good morning, beautiful people. Today, let's pray Matthew 6:1–4.

Be careful not to practice your righteousness in front of others to be seen by them. If you do, you will have no reward from your Father in heaven. So when you give to the needy, do not announce it with trumpets as the hypocrites do in the synagogues and on the streets to be honored by others. Truly I tell you, they have received their reward in full. But when you give to the needy, do not let your left hand know what your right hand is doing, so that your giving may be in secret. Then your Father, who sees what is done in secret, will reward you.

Father, thank you that you desire people to help others. Show us, Lord, where to help, when to help, and lead us to be a blessing to someone today, we pray. May we be an answer to someone's prayer today. May all your people be giving something of themselves.

This exchange of giving will look different for everyone. To some people, you will ask to give away a smile, some will give in monetary ways, and yet others may shake a hand. You see it all, Lord, and reward accordingly. Since it's all for your glory, Jesus, we thank you for allowing us the opportunity to be your hands and feet extended to a hurting world.

May the world know that you live because they witness the goodness of your people. May hope arise all across this globe today. Amen.

Have a blessed day, God's beautiful people. Hush is the word in your giving.

Are You Out of the Boat?

Good morning, beautiful people. Today let's pray together about being faithful.

What does scripture say? Abraham believed God, and it was credited to him as righteousness. (Romans 4:3)

But my God shall supply all your needs according to his riches in glory by Christ Jesus. (Philippians 4:19)

Consequently, faith comes from hearing the message, and the message is heard through the word about Christ. (Romans 10:17)

I can do all things through Christ who strengthens me. (Philippians 4:13)

Father, may we be found faithful. May our lives be marked by faithfulness and obedience to you. We stepped out of the boat and are walking on the water. As we continue to journey our walk by faith and not by sight, we are reminded of Abraham. Abraham believed God, and it was credited to him as righteousness.

All across this globe today, we join our faith and declare we are moving forward in you. The promises, the visions, and the dreams you have placed within us are already marked with your yes. Amen. We declare we are believing God. We declare whatever the cost to obeying you is well worth it. We are out of the boat. Amen.

Have a blessed day, beautiful people. Shout "I am out of the boat."

Believe in God's Timing

Good morning, beautiful people, good morning. I often asked God about his timing. Sometimes I have felt his answer to my prayer was slow in coming. When it finally came, I realized even one day earlier would have not been the right time. Learning to trust his timing is key in our journey with God. His clock, his seasons, and his calendar look different than ours. His answer, his timing is always right on time. Amen? Let's pray.

Father, thank you for your timing. As we journey life, you have given us the assurance that you will answer our prayers according to your will, your timing, and what is the very best for us.

Father, forgive us when we have complained at the tardiness of your answer. You always deliver at the right moment. We thank you for the confidence that we are never journeying life alone. Thank you that your watchful eye is always upon us.

Father, thank you for harvest time. We know the great commission (Matthew 28:18–20). As we go out and spread the good news to all the nations, we are assured you are the God with us. Amen.

Have a blessed day, God's beautiful people. Don't forget to believe and wait on his timing.

Then Jesus came to them and said, "All authority in heaven and on earth has been given to me. Therefore, go and make disciples of all nations, baptizing them in the name of the Father and of the Son and of the Holy Spirit, and teaching them to obey everything I have commanded you. And surely, I am with you always, to the very end of the age." (Matthew 28:18–20)

Are You Wearing the Wrong Glasses?

Good morning, beautiful people. I shared the dilemma of not being able to see out of my new glasses. A mistake was made, and I was given the wrong prescription. As I brought the message last Sunday at a church I was speaking at, I am sure glad I had a lot of scripture hidden in my heart. I couldn't read much of my notes, but I showed up for duty. I didn't know I had the wrong prescription at that point. Thank God, I was able to share the word of God with his power and his anointing. He always comes through. Did I say always?

I drove the two and a half hours to where I purchased the glasses to tell them I couldn't see through the lens correctly. I also had my eyes re-examined. In twelve days, I will have another pair of glasses. Until then, I am wearing my old set that has a cracked lens.

Another eyeglass store, we stopped at was going to be more expensive (I thought) so I went with my original plan. A friend that was with me tried on glasses. As I waited for her, I decided to try on more glasses. People were asking us our opinion as they were trying on their frames. We were all engaged in looking at each other's glasses.

Time was running out as I had plans to attend the annual Pregnancy Care Center Banquet that evening. We gave the ladies our opinions and left the store. As I looked in my rearview mirror to back out of the driveway, I couldn't help but yell, "I have the wrong glasses on." I hurriedly went back in the store, and someone had put my glasses with the cracked lens in with all the other glasses on one of the many shelves. Sometimes you just got to laugh.

We got everyone in the store we could engaged in looking for my glasses. I almost tripped over a chair as I was getting a bit excited about the time. One of the customers we had previously helped found them. Praise God, and we were ready for the marathon ahead.

As I backed out of the parking lot, my eye saw an elderly couple, and their car was going backward slowly. We stopped and waited as they kept going slowly toward an embankment. My friend jumped out to help them. The driver of the car got in with me and said quite excitedly, "I just reached up pulled down my arm like this and asked Jesus for help." She showed me what she had done with her arm as she was a bit shaken herself. I assured her God had heard her prayer, and here we were, cracked glasses and all. Her car had stalled, and because it was on a hill, it was rolling backward. She was unaware the car had stalled. My friend started the car as the elderly man in the passenger seat was quite excited as well, asking her to drive him home. She calmed him down, and we got them straightened out, and their car and them on their way home. Let's pray.

Father, thank you for changing our schedules. Give us your eyes, Lord, to see what's all around us. Thank you, God, even for the delays in our daily lives. Father, may many reach their arm up today and ask for help. Just like the woman didn't realize the car had been stalled, many among us are losing hope. You are their hope. You always, always care and desire the best for your people.

Father, for the person that doesn't know you or doesn't know you as the Good Father would you draw them by your spirit, we pray.

Father, use us today, cracked glasses and all. Amen.

Have a blessed day, beautiful people. Look for an opportunity to make life better for someone else.

"But now, Lord, what do I look for? My hope is in you" (Psalm 39:7).

Awakening, Revival, and Lobster

Good morning, beautiful people. Isn't it fun journeying with Jesus? Remember the young evangelist, Carl, I wrote about in my post, "Sometimes, I just forget?" I had scheduled a radio interview with him last week but had to cancel due to the rain. I tried to drive but decided to turn back for home. Well, does God have a timing for everything?

Friday evening, my brother and I attended a meeting at I Care Ministries, and who did I run into? This man's wife. I was finally able to interview him after the meeting. Dear, goodness, this man is also a lobster man. He had been selling lobsters down the road prior to the meeting. Guess what we were eating at a very late hour Friday night? Yummy lobster.

I celebrated Veterans Day with family, visited family along the way, and met with some friends, some new friends and some old. Don't you love friends? When we come together, it empowers us to take on the world. I enjoyed a muffin and coffee and took a napkin from the table as we were talking about vision for the future. As we continued to pray and write, I noticed the napkin in the holder, and it read, "What did you do to change the world today?" I brought that napkin home with me. I am a world changer and so are you! Don't you just love that he knows the way we should take? Let's thank him today.

Father, thank you for journeying life with us every day. Thank you that you know the way we should take. Thank you that we are world changers. Thank you for blessing abundantly the ministries you have called us too. We break off any small thinking, any lack. We are going higher with you, Jesus. We submit control of our lives to you.

Thank you for this awakening, this revival. Continue to pour out your Spirit, and we will continue to pray and give thanks. Thank you for making us world changers. Thank you for the traveling evangelist lobster man. Enlarge his territory, we pray. His fire is contagious. Amen.

Have a blessed day, beautiful people. Leave your mark on the world today.

Those who look to him are radiant; their faces are never covered with shame. (Psalm 34:5)

Nehemiah said, Go and enjoy choice food and sweet drinks, and send some to those who have nothing prepared. This day is sacred to our Lord. Do not grieve, for the joy of the Lord is your strength. (Nehemiah 8:10)

Are You Looking Up Today?

Good morning, beautiful people. Together, let's pray Psalm 121.
God the Help of Those Who Seek Him.

I will lift up my eyes to the hills—from whence comes my help? My help comes from the Lord, who made heaven and earth. He will not allow your foot to be moved; he who keeps you will not slumber. Behold, he who keeps Israel shall neither slumber nor sleep. The Lord is your keeper; The Lord is your shade at your right hand. The sun shall not strike you by day, nor the moon by night. The Lord shall preserve you from all evil; he shall preserve your soul. The Lord shall preserve you're going out and your coming in from this time forth, and even forevermore.

Father, thank you that you promise never to leave us nor forsake us. Your Word is yes and amen. Today, we do not need to worry or be afraid, we just need to keep looking up to the hills from where our help cometh. Our help cometh from the Lord.

All across this globe today, we have our eyes open and set on you, O God. We declare we are looking up! Amen.

Have a blessed day, God's beautiful people. Keep looking up!

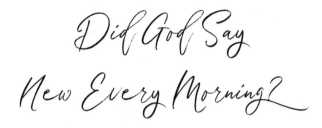

Did God Say New Every Morning?

Good morning, beautiful people. I am sure you are just like most folks; we are all waiting on the Lord for some answers. We wonder when the answer will arrive as we continue to put our trust in him. I continually need to remove any limitations (small thinking) I have placed on him. He will deliver his promise to us right on time. Until then, we stand on his faithfulness. Let's pray.

Father, Lamentations 3:21–25 tells us,

Yet this I call to mind and therefore I have hope. Because of the Lord's great love, we are not consumed, for his compassions never fail. They are new every morning; great is your faithfulness. I say to myself, "The Lord is my portion; therefore, I will wait for him." The Lord is good to those whose hope is in him, to the one who seeks him.

As we wait on you, Father, we give you praise. We seek you both day and night. Never forgetting our brokenness and how you turned our darkness into light. Great is your faithfulness. Amen.

Dancing…

My Lord, my God, my Redeemer, my Father, and yet my Friend, we wait upon you. We look to you, O Lord. Wisdom, yes, we lack. We ask of you, our Lord, healing waters. Yes, we do believe healing your people. Wholeness, that's what we so desire. You, O Lord, you are the one…the only one who can complete the deep work in me, removing pain, shame, deception, bringing truth to the light… Yes, Lord, that's what we need. Strongholds destroyed by the power of your name. Jesus, how do we say thank you? We want to worship you both day and night. Never forgetting the brokenness and how you turned our darkness into light. Dancing, dancing, we want to praise your name. Inside we are dancing both day and night. Jesus, our Lord, we just want you to know how much we love you. Jesus, our friend and yet our Lord, we wait on you. We feel like dancing as we wait on you. We feel like dancing as we wait on you…

Have a blessed day, beautiful people. His compassions never fail. They are new every morning.

Let Him Rain on You

Good morning, beautiful people, it's raining. God's healing rain is for everyone. I am so glad he doesn't pick just certain people. He wants the very best for everyone. You are the very best. He doesn't look at the color of your skin nor what side of the tracks you are from. God looks at what he created in his image.

I am so thankful for the healing waters of Jesus Christ. Receive it today. Let's pray.

Father, thank you for the healing that is in this rain. Thank you for the deliverance that is in this rain. Wash over our region like never before. Our ground, our hearts are prepared to receive the greatest outpouring of your spirit that this region has ever known. Maine, you will never be the same. (Pray for your state.)

Father, thank you for the healing waters; we receive it. Flood our lives with your love. The love that is beyond what we can only begin to comprehend.

We join our faith today for every person struggling with drugs, every alcoholic, every person bound to addiction, to every lost soul, to every beating heart without Jesus, we call you forth. Jesus has the freedom plan for your life. Believe! Your part of the rain. He welcomes you in today. Jesus paid the price, and he has the keys to your freedom. Oh, somebody shout freedom! Welcome to the kingdom of God. He is only one prayer away.

Father, for the ones who are believers, rain on us afresh today. Amen? Amen!

Have a blessed day, beautiful people, thank him for raining on you today. He loves you!

Read John chapter 1 today.

Even the Wind and Waves Obey

Good morning, beautiful people. Together, let's pray these scriptures and believe.

Wind and Wave Obey Jesus

Now it happened, on a certain day, that he got into a boat with his disciples. And he said to them, "Let us cross over to the other side of the lake." And they launched out. But as they sailed, he fell asleep. And a windstorm came down on the lake, and they were filling with water, and were in jeopardy. And they came to him and awoke him, saying, "Master, Master, we are perishing!" Then he arose and rebuked the wind and the raging of the water. And they ceased, and there was a calm. But he said to them, "Where is your faith? "And they were afraid, and marveled, saying to one another, "Who can this be? For he commands even the winds and water, and they obey Him!" (Luke 8:22–25)

Father, thank you that you are in charge and control. At any moment, you can speak to the storm, and it will be still. Today, we join our faith with every person around this globe going through a storm, and the wind is blowing hard, and they feel almost shipwrecked. We thank you for the grace to trust you more. Lord, today I pray faith would arise, and calmness would be their portion.

Today we declare peace to the storm. We know the master of the wind. He has us. He is in our boat. Storm subside in the name of Jesus. Amen.

Have a blessed day, for this is the day the Lord has made, and we will rejoice and be glad in it.

You Promised Us, O God

Good morning, beautiful people, good morning. I was thinking this early morning how many times we let our emotions dictate to us. That's an easy way to lose the battle. Our feelings are so fickle; they change quite quickly.

Sometimes we let how we feel or what we think overtake the promises of God. At the end of the day, it doesn't really matter what our emotions say, it is what God's Word says. Tomorrow we may feel differently, but God's Word never changes. It is the same yesterday, today, and forever. Jesus is the same yesterday, today, and forever (Hebrews 13:8). It is a great assurance that we can rest in his promises, knowing that he has a providential plan for our lives. Let's pray.

Father, "your eyes had seen our unformed substance; and in your book were written all the days that were ordained for us, when as yet there was not one of them" (Psalm 139:16). Your promises to us is where we put all our hope. "For in you, O God, we live and move and have our being" (Acts 17:28).

As we believe your promises, we will receive accordingly. Forgive us, God, when we were filled full of doubt, fear, and unbelief. Thank you for the grace to trust you more. You are not a God who you should lie (Numbers 23:19).

We declare the Word of our Lord God over our lives today. His promises are true and forever settled. We believe! Amen.

Have a blessed day, God's beautiful people. Believe in his promises. Surely they will come to pass.

And God Said and We Believe

Good morning, beautiful people, good morning. Did you ever know something so deep in your heart, mind, body, soul, and spirit that nobody could convince you otherwise? You know because you know because know. It's always your final answer, and nothing can make you change your mind. You know what I am talking about, right? Let's pray today from Genesis 1.

Father, thank you for that you created the heaven and the earth.

And the earth was without form, and void; and darkness was upon the face of the deep. And the Spirit of God moved upon the face of the waters. And, God, you said, let there be light: and there was light. And, God, you saw the light, that it was good: and you divided the light from the darkness. And you, O God, called the light day, and the darkness you called night. And the evening and the morning were the first day. And, God, you said, let there be a firmament in the midst of the waters, and let it divide the waters from the waters. And, God, you made the firmament and divided the waters which were under the firmament from the waters which were above the firmament: and it was so. And, God, you called the firmament heaven. And the evening and the morning were the second day. And, God, you said, let the waters under the heaven be gathered together unto one place, and let the dry land appear: and it was so. And, God, you called the dry land earth; and the gathering together of the waters called the seas: and God you saw that it was good. And, God, you said, let the earth bring forth grass, the herb yielding seed, and the fruit tree yielding fruit after his kind, whose seed is in itself, upon the earth: and it was so. And the earth brought forth grass, and herb yielding seed after his kind, and the tree yielding fruit, whose seed was in itself, after his kind: and, God, you saw that it was good. And the evening and the morning were the third day. And, God, you said, let there be lights in the firmament of the heaven to divide the day from the night; and let them be for signs, and for seasons, and for days, and years: And let them be for lights in the firmament of the heaven to give light upon the earth: and it was so. And, God, you made two great lights; the greater light to rule the day and the lesser light to rule the night. You made the stars also. And, God, you set them in the firmament of the heaven to give light upon the earth and to rule over the day and over the night and to divide the light from the darkness. And you, O God, saw that it was good. And the evening and the morning were the fourth day. And God said, Let the waters bring forth abundantly the moving creature that hath life, and fowl that may fly above the earth in the open firmament of heaven. And, God, you created great whales and every living creature that moveth, which the waters brought forth abundantly, after their kind, and every winged fowl after his kind: and you, O God, saw that it was good. And, God, you blessed them, saying be fruitful and multiply and fill the waters in the seas and let fowl multiply in the earth. And the evening and the morning were the fifth day. And, God, you said, let the earth bring forth the living creature after his kind, cattle, and creeping thing, and beast of the earth after his kind, and it was so. And, God, you made the beast of the earth after his kind and cattle after their kind and everything that creepeth upon the earth after his kind. And God saw that it was good. And, God, you said, let us make man in our image, after our likeness: and let them have dominion over the fish of the sea, and over the fowl of the air, and over the cattle, and over all the earth, and over every creeping thing that creepeth upon the earth. So, God, you created man in your own image, in the image of God created he him; male and female created he them. And, God, you blessed them, and God said unto them, be fruitful, and multiply, and replenish the earth, and subdue it: and have dominion over the fish of the sea, and over the fowl of the air, and over every living thing that moveth upon the earth. And, God, you said, Behold, I have given you every herb bearing seed, which is upon the face of all the earth, and every tree, in the which is the fruit of a tree yielding seed; to you it shall be for meat. And to every beast of the earth, and to every fowl of the air, and to everything that creepeth upon the earth, wherein there is life, I have given every green herb for meat: and it was so. And, God, you saw everything that you had made, and, behold, it was very good. And the evening and the morning were the sixth day.

Father, we believe. Amen.

Have a blessed day, God's beautiful people. Enjoy everything he has created and enjoy the fullness of your day. You are loved and created in the image of God. Believe because he said so.

Awaken Your Dream

Good morning, beautiful people. This morning, I was looking through my journal. This is what I penned one early morning.

Father, I believe in you. You always make me stand in awe of your goodness. You give me beyond what I could ever think or ask. You make a way for me where there seems to be no way. Oh, how you love me. I feel your presence. I feel your love and anointing. I am abundantly blessed.

Jesus, draw me closer. I cast down my idols. Draw me up higher. Take off all the limitations that others have placed on me or I have placed on myself. I want to walk out the plan you have for my life. I am going up higher. I declare today I am going higher.

Let's pray this prayer together.

Father, thank you for taking us to a new level in you. We thank you for removing all limitations and let faith arise in us today. Your love is amazing, and we thank you that you are a limitless God. Everything is possible in you and through you. Touch the world through us, God.

We choose to lay down our idols.

We declare today we are going up higher. Awaken the dream you placed inside us each of us, God. Forgive any unbelief that we allowed to enter in. All things are possible, all things. We will march to your heartbeat for your glory alone. Thank you for taking us up higher. Amen.

Have a blessed day, beautiful people.

"Where there is no vision, the people perish" (Proverbs 29:18).

"If you believe, you will receive, if you have faith" (Matthew 21:22).

Are You the Woman in the Pink Dress?

Good morning, beautiful people, good morning. This morning, my eyes were drawn to my pink baby dress I have hanging on my bedroom wall. It made me think of the portrait so beautifully framed as a gift to me from the Artist Gabriella from Central California. She was bringing forth a message through the gift she has been given by God. The sketch in which she titled, Oh No! What Have I Done, made my mind ponder the terrible mess this young artist was thinking about when she was painting this portrait.

Standing in muddy waters, this once beautiful girl now with a tattered pink dress had a look of despair. She was now glaring at her right hand as she realizes her life has been tainted by bad choices. She had gotten herself in a bad situation, a dark place, a frightening dilemma that was now beyond her own control. Only God himself could help her and put her life's journey on a better course.

On the back of the portrait were the Bible verses "Do not be deceived, evil company corrupts good habits" (1 Corinthians 15:33) and "And do not be conformed to this world but be transformed by the renewing of your mind, that you may prove that is good and acceptable and perfect will of God" (Romans 12:2).

These scriptures say it well if we only would have adhered to them. However, we all have made poor choices, bad decisions, and sometimes just plain old stupid mistakes. I am so thankful for a loving Heavenly Father that died on a cross for us when we were yet sinners.

I thank God for his grace; he so mercifully gives to each of us. Although I don't believe I wore a pink dress as a teenager; I had made some bad choices just like the girl in the portrait. It did leave its mark on my life, but years ago, I had met Jesus, my Redeemer.

I looked in the mirror the very next morning as I was preparing for work. Applying the makeup that would cover the tear-stained face from the painful words that were spoken; I talked to God, the Creator of the universe about how he saw me. I remember that morning just like it was this morning. Beautiful was his reply. I then quickly found a pen and paper to write, and this was what flowed.

Ashes No More

Jesus, Lover of my soul, Creator of my image, Lifter of my head. My name is Beautiful. Woman, pure, holy, undefiled. Sanctified, set apart, journeying with Jesus. A path, narrow and straight. Ashes, no more. Trusting her master, her maker, the lover of her soul. Skipping on the journey with childlike faith. Believing her Father knows what's best. The morning dew, the night's crisp air reminds her of the kisses from above. Jesus, the ultimate Man, the Lover of her soul. Beautiful, a receiver of his glory. Ashes, no more.

I am so thankful for a loving Heavenly Father who speaks to his children and sets the course of destiny for each of our lives. Today no matter what you have done, where you have been, or where you now find yourself, know that you are loved. Just like the girl with the tattered pink dress, whose sin had left its mark, today Jesus is saying, "Come journey with me and let me give you a new beginning. I am your redeemer."

Let's pray.

Father, we thank you for the Word of God (Bible). We thank you that you are our redeemer. Thank you for paying the ultimate price for our sins. Thank you for grace. Father, today we pray for every girl, every woman that is caught in a bad situation that needs intervention. For every person today, O God, that bad choices have left its mark, we pray by the power of your Holy Spirit, you draw them to yourself, and may they know you as their redeemer. We pray for shackles to be broken all across this globe. May the love of Christ flow freely to your people, we pray. Thank you for writing beautiful, created in your image (God) on their mirror this day. Jesus, the ultimate Man, the Lover of our soul, thank you for new beginnings this day for people all across this globe We pray. Amen.

Have a blessed day, God's beautiful people.

Do You Have Crying Eyes?

Good morning, beautiful people. Our God heals and dries up crying eyes.

Crying eyes, tears of sadness, in need of a warm embrace. Heartache, broken dreams, unfulfilled promise and vows. Never to return. A broken woman, a strong courageous woman, a woman of destiny.

Man cannot ruin me, for I belong to my Creator, Jesus, Lover of my soul. The storm blows. I feel the darkness trying to overtake me. The web, the snare that the enemy of my soul has spun.

The glory, the light, Jesus, the Lifter of my head, you came and rescued me. I see the sun starting through, although the clouds still seem dark and gray.

I see the light; now it's shining dimly again. Destiny awaits. Jesus come, walk with me day by day, hand in hand, moment by moment, one day, one step at a time.

Jesus come, Jesus come, Jesus, where from here? Jesus, no asking you why. Let's pray.

Father, together, we pray for every broken woman across this globe today. We pray your Word in Isaiah 61.

The Spirit of the Lord God is upon me because the Lord has anointed me to preach good tidings to the poor; he has sent me to heal the brokenhearted, to proclaim liberty to the captives, and the opening of the prison to those who are bound, to proclaim the acceptable year of the Lord, and the day of vengeance of our God; to comfort all who mourn, to console those who mourn in Zion, to give them beauty for ashes, the oil of joy for mourning, the garment of praise for the spirit of heaviness; that they may be called trees of righteousness, the planting of the Lord, that he may be glorified. And they shall rebuild the old ruins, they shall raise up the former desolations, and they shall repair the ruined cities, the desolations of many generations. Strangers shall stand and feed your flocks, and the sons of the foreigner shall be your plowmen and your vinedressers. But you shall be named the priests of the Lord, they shall call you the servants of our God. You shall eat the riches of the Gentiles, and in their glory, you shall boast. Instead of your shame, you shall have double honor, and instead of confusion, they shall rejoice in their portion. Therefore, in their land they shall possess double; everlasting joy shall be theirs. For I, the Lord, love justice; I hate robbery for burnt offering; I will direct their work in truth, and will make with them an everlasting covenant. Their descendants shall be known among the Gentiles, and their offspring among the people. All who see them shall acknowledge them, that they are the posterity whom the Lord has blessed. I will greatly rejoice in the Lord, my soul shall be joyful in my God; For he has clothed me with the garments of salvation, he has covered me with the robe of righteousness, as a bridegroom decks himself with ornaments, and as a bride adorns herself with her jewels. For as the earth brings forth its bud, As the garden causes the things that are sown in it to spring forth, So the Lord God will cause righteousness and praise to spring forth before all the nations.

Father, thank you that you will make every crooked way straight. I pray hope into every broken life. I pray you draw the readers today, and that this would be a word in season for them. When they look in the mirror today, O God, I pray they will see themselves as beautiful, for that is how you created them. They were created in your image, and you are waiting for them to ask you to make them whole again. Your answer is the same for every woman across this globe, yes and amen. Let it be so. We give you thanks. Destiny awaits.

Have a blessed day, God's beautiful people. Let him dry up your crying eyes.

Be a God Pleaser

Good morning, beautiful people. Let's pray about being a God pleaser.

Father, thank you for being above it all. You are above kings, rulers, and every aspect of government. You are worth more than any earthly possession. It truly is a treasure-journeying life with the Greatest Leader, Jesus Christ.

Today we pray for courage for all God's people to please him in difficult times. Lord, your Word states you chose the foolish things of the world to confound the wise. God, you chose the weak things of the world to shame the strong. God, you chose the lowly things of this world and the despised things—and the things that are not—to nullify the things that are so that no one may boast before you according to your Word in 1 Corinthians 1:27–29.

Father, we will choose to be God pleasers and not man pleasers. We will not try to win the approval of human beings but God himself. We desire to be true servants of the Most High God. Your Word states, "If I were still trying to please people, I would not be a servant of Christ" (Galatians 1:10).

Thank you, God, for being a God above it all. Amen

Have a blessed day, beautiful people. Be a God pleaser.

Do You Believe in Jeremiah 32:27? I Do

Good morning, beautiful people, good morning. This morning, I was praying over a situation that needs divine intervention from the Lord Jesus Christ himself. I joined my faith with another individual, and we prayed and believed the God of miracles would hear our prayer and answer accordingly this early morning.

I have had the privilege to witness miracles. I have interviewed people who have received miracles on my radio broadcast Destiny Moments. I have been part of prayer assignments in which God performed a miracle. I speak with people almost every day who have received miracles. I love the stories of how God uses ordinary people and circumstances to perform these miracles. Isn't life exciting?

I love the book, True Stories of the Miracles of Azusa Street and Beyond. The subtitle, Re-live One of the Greatest Outpourings in History that is Breaking Loose Once Again… Doesn't that get you excited to see to be a part, witness, or bring the miracle?

God's Word says Jesus Christ is the same yesterday, today, and forever (Hebrews 13:8). "Very truly I tell you, whoever believes in me will do the works I have been doing, and they will do even greater things than these because I am going to the Father" (John 14:12). He tells us in Mark 16:20, "Then the disciples went out and preached everywhere, and the Lord worked with them and confirmed his Word by the signs that accompanied it."

I love how he works with us. Someone today may need a miracle, and you may be the answer. Ask Jesus to show you an assignment today that will be beyond yourself that only could be accomplished through the power of the Holy Spirit.

If you are the one today that needs a miracle, ask him and thank him for your miracle. He is the God of miracles. He says in Jeremiah 32:27, "Behold, I am the Lord, the God of all flesh. Is there anything too hard for me?" Let's pray.

Father, for everyone needing a miracle today, we join faith together all across this globe for their miracle. We declare you are alive and well, and your spirit is moving across this land. God of miracles, we believe in you. Yes, yes, we do!

Father, thank you for divine connections and divine appointments. Thank you for ordering our steps into the next season of our destinies. Thank you for every miracle needed today; we receive it.

Father, thank you for using us today to bring a miracle to someone who needs it. Holy Spirit, thank you for leading us to them. You said you would confirm your Word with signs and wonders and miracles, and we believe. We take you, O God, at your Word. Let the river of miracles flow today through each of us. We pray. Amen.

Have a blessed day, beautiful people. Believe in Jeremiah 32:27: "I am the Lord, the God of all the peoples of the world. Is anything too hard for me?"

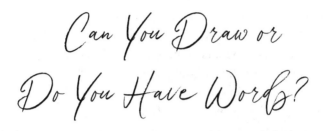

Can You Draw or Do You Have Words?

Good morning, beautiful people. I wanted to share this experience with you today. I have been attending classes for a certificate in care counselor training. One particular class, we were given an assignment that really has stayed etched in my mind. We were setting around a table with seven people at each table. We were given a certain amount of time to draw on a large sheet of paper anything that we desired to draw. Then we were to move to the next chair and add something to the next person's picture. We continued to do this until we had an opportunity to add something on each person's picture around our table. At first, I panicked as I don't draw well, but when I moved to the first chair, I couldn't seem to draw anything but a red heart for the heart of Christ for that person.

However, words kept coming to my mind. So I wrote words on the picture. Then we all moved to the next chair, and the same thing happened. I drew the heart, and words came very quickly to me. Once again, I penned them on the paper. After about the third chair, I raised my hand to make sure this was okay as I prayed, O God, I hope I'm not messing up the people's pictures. I just kept getting words when I would sit in their chair and look at their picture. They assured me it was all okay.

After I sat back in my own chair, and I looked at my picture and what the other six people had drawn on my paper, I was very touched. Some of these folks I knew fairly well and some I barely knew at all. They sure had made my picture beautiful. I smile every time I look at it. It reminds me of that special class with six people drawing on my life. Can you imagine what the world would be like if we drew something nice, kind, beautiful on people's lives around this globe? What if the words we spoke and the pictures we drew on each other's lives today were of the same nature? Encouraging, uplifting, kind, loving, and truly showing the love of Christ.

We don't go around with a large piece of paper around our necks for others to draw on; however, we have the opportunity to make an impact on every life we meet each and every day. It brings to my mind the scripture in 1 Peter 3:8, "Finally, all of you, be like-minded, be sympathetic, love one another, be compassionate and humble."

Another favorite scripture that reminds us to be kind, compassionate, and loving toward all people is Hebrews 13:2, "Do not forget to show hospitality to strangers, for by so doing some people have shown hospitality to angels without knowing it."

Today, go out of your way to be kind. Do a good deed for someone. Everyone you meet today, treat them as they could be an angel. You never know who God will entrust you with this day. Draw a heart on their life to reflect the love of Christ. You may be the only hope they have, and he has entrusted you to draw or write hope and love on their picture (life) today.

Share the love of Christ all across this globe today, even if you need to use words.

Have a blessed day, God's beautiful people. Make a difference in the world today.

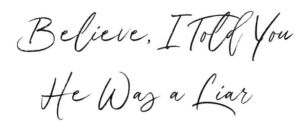

Believe, I Told You He Was a Liar

Good morning, beautiful people, good morning. I was rereading my post, "Fear Is Not Your Portion," this morning. I need to add to it—I just need to.

We have a real enemy. He is a thief, and he comes to kill, rob, steal, and destroy. Jesus came to give us life and life more abundantly (John 10:10).

This thief called fear embeds itself in our thoughts and makes us feel stuck. That is not our portion. We need to get Jesus involved. Ask him, what do you say about this situation, Jesus? Find scripture that pertains to the issue you are dealing with and believe it.

The enemy will use people to try to make us believe that we are not worthy of anything. Sometimes the enemy uses people close to us. He may even try to convince you that you're not even worthy of waking up in the morning. He is a liar, and you need to tell him so.

Today serve notice on fear. Declare today that fear is not my portion. It doesn't matter what tries to come against you. You have God's Word. Take these Holy Scriptures and wield them right back at the enemy. Renew your mind with them every day, and it will keep your mind strong even in the most difficult circumstances.

Pray and ask God for a way of escape out of any negative situation, and he will be right on it. He hears you when you call. Psalm 34:17 tells us the righteous cry out, and the Lord hears them; he delivers them from all their troubles. Yes! He is a Good Father.

"Trust in the Lord with all your heart, do not depend on your own understanding, in all your ways acknowledge Him, and he will make your path straight" (Proverbs 3:5–6).

If the enemy speaks through someone today and tells you that you are not worthy, you're not good enough, you're fat, you're ugly, you're hopeless, you're rejected, you're less than, you're not smart enough, nobody would ever want you, you will never win, you shouldn't be around people, you need to be put in an institution, and the list is endless. You tell the enemy what Jesus says. He will flee.

Beautiful people, "be strong and courageous and do not be afraid, do not be discouraged, for the Lord your God will be with you wherever you go" (Joshua 1:9). His love is for you. "There is no fear in love. But perfect love drives out fear because fear has to do with punishment. The one who fears is not made perfect in love" (1 John 4:18). He loves you, he loves you, he loves you. Believe!

Have a blessed day, God's most beautiful people. Fear is not your portion. You are loved!

Somebody shout victory!

Cancellations

Good morning, beautiful people, good morning. A winter storm warning was announced yesterday for our area. My first thought this morning was: I wonder what has been cancelled for today. As I sit to write my prayer this morning, I just couldn't help thanking God for cancelling the debt I owed through his son, Jesus Christ. We all owed a debt we could not pay.

Isaiah 1:18 says, "Though your sins are like scarlet, they shall be as white as snow."

As I looked out my window, I saw white everywhere. Yes, that's what Christ has done for us. He puts us on a journey that leaves our past behind, and we press on toward the mark for the prize of the high calling of God in Christ Jesus (Philippians 3:14).

Father, thank you for the freshness of the white snow. Thank you for forgiveness of our pasts and for making our lives into more of your image. For anyone that needs a new beginning, today is your day.

You said, "There is therefore now no condemnation for those who are in Christ Jesus" (Romans 8:1). May many receive it today. Amen.

Talk with him today, leave the past in the past, and press on. Begin to prepare for greater new beginnings.

Have a blessed day, beautiful people. Press on.

Covered and Justified

Good morning, beautiful people. This morning, I was reading from 1 John 2 once again. I am so thankful for Jesus Christ. I am so thankful for the price he paid that we can live out our lives with such victory. He truly has our lives covered. Oh, thank him today for mercy and grace. He is so worthy.

My dear children, I write this to you so that you will not sin. But if anybody does sin, we have an advocate with the Father—Jesus Christ, the Righteous One. He is the atoning sacrifice for our sins, and not only for ours but also for the sins of the whole world. (1 John 2:1–2)

Father, thank you for mercy. Thank you for grace. You paid a great price because of your great love for us. Thank you hardly seems adequate. Today help us to love what you love. Empower us to see beyond the actions of man and see the lost soul for what it is…lost.

Thank you for removing the veil that "the god of this age has blinded the minds of unbelievers so that they cannot see the light of the gospel that displays the glory of Christ, who is the image of God" (2 Corinthians 4:4). Thank you that "everyone who calls on the name of the Lord will be saved" (Acts 2:21).

Today we join our faith together all across this globe and declare your Word over the nations. You are the one true God in who man can be saved. May many today hear and see the truth in your Word and believe. Amen.

Have a blessed day, beautiful people. Talk with him today; he has you covered. He loves journeying life with you.

Born to Love

Good morning, beautiful people. Today let's pray about when love came to earth.

In those days Caesar Augustus issued a decree that a census should be taken of the entire Roman world. (This was the first census that took place while Quirinius was governor of Syria.) And everyone went to their own town to register. So Joseph also went up from the town of Nazareth in Galilee to Judea, to Bethlehem the town of David, because he belonged to the house and line of David. He went there to register with Mary, who was pledged to be married to him and was expecting a child. While they were there, the time came for the baby to be born, and she gave birth to her firstborn, a son. She wrapped him in cloths and placed him in a manger, because there was no guest room available for them. And there were shepherds living out in the fields nearby, keeping watch over their flocks at night. An angel of the Lord appeared to them, and the glory of the Lord shone around them, and they were terrified. But the angel said to them, "Do not be afraid. I bring you good news that will cause great joy for all the people. Today in the town of David a Savior has been born to you; he is the Messiah, the Lord. This will be a sign to you: You will find a baby wrapped in cloths and lying in a manger." Suddenly a great company of the heavenly host appeared with the angel, praising God and saying, "Glory to God in the highest heaven, and on earth peace to those on whom his favor rests." When the angels had left them and gone into heaven, the shepherds said to one another, "Let's go to Bethlehem and see this thing that has happened, which the Lord has told us about." So, they hurried off and found Mary and Joseph, and the baby, who was lying in the manger. When they had seen him, they spread the word concerning what had been told them about this child, and all who heard it were amazed at what the shepherds said to them. But Mary treasured up all these things and pondered them in her heart. The shepherds returned, glorifying and praising God for all the things they had heard and seen which were just as they had been told. (Luke 2:1–20)

Father, thank you for bringing love to the world through your Son, Jesus. The good news of the gospel, a Savior was born. This is the greatest love story this world has ever known. The perfect child brought love to a hurting world. So hard for the human mind to comprehend, but we believe.

Father, today we just want to say thank you for when love came down. All across this globe today, we declare he is our king. Amen.

Have a blessed day, beautiful people. You were born to love.

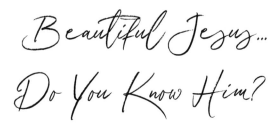

Beautiful Jesus... Do You Know Him?

Good morning, beautiful people. Today, let's pray together from 2 Peter 1:3–11.

His divine power has given us everything we need for a godly life through our knowledge of him who called us by his own glory and goodness. Through these he has given us his very great and precious promises, so that through them you may participate in the divine nature, having escaped the corruption in the world caused by evil desires. For this very reason, make every effort to add to your faith goodness; and to goodness, knowledge; and to knowledge, self-control; and to self-control, perseverance; and to perseverance, godliness; and to godliness, mutual affection; and to mutual affection, love. For if you possess these qualities in increasing measure, they will keep you from being ineffective and unproductive in your knowledge of our Lord Jesus Christ. But whoever does not have them is nearsighted and blind, forgetting that they have been cleansed from their past sins. Therefore, my brothers and sisters, make every effort to confirm your calling and election. For if you do these things, you will never stumble, and you will receive a rich welcome into the eternal kingdom of our Lord and Savior Jesus Christ.

Father, thank you for your Word of instruction. Today we pray for increase of goodness, knowledge, self-control, perseverance, godliness, mutual affection, and love to rule our hearts. We pray, beautiful Jesus, for effective lives. We desire to be world changers and not have the world change us.

We declare we will live our lives according to the Word of our Lord and Savior, Jesus Christ. There is only one true God in whom man can be saved.

We will let our yes be yes and our no be no. Today, all across this globe, we will together declare we are followers of Jesus Christ. Amen.

Have a blessed day, beautiful people. Praise beautiful Jesus!

Broken Heart?

Good morning, beautiful people. If you have brokenness in your heart today, let me introduce you to Christ the Healer.

Today, let's pray scriptures together for the brokenhearted.

The Lord is near to the brokenhearted and saves the crushed in spirit. (Psalm 34:18)

He heals the brokenhearted and binds up their wounds. (Psalm 147:3)

My flesh and my heart may fail, but God is the strength of my heart and my portion forever. (Psalm 73:26)

Come to me, all who labor and are heavy laden, and I will give you rest. Take my yoke upon you, and learn from me, for I am gentle and lowly in heart, and you will find rest for your souls. For my yoke is easy, and my burden is light. (Matthew 11:28–30)

He sent out his word and healed them, and delivered them from their destruction. (Psalm 107:20)

Father, thank you for healing our hearts when it was broken. Thank you for sending the body of Christ to intercede on our behalf. We received the victory.

Today we pray for the brokenhearted all across this globe. You are ever so close to them. We join our faith from the north, south, east, and west and declare your Word over every broken life.

We thank you that you came to bind up the brokenhearted and set the captives free. Today, may the healing oil of Gilead be poured out and hearts be made whole again all across this land.

Weeping may endure for the night, but joy comes in the morning. Amen.

Have a blessed day, God's beautiful people. This is the day the Lord has made, and we will rejoice and be glad in it. Now take your whole heart and go help someone with a wounded heart.

Caring

Good morning, beautiful people, good morning. Today, let's pray about caring for others.

Not looking to your own interests but each of you to the interests of the others. (Philippians 2:4)

Let us not lose heart in doing good, for in due time we will reap if we do not grow weary. So then, while we have opportunity, let us do good to all people, and especially to those who are of the household of the faith. (Galatians 6:9–10)

Be kind and compassionate to one another, forgiving each other, just as in Christ God forgave you. (Ephesians 4:32)

Whoever shuts their ears to the cry of the poor will also cry out and not be answered. (Proverbs 21:13)

Father, today we pray you pierce our hearts once again for the needs of your people. Use us today to make a difference in our world. Thank you that you change the hearts of man. Today we ask you to turn hearts of stone to be hearts soft and pliable, ready for the master's use. We say yes, Lord, use us today. Amen.

Have a blessed day, beautiful people. Show the world you care.

Can He Have It All?

Good morning, beautiful people, good morning. Today let's pray about surrendering our lives.

Father, thank you for the grace to surrender our whole lives to you. You don't want just a part of our lives, you want all of it. You hold the whole world in your hands. You take our surrendered hearts and line it up with your will.

Oh, Heavenly Father, you know what is best for us. As we surrender our hearts totally to your will, your plan for our lives unfolds according to your master plan. Thank you for destiny.

Today we just want to say, "God you can have it all." (Can you honestly say that?) Every plan, every dream, every desire, every thought, and every part of our hearts and lives, we surrender it all.

Do with our lives as you will, O God. Your plan is our heart's desire. We will continue to keep our eyes focused on your Word as you lead us each and every day. Unfold your will, O God, for our lives, we pray. You can have it all. Amen.

Have a blessed day, beautiful people. Surrender it all to Jesus and believe. Today take time to read John 13.

"Be still, and know that I am God. I will be exalted among the nations, I will be exalted in the earth!" (Psalm 46:10).

Can You Get Out of the Way?

Good morning, beautiful people, good morning. We have so much to celebrate every day. I love kids; they are so innocent and pure hearted. The Bible says a child shall lead them (Isaiah 11:6). How can we not stand with them and for them? Keep us humble and on the straight and narrow path, God. May we truly be fit for the master's use. We pray. Amen.

Jesus answered, I am the way and the truth and the life. No one comes to the Father except through me. (John 14:6)

Yet to all who did receive him, to those who believed in his name, he gave the right to become children of God. (John 1:12)

Whoever believes in the Son has eternal life. (John 3:36) For there is one God and one mediator between God and mankind, the man Christ Jesus. (1 Timothy 2:5)

Father, thank you that you provided the only way to forgiveness of sin and eternal life. Everyone must decide for themselves what they will believe. Lord, we admit today. Without you, we have nothing. But with you, we have everything. As much as we desire to see others come to the saving knowledge of Jesus Christ, only they themselves can choose to believe.

There are a lot of voices in our world today. However, the Bible (God's Word) is the only book that provides the steps to peace with God. Jesus the ultimate sacrifice for the sins of mankind. He is the one true God in whom man can be saved.

If people choose religion, they have nothing but rules and regulations that will keep them shackled. If they choose relationship, it's a journey of freedom. For your Word says that You have come to give us life and life more abundantly (John 10:10).

God, today we join our faith all across this globe and thank you for the outpouring of your spirit that has already started. We declare we are beginning to see the greatest awakening this land has ever known. For you said, O God, it's not by might nor by power but by your spirit (Zechariah 4:6) You also said if we prayed and believe, we would receive (Mark 11:24).

Thank you, Father, for many coming to know you all across this globe today. Thank you for the awakening that has already begun in our nation. Amen. Have a blessed day, beautiful people, for this is the day the Lord has made, and we will rejoice and be glad in it. Tell him you are ready to get out of the way and give yourself to him.

Come to the Beautiful River

Good morning, beautiful people, good morning. I went to the airport last week to pick up a friend. As I watched the screen of pictures of Aroostook County where I live, I became so excited as it showed pictures of the river. Aroostook means beautiful river. Oh, how I love the river. Everything we need is in the river. I just had to declare it once again. From the Crown of Maine to seven continents of the world, we declare the river is flowing. This beautiful river has refreshing like you have never experienced before.

I have heard many times over my life. Now don't put all your eggs in one basket, Angel. Well, I can tell you. I have put all of my eggs in this basket. I can tell you without a doubt, the river is here, and it is flowing. Everything we need or will ever need is in this river. It is the river of God. What a beautiful river. Doesn't that make you want to go to the river?

Once you have experienced the love of Christ for yourself and have been set free, once you have been to the river, it changes life, it just does. My prayer is that you will come to the river often. You can come as many times as you need to, and Jesus Christ will always meet you there. He paid the price with his precious blood, and there is nothing that he can't and won't do for you according to his will. Let's pray.

Father, thank you for the river. Thank you for taking broken lives and making them whole again. Jesus, you truly are the river of life. Wash over us and bring cleansing, refreshing newness and destiny. As we come to the river today, break up any stones in our heart and make us pliable and fit for our master's use. Oh, how we love to meet you at the river.

Yesterday is gone, and our today is bright, and our future is in your hands. Every day is a new beginning, and for every person who will come to the river and talk (pray) with you all across this globe, they can be washed by the same blood. I have experienced a lot of things in my life but nothing like being washed by the blood of Jesus Christ. Oh, I just love to meet you at the river, Jesus.

You rebuild lives, set people free, and put us on the path of life that you had for us before the foundations of the earth (Psalm 139). There is so much joy in this river; we can hardly contain it. Oh, I love how the river is flowing, the most beautiful river I know. Amen and amen.

Somebody shout, "Aroostook!" Somebody shout, "Beautiful river!" Somebody shout, "The beautiful river is flowing from Aroostook County, Maine!"

Have a blessed day, beautiful people. Fill your day with much love, laughter, and joy at the river, the river of our God.

"There is a river, the streams whereof shall make glad the city of God, the holy place of the tabernacles of the most high" (Psalm 36:4).

Choices, Decisions, and Peace

Good morning, beautiful people, good morning. Today let's pray about the door to our heart, the choice we make, and the peace we all can have.

Here I am! I stand at the door and knock. If anyone hears my voice and opens the door, I will come in and eat with that person, and they with me. (Revelation 3:20)

Jesus answered, I am the way and the truth and the life. No one comes to the Father except through me. (John 14:6)

Yet to all who did receive him, to those who believed in his name, he gave the right to become children of God. (John 1:12)

Whoever believes in the Son has eternal life. (John 3:36)

For all have sinned and fall short of the glory of God. (Romans 3:23)

Therefore, since we have been justified through faith, we have peace with God through our Lord Jesus Christ. (Romans 5:1)

For what I received I passed on to you as of first importance: that Christ died for our sins according to the Scriptures, that he was buried, that he was raised on the third day according to the Scriptures. (1 Corinthians 15:3–4)

For there is one God and one mediator between God and mankind, the man Christ Jesus. (1 Timothy 2:5)

Father, thank you that you provided the only way to forgiveness of sin and eternal life. Everyone must decide for themselves what they will choose. Lord, we admit today, without you, we have nothing, but with you, we have everything. As much as we desire to see others come to the saving knowledge of Jesus Christ, only they themselves can choose.

There are a lot of voices in our world today. There is a lot of talk about embracing other faiths. However, the Bible (God's Word) is the only book that provides the steps to peace with God. Jesus the ultimate sacrifice for the sins of mankind. He is the one true God in whom man can be saved. If people choose religion, they have nothing but rules and regulations that will keep them shackled. If they choose relationship, it's a journey of freedom. For your Word says that "you have come to give us life and life more abundantly" (John 10:10).

Father God, today we join our faith all across this globe and believe for an outpouring of your spirit. We declare we will see the greatest awakening this land has ever known. For you said, O God, it's not by might nor by power but by your spirit (Zechariah 4:6). You also said, O God, if we prayed and believe, we would receive (Mark 11:24). Thank you for many coming to know you all across this globe today. Amen.

Have a blessed day, beautiful people. For this is the day the Lord has made, and we will rejoice and be glad in it

Cut It Loose, Give God Control

Good morning, beautiful people, good morning. Today let's cut loose areas in our lives that we have no control over.

But I gave them this command: Obey me, and I will be your God and you will be my people. Walk in obedience to all I command you, that it may go well with you. (Jeremiah 7:23)

Be still, and know that I am God: I will be exalted among the nations, I will be exalted in the earth. (Psalm 46:10)

Father, thank you that you, O God, are in control. Today we release everything that keeps us bound (relationships, worry, fear, children, and future). We cut the cords of control and put our trust in you. Your Word states, "For the which cause I also suffer these things: nevertheless I am not ashamed: for I know whom I have believed, and am persuaded that he is able to keep that which I have committed unto him against that day" (2 Timothy 1:12).

Today we realize not everyone is going to like us, and we are not going to agree on every issue. What are our own personal convictions and the way we live our lives according to your Word will cost us. We cut loose every hindrance and declare we are on the narrow path of following Jesus.

Matthew 7:21 states, "Not everyone who says to me, 'Lord, Lord,' will enter the kingdom of heaven, but only the one who does the will of my Father who is in heaven."

All across this globe today, let's be obedient to do the will of our Father. Amen.

Have a blessed day, beautiful people. For this is the day the Lord has made, and we will rejoice and be glad in it.

Agree? Yes or No?

Good morning, beautiful people. Some friends and I set up a simple prayer booth at our local fair. It is so exciting to see God answer the prayers. One lady we prayed with yesterday. Before she even got to her car, the answer came. She was so excited she brought a friend and came back to tell us how God had answered the prayer that we prayed together and have us pray for the needs of her friend.

One thing I have learned, God answers prayer. We lift up the requests, and he sends down the answer, Jesus style. I love to pray the Holy Scriptures because they are powerful. Let's pray for your needs today.

Father, thank you for hearing and answering prayer. You said in Jeremiah 29:12, "Call on me and come and pray to me, and I will listen to you." In Mark 11:24, "Therefore, I tell you, whatever you ask for in prayer, believe that you have received it, and it will be yours."

We lift up every reader (tell him your situation and what you have need of), and we come praying in agreement for the answer. "Says we have not because we don't ask God" (James 4:2). We are asking today and receiving according to the Holy Scriptures. Amen.

Have a talk with him (pray). He will journey life with you. If you don't know him, invite him into your heart. Just ask, have a heart to heart chat with him. Since you were created in his image anyway (Genesis 1:27). He knows you best.

Have a blessed day, beautiful people. Pray, believe, and receive (Mark 11:24).

Always a Great Day

Good morning, beautiful people. This morning, I was glancing through one of my journals. As a writer, I pen my thoughts on pages of paper all the time. This morning, I ran across this writing I penned years ago. I wanted to share it with you today.

My Days…

My days are filled with peace when anxious thoughts arise. You sent me your Word to speak.

My days are filled with joy. You, O God, are my strength and joy.

My days are filled with so many questions. You, O Lord, are my wisdom.

My days are filled with planning. You, O Lord, order my footsteps.

Jesus, you are the way maker. Your love for me goes beyond what I know.

You turn my sorrow into gladness. You turn my shame into honor.

You turn my suffering into joy.

Where you are is where I want to be. In your presence, O Lord.

Teach me to pray, O God. Teach me to prophesy. I want to fulfill your plan.

Let's pray. Father, thank you for your love. We love your presence. O God, thank you for being the most loving Father ever known to mankind. Thank you for hearing our many prayers and always being for us and saying yes to every prayer that is best for us.

As we continue to put our trust in you, you will bring to pass every plan, purpose, and destiny for our lives.

Have a blessed day, beautiful people. He's working out his plan. Believe.

"You are a chosen generation, a royal priesthood, a holy nation, his own special people, that you may proclaim the praises of him who called you out of darkness into his marvelous light" (1 Peter 2:9).

America, Do You Believe in the God of Miracles?

Good morning, beautiful people, good morning. Let's pray for America today.

Father, thank you that you are a God of miracles. No matter what it looks like, we will see the greatest outpouring of your spirit in America. Why? How can we be sure? Because you said it, and your Word does not lie. Forgive our unbelief, O God, we believe. Amen.

In the last days, God says, I will pour out my Spirit on all people. Your sons and daughters will prophesy, your young men will see visions, your old men will dream dreams. Even on my servants, both men and women, I will pour out my Spirit in those days, and they will prophesy. I will show wonders in the heavens above and signs on the earth below, blood and fire and billows of smoke. The sun will be turned to darkness and the moon to blood before the coming of the great and glorious day of the Lord. And everyone who calls on the name of the Lord will be saved. (Acts 2:17–21)

Have a blessed day, beautiful people. Believe in the God of miracles. You will see the greatest outpouring of his spirit this world has ever known. Yes, yes, we will!

America's Passion

Good morning, beautiful people. Let's pray America's passion would be prayer.

Father, America is in your hands. We don't need to operate in a spirit of fear. We either belong to the kingdom of darkness or the kingdom of light. Every person on this planet can ask and come into the kingdom of light, and you will change the course of their destiny. That's your heart according to John 3:16.

No political hype or scare tactics can change the Word of the Lord. We will put our trust in you. America was such a proud country, and we all have been humbled by the need of our risen Savior, Jesus Christ.

Prayer is going up to your throne room in every state for our country. Churches, groups of praying people, and various meetings have ignited. The all-consuming fire of God is moving. We say here in Maine (name your state), "Blaze, Spirit, blaze. Blaze across this land."

We will not be afraid. God you are right on time in every situation. In God, we place our complete trust. We continue to stand on "the earth is the Lord's, and everything in it, the world, and all who live in it" (Psalm 24).

We are in the best hands ever known to mankind, the hands of the Lord.

Have a blessed day, beautiful people, and don't be afraid. Jesus is working on our behalf.

"God opposes the proud but shows favor to the humble" (James 4:6).

An Indescribable Gift For You

Good morning, beautiful people, good morning. Together let's pray these Holy Scriptures.

Thanks be to God for his indescribable gift! (2 Corinthians 9:15)

For the wages of sin is death, but the gift of God is eternal life in Christ Jesus our Lord. (Romans 6:23)

For it is by grace you have been saved, through faith—and this is not from yourselves, it is the gift of God. (Ephesians 2:8)

A man's gift makes room for him, and brings him before great men. (Proverbs 18:16)

Father, thank you for this free gift of salvation (totally unearned and undeserved). Thank you for the gift you have placed inside every person in whom was created in your image. Today we join our faith together and believe many will come to know you this day. The greatest love story... the cross.

We join our faith together all across this globe today and declare the gift you have given us will make room for us. You said you would give us the words to speak in front of kings and rulers. Together we will walk out your Word. Thank you for open doors. Amen.

Have a blessed day, for this is the day the Lord has made, and we will rejoice and be glad in it.

And God Said, and We Believe

Good morning, beautiful people, good morning. Did you ever know something so deep in your heart, mind, body, soul, and spirit that nobody could convince you otherwise? You know because you know because know. It's always your final answer, and nothing can make you change your mind. You know what I am talking about, right? Let's pray today from Genesis 1.

Father, thank you for that you created the heaven and the earth. And the earth was without form, and void; and darkness was upon the face of the deep. And the Spirit of God moved upon the face of the waters. And, God, you said, let there be light: and there was light. And, God, you saw the light, that it was good: and you divided the light from the darkness. And you, O God, called the light day, and the darkness you called night. And the evening and the morning were the first day. And God you said, let there be a firmament in the midst of the waters, and let it divide the waters from the waters. And, God, you made the firmament and divided the waters which were under the firmament from the waters which were above the firmament: and it was so. And, God, you called the firmament heaven. And the evening and the morning were the second day. And, God, you said, let the waters under the heaven be gathered together unto one place, and let the dry land appear: and it was so. And, God, you called the dry land earth; and the gathering together of the waters called the Seas: and, God, you saw that it was good. And, God, you said, let the earth bring forth grass, the herb yielding seed, and the fruit tree yielding fruit after his kind, whose seed is in itself, upon the earth: and it was so. And the earth brought forth grass, and herb yielding seed after his kind, and the tree yielding fruit, whose seed was in itself, after his kind: and, God, you saw that it was good. And the evening and the morning were the third day. And God you said, let there be lights in the firmament of the heaven to divide the day from the night; and let them be for signs, and for seasons, and for days, and years: And let them be for lights in the firmament of the heaven to give light upon the earth: and it was so. And God you made two great lights; the greater light to rule the day, and the lesser light to rule the night: you made the stars also. And God you set them in the firmament of the heaven to give light upon the earth, and to rule over the day and over the night, and to divide the light from the darkness: and you O God saw that it was good. And the evening and the morning were the fourth day. And God said, Let the waters bring forth abundantly the moving creature that hath life, and fowl that may fly above the earth in the open firmament of heaven. And God you created great whales, and every living creature that moveth, which the waters brought forth abundantly, after their kind, and every winged fowl after his kind: and you, O God, saw that it was good. And, God, you blessed them, saying, be fruitful, and multiply, and fill the waters in the seas, and let fowl multiply in the earth. And the evening and the morning were the fifth day. And, God, you said, let the earth bring forth the living creature after his kind, cattle, and creeping thing, and beast of the earth after his kind: and it was so. And, God, you made the beast of the earth after his kind, and cattle after their kind, and everything that creepeth upon the earth after his kind: and God saw that it was good. And, God, you said, let us make man in our image, after our likeness: and let them have dominion over the fish of the sea, and over the fowl of the air, and over the cattle, and over all the earth, and over every creeping thing that creepeth upon the earth. So, God, you created man in your own image, in the image of God created he him; male and female created he them. And, God, you blessed them, and God said unto them, be fruitful, and multiply, and replenish the earth, and subdue it: and have dominion over the fish of the sea, and over the fowl of the air, and over every living thing that moveth upon the earth. And, God, you said, Behold, I have given you every herb bearing seed, which is upon the face of all the earth, and every tree, in the which is the fruit of a tree yielding seed; to you it shall be for meat. And to every beast of the earth, and to every fowl of the air, and to everything that creepeth upon the earth, wherein there is life, I have given every green herb for meat: and it was so. And, God, you saw everything that you had made, and, behold, it was very good. And the evening and the morning were the sixth day.

Father, we believe. Amen.

Have a blessed day, God's beautiful people. Enjoy everything he has created and enjoy the fullness of your day. You are loved and created in the image of God. Believe because he said so.

Everything Plus More

Good morning, beautiful people, good morning. This morning, I reflect back on this past weekend at the ACTS retreat at the Christian Life Center in Frenchville, Maine. God was everything plus more. I love to be with God's people, and I love how he showers his people with his presence and love. The theme, "With God, all things is possible" (Matthew 19:26), empowers me once again to believe him to be everything I need in life. He always gives to me beyond my expectations.

Today wherever you are on the journey, and whatever you are experiencing in life, please know that God loves you, and he wants to be your everything. He wants to journey life with you. He wants to show himself as Father Abba and shower you with his agape love. It's everything plus more. Let's pray.

Father, thank you for being everything to us. You truly make our hearts overflow with your goodness. You touch hearts and bring healing in ways only you, our Creator can do.

Father, thank you for "John 3:16." Your presence on the earth makes our hearts overflow. Your abundant love resonates in our hearts because you have touched our lives. You take impossible situations and set us free.

Father, as we journey the day, continue to remind us that with you all things are possible. Because of your great love, we can believe and know that you are working all things out for good in our lives. Amen.

Have a blessed day, God's beautiful people. Make him your everything.

Face-to-Face, a New Hallelujah!

Good morning, beautiful people, good morning. I was remembering this morning as a child going to visit the church in Allagash, Maine. A young girl named Molly would stand and say she couldn't wait to see Jesus face-to-face. It seemed every time I was there. She would stand and say that. Although I didn't understand until many years later what she meant, it stayed with me. Oh, how I long to know him deeper and see him face-to-face.

As I interview people face-to-face almost every day, I feel the need for people to feel valued, cared for, understood, and loved. Isn't it great that we have a man who journeys life with us face-to-face? The many facets of his love are beyond what we can even imagine. His tender care that says, "I am the good shepherd. I know my sheep and my sheep know me" (John 10:14). Let's pray.

Father, 1 Corinthians 13:12 tells us, "For now we see through a glass darkly, but then face to face now I know in part, but then shall I know even as also I am known."

Father, we want to know you more. We want to know the many facets of your love. New dimensions, trading religion, and rules made by man for relationship with our God. Strip away everything that keeps us from face-to-face with you, God.

Father, your tender care and freedom for every race and every nation moves us to worship you each and every morning. Arise is us today, O God, face-to-face that's our heart's desire.

Awaken, world, and prepare the way of the Lord. Everything belongs to him (Psalm 24:1–3).

Have a blessed day, beautiful people. Together, let's seek his face.

For Everything You Need

Good morning, beautiful people, good morning. This morning, I was thinking about prayers God answered for me recently. I have had some big projects I have been working on for some time. I had trusted people who let me down. They overstepped boundaries and tried to control God's plan. Isn't it funny sometimes as people, we all feel we know what's best for others at times, but we need to allow God to lead and instruct his own people. He is well able. After praying about the issue, God sent me people that assisted me in completing what needed to be done. Forever I will be grateful.

One thing about God, he always wants what's best for us. He isn't controlling and he is there moment by moment to lead the way. Today, sit a while with him, let him lead you beside the still waters. It is there you will find rest for your soul. You can always take him at his Word. He is a gentle Father, not overbearing, full of kindness, goodness, and love toward us. Let's pray.

Father, thank you that you hear every prayer. You tell us you hear us when we call. "I love the Lord, because he hath heard my voice and my supplications. Because he hath inclined his ear unto me, therefore will I call upon him as long as I live" (Psalm 116:1–2).

Father, you know every detail about every person you created. You know what's best for each of us. Thank you for leading us today and every day. Thank you for answering our prayers. We continue to put our trust in you. Amen.

Have a blessed day, God's beautiful people. He is there for everything you need.

Aren't You Excited, People?

Father, thank you that everything comes alive in the river. Thank you for pouring out your spirit. Thank you for rising up the church with power. You always have and always will have the final say. I get so excited, God.

Thank you, Father, that the earth belongs to you (Psalm 24). You created it, and you know how to make every crooked way straight. Yes, you do!

As born-again believers and followers of Christ, we truly are sons and daughters of a King (2 Corinthians 6:18). Doesn't that get you excited, people? Everything we have need of is found in him. He is the best Father. Father Abba, there is nothing that's impossible with you (Luke 1:37).

Our hearts are so full of love, joy, and peace in the Holy Ghost (Romans 14:17). Thank you that you said if you be lifted up, you will draw all men unto yourself (John 12:32).

All across this globe today, lift Jesus higher. Amen.

Have a blessed day, beautiful people. He loves you. Talk with him today and get in the river.

Get Out of Mind Prison

Good morning, beautiful people, good morning. Time to get released from the cages.

Father, we pray for every person who needs to get out of prison in their mind today. We recognize the hurts, the pain they are in, and we know you are the answer. Holy Spirit draw them to yourself today, we pray. The Bible tells us in Romans 10:8.

The word is near us; it is in our mouth and in your heart," that is, the message concerning faith that we proclaim: If we declare with your mouth, "Jesus is Lord," and believe in our hearts that God raised him from the dead, you will be saved. For it is with your heart that you believe and are justified, and it is with your mouth that you profess your faith and are saved. As Scripture says, "Anyone who believes in him will never be put to shame." For there is no difference between Jew and Gentile—the same Lord is Lord of all and richly blesses all who call on him, for, "Everyone who calls on the name of the Lord will be saved."

Also in Psalm 68:5–8, it says,

It says that you are a father of the fatherless, and a judge of the widows, is God in his holy habitation. God setteth the solitary in families: he bringeth out those which are bound with chains: but the rebellious dwell in a dry land. O God, when thou wentest forth before thy people, when thou didst march through the wilderness; Selah: The earth shook, the heavens also dropped at the presence of God.

Doesn't that make you want to do a little happy dance this early morning? These holy scriptures are true. Don't take my word for it, try it out for yourself. I'll try not to say I told you so!

Have a blessed day, beautiful people. Read your Bible and believe. Ask the Holy Spirit to teach you. His answer is the same to everyone all across this globe. Yes!

Who Is Lying to You?

Good morning, beautiful people, good morning. Whatever the enemy of your soul is saying to you today, you speak the Word of God. You tell fear to take a hike. Snap your finger and tell stress, anxiety, fear, and anything, and everything else that's trying to take the life right out of you to be gone in the powerful name of Jesus. Depression flee, be gone. This is not my portion. Stress, you take a hike. You're not on my agenda today. I am a child of God. Today is the last day, enemy of my soul, you lie to me. I will win this fight. You declare that over your life and live in peace every day, my friend. Peace, sweet peace is a good trade for an anxious mind.

Believe me, the enemy of your soul will try to come back and steal your peace. If he can't get you on one level, he will try another. Your position walking in the peace of God makes him angry. So many people take medication just to have an ounce of peace. I am not against medication, take it if you need it, but learn to fight the good fight of faith journeying with Jesus as well. You only have one enemy, and you can defeat him at every level. Jesus made a public spectacle of him, and you can too. God gave us the tools. It is the Word of God.

If this demonic spirit can't get you at this level, it will try to capture you in another way. Fight, beautiful people, fight. Believe these holy scriptures and declare them over your life every day. I get talked about sometimes by people. They ponder my heart's motives. They wonder how I get to do what I do. They wonder who I think I am. Some think I need more schooling. Some think I need to do this. Some say I should do that. Some see my shortcomings and expound about that. Some just downright lie about me. If I listened to everybody, if I listened to the lies, I would never do anything, and I would be defeated. Some people are jealous of me. Some wish I was dead. Dear God, if the enemy of your soul can't get you on one level, he will try another. Learn to fight beautiful people, fight.

Jesus said, "I have come to give you life and life more abundantly" (John 10:10). I didn't say it, Jesus did. What does that abundant life look like, you may ask? It's not the sports car in your garage that makes you work eighteen hours a day to pay for it. It's not keeping up with Jones's. It's not in the things you own, it's a matter of the heart. Stop striving, beautiful people, and live life according to the plan of God for your life.

Live in the peace of God that transcends all understanding (Philippians 4:7). Fight for it and keep it. Fight!

"He has shown you, O mortal, what is good. And what does the Lord require of you? To act justly and to love mercy and to walk humbly with your God" (Micah 6:8).

Not Debatable, Life

Good morning, beautiful people. Today let's pray for the unborn.

Yet you brought me out of the womb; you made me trust in you even at my mother's breast. From birth, I was cast upon you; from my mother's womb you have been my God. (Psalm 22:9–10).

For you created my inmost being; you knit me together in my mother's womb. I praise you because I am fearfully and wonderfully made; your works are wonderful, I know that full well. My frame was not hidden from you when I was made in the secret place. When I was woven together in the depths of the earth, your eyes saw my unformed body. All the days ordained for me were written in your book before one of them came to be. (Psalm 139:13–16)

This is what the LORD says—he who made you, who formed you in the womb, and who will help you. (Isaiah 44:2)

The word of the LORD came to me, saying, "Before I formed you in the womb, I knew you, before you were born, I set you apart; I appointed you as a prophet to the nations." (Jeremiah 1:4–5)

Father, we thank you for life. Today we join our faith across this globe and pray for the unborn. God, you are a God who loves children. Today we pray you strengthen the women who are carrying child.

Father, we join our faith and declare safe houses for women and children will open all across this globe. We pray a hedge of protection around the unborn. Give every woman wisdom, Lord, and send them help from on high. May they know the truth and don't buy into the world's lies.

Father, for women who have suffered from abortion and the aftermath and all the devastation that came to them from that choice, we bring them to the healing waters of Jesus Christ today. Lord, thank you for making your women whole again. "There is therefore no condemnation for those who are in Christ Jesus" (Romans 8:1). Only you, O God, can accomplish this in a woman's life, only you.

Father, you are our Father, and you know every detail of our lives, even to the number of hairs on our heads (Matthew 10:30). You know what your people need to be whole again. Thank you for setting this up for your people who have bought into the lie– it wasn't a life. Your Word is not debatable.

Thank you for hearing and answering our prayer today. Amen.
Have a blessed day, God's beautiful people. Life is not debatable.

April Showers Bring?

Good morning, beautiful people. April showers bring May flowers. Yes, they sure do. As I glance out my window this morning, this rain is washing away our snow. Yes! Soon the flowers will bloom once again.

I was reminded this morning of a sketch that an elderly woman gave me at the Healing Waters Conference last weekend. It was a beautiful flower with a bird and a heart. A vision she had while I was speaking. She apologized for her not so good drawing. The lady doesn't even realize she is an artist. Her prophetic gifting and encouragement were such a great blessing to me personally. I love how God uses the gifting in each of us to be a blessing to the world.

As we are winding down the days of this month, let's thank God for his rain. May we see lives bloom once again.

Father, thank you for heaven's rain. Let the healing balm of Gilead rain down on your people, O God. May lives bloom again where there has been hurt, pain, and injustice. Your grace is enough for us all. Cleanse us, Holy Spirit, from the inside out.

Thank you for rain, O God. Wash over us with your healing rain so that new life can bloom once again in our lives. Wash over our regions like never before. Our ground, our hearts are prepared to receive it. May our lives bloom just like the wildflowers.

April showers bring may flowers. Maine, you will never be the same. Your days have never looked like this before. Father, thank you for this rain that is bringing the greatest move of God to our region. We so receive it. Faith matters in Maine, yes, it sure does. Pour it down on us like never before, O God.

We pray for every beating heart without Jesus; we call you forth. Jesus has the freedom plan for your life. Believe! You are part of the latter rain. He welcomes you in his kingdom today. Jesus paid the price, and he has the keys to your freedom and the plan for your life. Amen.

Oh, somebody shout freedom! Talk with him today (pray), beautiful people. He loves you and desires to make the sun shine in your life once again.

"But by the grace of God I am what I am, and his grace which was bestowed upon me was not in vain" (1 Corinthians 15:10).

Are We Hearing Correctly?

Good morning, beautiful people. Today let's pray about hearing God's voice.

My sheep listen to my voice; I know them, and they follow me. (John 10:27)

For all who are led by the Spirit of God are children of God. (Romans 8:14)

In those days when you pray, I will listen. If you look for me whole-heartedly, you will find me. (Jeremiah 29:12–13)

Trust in the Lord with all your heart; do not depend on your own understanding. Seek his will in all you do, and he will show you which path to take. (Proverbs 3:5–6)

Father, thank you that we can hear your voice. Today we ask you to remove anything and everything that is not allowing us to be in tune with your Holy Spirit. We commit everything we do to you, O God. Lead us this day, we pray.

Thank you for divine appointments, and may our ears be open to hear what the spirit of the Lord is saying. Nothing compares to the promise we have in you. Amen.

Have a blessed day, God's beautiful people. Make sure you are hearing your Heavenly Father's voice.

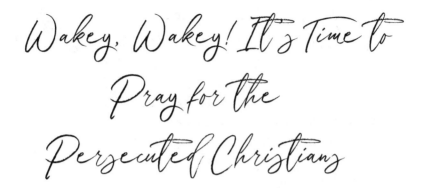

Wakey, Wakey! It's Time to Pray for the Persecuted Christians

Good morning, beautiful people, good early morning. Last evening, I attended a prayer gathering for the persecuted Christians. We joined faith here in Maine for different countries that are experiencing persecution for their faith. The gathering was well organized and was a full house. Thank God he hears us when we call.

I get undone at injustice. Hearing stories of what is happening to people because of their faith moves me this early morning to hit my knees in prayer. What is happening to women and girls in Africa and other parts of the world is just unacceptable. We cannot be silent anymore. We have a voice, and we must speak out. Why do I sense time is running out? Together, let's join faith and pray this morning for our world.

Father, thank you that we can still share our faith, and it doesn't cost us our lives. Father, forgive us when we haven't been diligent to pray for the persecuted Christians. Forgive us God when we were too timid to share our own faith with people who are perishing all around us.

Words are hard to come by this morning God as I know your heart is that none would perish. You said in Matthew 24:14, "The Gospel of the Kingdom shall be preached in all the world as a witness to all nations and then the end will come. Why do I sense time is running out?"

Father, thank you for the army of God that you have raised up for such a time as this. Strengthen them, may they be bold as a lion and gentle as a dove. Your kingdom come, your will be done, O God. The world belongs to you. You created it, and you will have the final say. Amen.

Have a blessed day, beautiful people. Share your faith and pray for the persecuted Christians.

Push Through the Opposition

Good morning, beautiful people. We all face opposition in our lives. We have circumstances we face each and every day that keeps us dependent on the one who created us. It keeps us on the potter's wheel as he continues to shape our lives. He will remove all our insecurities as we put our trust in him.

No matter what the opposition is, we have the victory. We must stay focused, stay in prayer and in his Word. As we push through each day, we build strong faith muscles as we see his plan unfold.

Push through any challenge you have to complete the assignment he has given you. Don't lose momentum on the last lap before the victory. He already won the battle for you. Push, push, push through. You got this!

"We are hard pressed on every side, but not crushed; perplexed, but not in despair; persecuted, but not abandoned; struck down, but not destroyed" (2 Corinthians 4:8–9).

Father, thank you that no matter what opposition comes our way, we have the victory through you. We continue to fight the good fight of faith believing the Holy Scriptures and every promise you have given us. We will complete our God-given assignments. Amen, beautiful people?

Thank you, Father, for the joy in the journey as we strengthen and enlarge our tent pegs. We are pushing through. Amen.

Have a blessed day, God's beautiful people. Push, push, push again, keep pushing. You will look back soon and say wow, I completed my God-given assignment.

Somebody shout victory!

I Just Gotta Tell You

Good morning, beautiful people, good morning. God is so good, so faithful, and so true to his Word. He is a good God, and his love is just downright amazing. I love the heart of my Heavenly Father. The double heart brings back to remembrance this early morning of Job and how he received double from God (Job 42).

"For your shame ye shall have double" (Isaiah 61:7). Who could ever give us that but God himself. In the prayer room at Whited Bible Camp in the little town of Bridgewater, Maine, last Thursday evening, I lay prostrate on my face before my God to see what he would have me say to his people. This is what I penned.

Tell Them...

Tell them I love them... Tell them they are mine... Tell them I will never leave them nor forsake them. Tell them they are precious gems... Tell them I see them as perfect... Tell them they reflect my image... Tell them not to look back. Tell them to look straight ahead... Tell them I laid out the red carpet for them... My blood is enough... Tell them, tell them, tell them again!

Tell them I love them... Tell them they are mine... Tell them I will never leave them nor forsake them. Tell them they are precious gems... Tell them I see them as perfect... Tell them they reflect my image... Tell them not to look back. Tell them to look straight ahead... Tell them I laid out the red carpet for them... My blood is enough...

Tell them, tell them, tell them again!

So there you have it. I told you, and I told you again.

"It is the goodness and kindness of God that leads man unto repentance" (Romans 2:4).

You just gotta know him for yourself. Read the book of John in your Bible and ask God for revelation. He loves you, beautiful people. Yes, it is true. He gives you back double. Oh, the heart of our Father!

Take Me to the King

Good morning, beautiful people. I am awake early this morning to speak with the King. It seemed yesterday I kept singing the song, "*Take Me to the King.*" I'm not sure where I heard it before, but this early morning, I'm looking the lyrics up on YouTube. All I know is we are in need of the King of Glory.

Last evening, I attended a public prayer night at the local middle school here in Presque Isle, Maine. A town that is in need of the King. Many churches, pastors, and parishioners, including a group of young people, attended from across Aroostook County to petition the King for their towns, cities, churches, leaders, business, etc. In unity, we joined our faith as pastors both men and women alike prayed a burden that the Lord had laid on their heart. Our world is in need of an awakening, and I believe it has begun here in the crown of Maine.

So this morning I ask you to join your faith with mine and let's believe for your town, your city, your leaders, and your business all across this globe. Let faith arise, O God, in your people to believe you have not forsaken our nation. You will awaken us, and we will see the greatest shaking this world has ever known. To that, we all say amen. We are ready to receive from our King. Let's pray.

Father, we thank you for your grace. It truly is amazing. We come before you today with a burden for our nation and nations across this globe. Lord, you paid a dear price on a cross for us, and we need your help. You said in your Word, the Holy Bible, you hear a prayer. So thank you, King of Glory, as we join our faith today for our president, for our leaders now and to be in the future. God, you are over the government, and our eyes and prayers are fixed on you. We pray for our schools, military, churches, business, and homes. Lord, we need you.

We cry, Father Abba, come heal our land. Today, Lord, we pray for the poor, the needy, the homeless, and the broken. Lord, I ask you to meet their need. I know you to do this through everyday ordinary people just like me and every reader across this globe. Lord, help us all to harken unto your voice. Father, we pray we would be a people who you would use for your glory. Help us to share our portion, our talents with another.

Forgive me, forgive us, Lord, for when we had plenty and not shared our abundance. Father, change our mind-sets, our vision. Father, thank you for opportunities. I thank you I will work today on a job that's motto is to listen, to learn, to care, and to respond. Your great love for humanity cost you everything, and today I pray we all will do our part. I pray you bless our land, God. Bless our crops and the work of our hands.

O God, thank you for hearing and answering our prayer. We believe, we receive. Together, we pray the Lord's Prayer.

Our Father, who art in heaven, hallowed be thy name. Thy Kingdom come, thy will be done on earth as it is in heaven. Give us this day our daily bread. And forgive us our trespasses, as we forgive them that trespass against us and lead us not into temptation, but deliver us from evil. For thine is the Kingdom, the power and the glory for ever and ever. Amen. (Matthew 6:9–13)

Have a blessed day, God's beautiful people.

Thanks, God

Good morning, beautiful people, good morning. Let's give our God some thanks today.

Father, today we just want to say thanks for all you have done for us. You are a good Father, and you take good care of us. You are not only a good Father but the best friend any person could ever have. We just want to say thanks.

You walk with us through the trials of life, and you bring us to the other side. No matter what a person is going through, you want to journey with them every day through your Word and the power of your Holy Spirit. We just want to say thanks.

Thanks for believing in every life, for having purpose, destiny, and a plan for every person today. We just want to say thanks.

Have a blessed day, beautiful people. Give him some thanks.

"And whatever you do, whether in word or deed, do it all in the name of the Lord Jesus, giving thanks to God the Father through him" (Colossians 3:17).

The Baby That Changed the World

Good morning, beautiful people. Life is a precious gift to enjoy. Every day we can choose how we will live it. It is such a blessing journeying life with Jesus Christ. His birth changed the world forever. Some people are looking for a sign, a reason to believe. The sign was given years ago, the birth of Jesus Christ. The baby who changed the world and changes lives forever. You haven't lived until you have journeyed life with him. Let's pray.

Father, thank you for Jesus the baby who changed the world. Our lives have forever been touched because of your great love for humanity. Thank you for the Holy Spirit who leads and guides us each and every day. You came to give the world life and life more abundantly (John 10:10). Oh, how we thank you.

Father, thank you for the opportunity to share the good news of the birth of Christ, his death and resurrection so that the world may know that he lives. He is the one true living God. May people experience the love, the joy, the happiness, his healing power, and the peace of journeying life every day with him.

Father, may the love that you have for us be enough to satisfy every longing of our heart. May your life you so willingly laid down at the cross be enough for people to believe today. Amen.

Have a blessed day, God's beautiful people. Believe in the name of the Lord Jesus Christ and be saved.

"If you declare with your mouth, Jesus is Lord, and believe in your heart that God raised him from the dead, you will be saved" (Romans 10:9).

The Battle Belongs to the Lord

Good morning, beautiful people, good morning. Today let's pray scriptures on spiritual warfare.

God is just: he will pay back trouble to those who trouble you and give relief to you who are troubled, and to us as well. This will happen when the Lord Jesus is revealed from heaven in blazing fire with his powerful angels. (2 Thessalonians 1:6–7)

The Lord will rescue me from every evil attack and will bring me safely to his heavenly kingdom. To him be glory for ever and ever. (2 Timothy 4:18)

The weapons we fight with are not the weapons of the world. On the contrary, they have divine power to demolish strongholds. We demolish arguments and every pretension that sets itself up against the knowledge of God, and we take captive every thought to make it obedient to Christ. (2 Corinthians 10:4–5)

Father, thank you that you made a public spectacle of our enemy. Today we thank you that no weapon formed against your children will prosper according to your Word.

Father, today we declare "no weapon formed against us will prevail, and you will refute every tongue that accuses us. This is the heritage of the servants of the Lord, and this is their vindication from you, declares the Lord" (Isaiah 54:17).

Father, thank you that we need fret not because we are overcomers by the blood of the lamb and the Word of our testimony.

Today we declare victory, for the battle belongs to you. Amen. Have a blessed day, God's beautiful people. The battle belongs to the Lord.

The Believe Calendar

Good morning, beautiful people. No matter what you are believing for, don't give up.

I love Christmas. Oh, how I love the spirit of Christmas. There is nothing that can snuff out my love for Christmas, no nothing. I learned the true meaning of Christmas years ago. Journey with me from now to Christmas, and let's pray, let's believe, and let's receive together.

I was writing my daily post last week and remembered a gift from my secret Santa (a former coworker) a few years ago. It was a believe calendar. I loved that calendar. I enjoyed the pictures, the verses, and all the different sayings. It was from a local church, which made it quite special.

I love to believe. I love to pray and believe God for big things. I must say, it's mostly thing's money can't buy. I pray and believe for people to know Christ intimately. I believe for people to be warm on cold nights. I believe for food for people that may be hungry. I believe for hurting hearts to be made whole again. I believe for miracles from the creator of the universe to whomever needs it. That takes me to my next point.

Miracles happen every day; they really do. However, I believe this time of year, we experience more of the miraculous. Maybe I'm just more sensitive to it, or I'm looking closer for it, I don't know, but I believe it's miracle season. Can you believe with me too?

The whole miraculous birth of Jesus, who can deny it was anything but ordinary. Jesus was humble and meek, a true servant, a foot washer. So must we. However, we serve; we must try hard to do it unto the Lord. Whether behind a desk in a hidden cubicle or in the public's eye, we work unto him. He is a God who sees it all, and it's all for his glory anyway. I want to be found faithful to the miracle maker. How about you? Aren't you excited about the journey?

I remember years ago now, I was cleaning in my kitchen and felt impressed to take half of my groceries to a particular family. I argued with the thoughts I was having as that didn't make sense. My sister, Flo, had just gone to Sam's and blessed me with a whole trunk load of groceries. Surely this couldn't be God asking me to give half away.

I decided to go polish the dining room table and get out of the kitchen. As I glanced up, I saw a candle I had in the China cabinet. I had purchased some candles from my daughter, Brooke's, class at school as they were raising money. I so heard *tell her I love her*. I was beginning to realize this was real. This was an assignment from the Creator himself. I hurriedly packed up the groceries and the candle and went to this family's house. At first, there was no answer, and I was just going to leave it by the door. As I turned to leave, the woman came out, and I told her my wild story. She invited me in and showed me her bare refrigerator. I was humbled. I was excited that I heard the voice of the Lord and humbled he wanted to use me to be his hands and feet extended. I asked God to forgive me for arguing about the food (it was never about the food anyway) and promised I would try to be a better servant. I so want to be a vessel in which he can trust. How about you? Are you ready and willing to be used by God himself?

God speaks to us. Do you hear him? I listened to a pastor's sermon, *"Ears to Hear,"* recently, and it sparked a fire to listen for God's voice more closely. Are you tuned in? Together, let's agree to listen for any assignments he may give us. Are you available? Let's pray.

Father, your Word is full of miracle stories. Today, O God, we join our faith across this globe and pray for eyes to see and for ears to hear and courage to obey. We believe (what miracle do you need? Ask and *believe* if you need one). Lord, you came as a servant, and may we serve wherever you may ask of us. Count us in, God, we totally give 100 percent of our lives to you (tell him honestly right where you are at. He will get you to the next level). Lord, use your body today (the body of Christ, that's us), and may we be found faithful. Let the miracles unfold for your glory, Lord, your glory alone. Amen.

Have a blessed day, God's beautiful people. Believe in Jesus. Believe in miracles. Amen.

"My sheep listen to my voice; I know them, and they follow me" (John 10:27).

This Love Never Fails

Good morning, beautiful people, good morning. Today let's pray and believe these scriptures on love together.

For God so loved the world, that he gave his only Son, that whoever believes in him should not perish but have eternal life. (John 3:16)

No, in all these things we are more than conquerors through him who loved us. For I am sure that neither death nor life, nor angels nor rulers, nor things present nor things to come, nor powers, nor height nor depth, nor anything else in all creation, will be able to separate us from the love of God in Christ Jesus our Lord. (Romans 8:37–39)

But God, being rich in mercy, because of the great love with which he loved us, even when we were dead in our trespasses, made us alive together with Christ— by grace you have been saved. (Ephesians 2:4–5)

But God shows his love for us in that while we were still sinners, Christ died for us. (Romans 5:8)

But you, O Lord, are a God merciful and gracious, slow to anger and abounding in steadfast love and faithfulness. (Psalm 86:15)

Father, thank you for your love. Today all across this globe, may love abound. We pray that people who struggle to receive your love would have a deep revelation. You loved us while we were yet deep in our sin, even to die for us. Thank you for your Word and changing us more into your image each day. Oh, how you love us. So much you have us etched on the palm of your hands (Isaiah 49:16). Amen.

Have a blessed day, beautiful people. You are loved, people, you are loved.

Is God Over the Government?

Good morning, beautiful people, good morning. Praying for the appointment of the next supreme court justice has been on my mind once again. Maybe because it has been all over the news. Today let's petition our God to put in place his choice for the next supreme court justice. Let's thank him for hearing and answering our prayer for such a time as this.

Father, your Word tells us that you are over the government. Psalm 22:28 tells us that "dominion belongs to the Lord and he rules over the nations." Thank you, Father, that the next supreme court justice is a man or woman who you have ordered according to your plan for America. You are rebuilding the ancient ruins and places of devastation according to Isaiah 61. America's days are in your hands.

We join our faith around this globe for your appointee. We pray in agreement this morning, Matthew 18:19 for the next official supreme court justice. You said we have not because we do not ask God (James 4:2). So today we are asking you, and we are thanking you for hearing our prayer and putting into place the right person. Lord, the person who has a passionate heart for you and a passion to see America restored.

Thank you, God, for raising him or her up for such a time as this. Thank you for ordering their footsteps right up the steps of the supreme court (Psalm 37:23). We are ready to receive your appointment. Amen.

Have a blessed day, God's beautiful people. Thank him today for life.

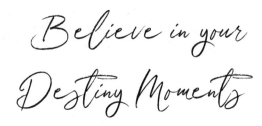

Believe in your Destiny Moments

Good morning, God. Good morning, beautiful people. Isn't it great to be journeying life with a man who can part a Red Sea? A man who can change a life, a direction in an instant. I am always so blessed when I see God himself interacting with everyday ordinary people. I always pray they can see it too.

There is nothing he won't do for his people who he loves. I don't believe in coincidences; I believe in destiny. I believe the Holy Scriptures are life to our very bones. I believe he holds every one of our days in his hands. Today let's thank him once again for destiny. Every breath we take is a destiny moment to enjoy according to his Word.

Father, thank you that all the days ordained for us were written in your book before one of them came to be (Psalm 139:16). You know the beginning from the end. Thank you that we were your idea before anyone else's. You created us in your image (Genesis 1:27).

Today we just simply come in your presence to tell you we love you and pray and join our faith all across this globe today and pray this prayer together, the Lord's Prayer from Matthew 6:9–13.

Our Father which art in heaven, hallowed be thy name. Thy kingdom come, thy will be done in earth, as it is in heaven. Give us this day our daily bread. And forgive us our debts, as we forgive our debtors. And lead us not into temptation, but deliver us from evil: For thine is the kingdom, and the power, and the glory, forever. Amen.

Gives us eyes to see the many miracles you perform every day. You truly are the God of miracles.

Have a blessed day, God's beautiful people. Thank God for the blessings and miracles he gives us every day.

Happy People Talk

Good morning, beautiful people. In March of 2015, I had the opportunity to be one of the representatives to attend the fifty-ninth session of the Commission on the Status of Women at the United Nations in New York. As I was standing in line, I found myself talking to some of the most interesting people I have ever met. Several young women asked me to attend a parallel event, Women and Girls Across the Generations, in which I did. It really was very touching, and I was blessed by their stories and music from this woman's organization. They then inquired if I would agree to do an interview. As a radio talk show host, I know how nerve-racking this can be when you are asked right on the spot, but I agreed. I shared some of my story from a poor decision in my teenage years.

A few days ago, I was searching the internet for freelance writing positions for women's magazines. I spoke with Jeannette Bennett from Bennett Communications. Jeannette told me she had put together this video, in which I was included, Happy People Talk, from my interview in New York.

Yes, Happy People Talk. For me, my voice came alive when I talked about my abortion to another safe person. I found deeper healing through a post-abortion Bible study, Forgiven and Set Free by Linda Cochrane. I completed this Bible study with another post-abortive woman at our local pregnancy care center. My voice became stronger, and today, yes, I can say I am happy.

Please don't suffer in silence. If you have been affected by the trauma of abortion, allow me to introduce you to the healing waters of Jesus Christ. I am a woman who has touched the hem of his garment, and you can too. He is no respecter of persons. My life verse: "So if the Son sets you free, you will be free indeed" (John 8:36). You do not need to suffer in silence any longer.

You were made to enjoy life. Have a voice and be free. Yes, happy people talk.

Have a blessed day, God's beautiful people… Be happy and share your faith.

Has God Ever Failed You?

Good morning, beautiful people, good morning. As I was reflecting back this morning on some events, trials, and loss in my own life, it brought me to ask myself some tough questions. Do I feel that God has failed me in any area of my life? I like to talk things over with God, to tell him what I am experiencing. I want to know how he sees things.

Do you feel God has ever failed you? Maybe he didn't answer the prayer like we thought he would. Maybe the answer looked differently than what we expected, but God's Word tell us in Romans 8:28, "All things work together for good for those that are called according to his purpose. He did say all things?" The call of God causes us to see the work of God in our hearts and to awaken us to his Word. So yes, you are called of God.

As I reflect back, I can honestly say I am thankful that God didn't answer the prayer according to my thoughts or wishes. He answered what was best for me. Some people say he will give you only what you need. I don't believe that either. I have so much more than what I need. He blesses our lives as we surrender our wills, desires, and believe that he knows what is best. He is and will always be the good Father. Let's pray.

Father, thank you for your love, goodness, mercy, grace, joy, happiness, peace, and all that we have journeying life with you. Your Word tells us in Deuteronomy 31:6 to be strong and courageous. Do not be afraid or terrified because of them, for the Lord your God goes with us; he will never leave us nor forsake us.

Thank you that our life is in your hands, and our good Father knows what's best. You always answer our prayers according to your will and desire. It is beyond what we can think or imagine. It's called the abundant life (John 8:36).

Have a blessed day, God's beautiful people. God never fails us!

Are You Reaching Higher?

Good morning, beautiful people. Just as the caterpillar transforms into a beautiful butterfly, that is what God is desiring to do in each of our lives. As we surrender our will, overcome our fear, God releases us into our destiny.

Today let's ask God for the grace to surrender everything we are or will ever become to him. Let's pray.

Father, thank you for the grace to surrender our lives to you. We want to walk in the perfect plan you have for our lives. Please instill your will in our heart today. Heavenly Father, you know what is best for us. As we give up control and let your plan come forth, destiny will unfold.

Today we recommit our surrendered lives to you. Every plan, every dream, and every desire, we bring before you today. We submit to the plan you have predestined for us. Do with our lives as you will, we pray. Fulfilling your plan is our heart's desire as we journey each and every day with you.

Father, transform our lives more into your image and cause us to soar higher than the eagles. Amen.

Have a blessed day, God's beautiful people. Reach higher, surrender, and soar.

Every Heart Is Hungry for This

Good morning, beautiful people, good morning. I am blessed to meet so many of God's beautiful people. One thing I discovered is that everyone has a need to be loved and cared for. Everyone wants to feel like they matter. Every breathing life has a soul that is hungry to be filled.

I attended a prayer meeting Saturday night, and this morning, I smile as I reflect back on that evening. I turned around in my chair to pray with an elderly couple for the persecuted Christians. The dear couple shared their names, and then the sweet lady went on to tell me how much in love they are. "Married for fifty-four years and never had an argument," she went on to share.

I laughed and said, "This must be what they call marital bliss."

She chatted a bit more, and my serious nature was concerned we wouldn't have enough time to pray our assignment. Somehow time stood still, and we got it all done. His yellow Hawaiian shirt and his head nodding into agreement as she chatted about the love between them left an impression on me. I asked God that night to allow me to meet up with them again the next day as I attended one of their two morning Sunday services.

Out of the corner of my eye, I saw them. She had gotten a bit lost trying to find her seat after returning from the ladies' room. He was half standing and waving her in the right direction as the pastor continued to speak. It was the cutest sight to behold. After service, I met them once again in this quite large auditorium full of people. He came up and thanked me for my prayers the prior evening and said I was quite inspirational. The last sight I saw as I drove away from that beautiful church that morning was this elderly couple driving off in their antique car. They really touched my heart. Let's pray.

Father, thank you that love is like a river. Thank you for your love for us, your gentle care. You draw us back to yourself when we have gone astray. When we understand the love of God, it changes everything. You are the best Father, and we ask you, O God, to be in driver's seat of our lives. Fill every empty place today in our hearts, good Father, so like a river, we can let it flow from one to another. Amen.

Have a blessed day, God's beautiful people. Share some abundance of love from your heart today. The world needs it.

"Let love and faithfulness never leave you; bind them around your neck, write them on the tablet of your heart" (Proverbs 3:3).

What Is Your Greatest Asset?

Good morning, beautiful people. Today let's pray Psalm 119:105–112 together.

Your Word is a lamp for my feet, a light on my path. I have taken an oath and confirmed it, that I will follow your righteous laws. I have suffered much; preserve my life, Lord, according to your Word. Accept, Lord, the willing praise of my mouth, and teach me your laws. Though I constantly take my life in my hands, I will not forget your law. The wicked have set a snare for me, but I have not strayed from your precepts. Your statutes are my heritage forever; they are the joy of my heart. My heart is set on keeping your decrees to the very end.

Father, thank you for the Word of God. It is alive and active. It is sharper than any double-edged sword. It penetrates even to dividing soul and spirit, joints and marrow; it judges the thoughts and attitudes of the heart (Hebrews 4:12). We submit our lives to your Word. (Tell him if that's true.) No matter what situation or circumstance we find ourselves in, your Word is our greatest asset.

Today, Lord, we pray for our words. May they build another person up, encourage someone that may be losing hope, and bring the love of Christ to people all around us today. Help us to be silent when we need to be silent, speak when we need to speak. Help us to speak life words.

Holy Spirit, help us to remember what we read in the Holy Scriptures and keep this book of the law always on our lips, meditate on it day and night so that we may be careful to do everything written in it. Then we will be prosperous and successful according to Joshua 1:8. Amen.

Have a blessed day, beautiful people. The Word of God is your greatest asset.

Do You Know the King?

Good morning, beautiful people, good morning. Today I wanted to share a journey I went on several years ago. I believe it was a supernatural journey. It was on a Saturday evening, and I went to a local church here in Presque Isle, Maine, for their evening service. Allison, a dear friend, came running up to me and said, "You need to be at the world conference in Orlando, Florida, in January."

I never heard of such an event and got excited when I get to go anywhere past Houlton, Maine, (which is only an hour away). She's a dear friend and always laughing and bringing joy to everyone around her. I thought she was just being giddy or something. She noticed I wasn't taking her seriously and said, "*Oh, no, Angel*, I'm serious. I spoke to Jeff and Judy about this, and they agreed *you need to be at this world conference in January."*

So I did the only thing I knew what to do, pray. I admit though, I just prayed a prayer something quick like "Jesus, you want me to go to the world conference? Set it up." I really never thought too much about it in the days that followed.

Then an acquaintance from another local church called to tell me about a brochure in the mail they received about the world conference in Orlando, Florida. She thought I should consider it. She further explained they had a time-share that would be available for my use. I was getting a bit excited. I was really beginning to believe there was a purpose for my attendance at this world conference. I asked for some time off from my job here at the local community action program. Believe me, in the winter months, it's action okay. Leaving for a week in January, one of our coldest and busiest times of the year when another coworker would be in Israel, seemed almost like a no brainer. Somehow I got a yes, and I knew this had to be a God thing.

I didn't buy Christmas gifts that year and saved my money to buy airline tickets as I wanted to take my family along. Every day, several times a day, I would check the prices of airline tickets. Finally two days before Christmas, I had enough money to book the tickets. My oldest daughter had decided she wasn't going to go (she likes to plan ahead, and this last-minute planning isn't her cup of tea). Sometimes when you are operating on faith, you don't have the money nor the plan until the very last minute. I told God he should change that because it isn't easy, but he makes the rules, and it's called faith.

I tried at the office I was working at to book the tickets, and a blue line would go through it when I would hit the final button to order the tickets. I tried hard to no avail. I went to the public library and tried to book the tickets; the very same occurrence (the blue line) hanging it up, and it wouldn't go through. The librarian kindly tapped my shoulder and said "We are closing early today, and we close the computers down fifteen minutes early."

Every day those airline tickets rise in price, and I just barely had enough money. I was getting a bit anxious.

That afternoon, a dear sister in Christ called to see if I was going to the candlelight service at the local Church. I told her if I went, I would be going by myself, and I didn't like that very much. She excitedly told me how the year prior, she went all by herself, and it was just pure worship. I hung up the phone and prayed a little prayer asking for forgiveness about thinking of myself and not desiring to go to worship him. I told her about this world conference. It seemed like I would be attending, and she agreed to pray for me.

The candlelight service was a beauty to behold. The presence of God with all the beautiful candles still makes my heart leap as I pen this. As I entered the church, the lady from the other church inquired if she could speak to me after service. I tried not to fret about it too much, although I caught my mind wondering at times. After the beautiful candlelight service, a sweet couple walked over and gave me a check toward this trip. I was humbled but blessed. Then the lady from the other church, God had impressed on her heart on Thursday to help book the tickets and inquired if I needed a rental car from Bangor to Boston? (My dear sisters, Flo and Dee, always agree to take me to Bangor.) Well, it sure seemed like this was a God setup.

I was at this meeting at the world conference at the Swan and Dolphin Hotel and was leaving the first session. A lady, pushing a woman in a wheelchair, who was a diabetic, inquired if I knew where they could get a snack. I did not but offered my banana and yogurt. They accepted, and now I was the one in need of a snack as I was hungry.

There were thousands of people all over, and I walked up to a lady sitting near a window and inquired of her the same, "*Do you know where I can get a snack?*" She tried to tell me but must have seen my puzzled look and decided to go with me. As we were chatting, she told me she had a house for sale in Oceanside, California. I prayed with her to sell her house, and we exchanged our address and phone numbers.

It was there in the prayer room at the Swan and Dolphin Hotel in Orlando, Florida, that I inquired of my King why he wanted me there. This is what I penned.

To write, teach, and deliver the message of inner healing for women based on the Word of God. To have a safe house, a place of refuge to meet the physical, mental, emotional, and spiritual needs of women in crisis. A place of refreshing, a place of ministry to bring hope, healing, and deliverance to the women of Aroostook County and Western New Brunswick. Also, I penned this: To journey with, encourage and equip women to fulfill the purpose of God in their lives using the gifts and talents they have been given. This looked quite an exciting assignment.

A short time went by, and the lady from California mailed me a letter stating her house had sold and enclosed was a check for $150.00. I put the check in an account under Healing Waters Women's Ministry. Each month, I felt inspired to send in a monthly donation to the Inspiration Television channel. I also sent a small donation to a ministry in the United Kingdom. It didn't take too long to empty out the account. I really had very little idea of what I was doing but wanted to do the right thing. I knew it was God money, not mall money.

Today I embark on the next step in founding the ministry of Healing Waters Women's Ministry, I covet your prayers. I closed the bank account but took out a pen and began to journal my journey of inner healing with my King. I soon will be publishing my life story and plan to publish devotionals and Bible studies as well. Through all of this, I discovered I had a gift; God himself gifted me to write.

What talent and gifts have you been blessed with? Today, inquire of the King if you do not know. He has a way of setting things up. Get ready to take your next step in fulfilling your greatness for Christ. Let me take you to the King.

I sense the day has come that the Esther's and the Deborah's will arise and make a great impact on this nation and the nations around this globe.

There's a whole lot more to this journey, but I must end for now. I need some rest before the morning dawn, and it's time to go corporately go worship my king, but first let's pray together.

Father, Creator, Jesus, and our King, we worship you. Today we want to know you more. We seek your face and desire to use the gifts and talents you have placed within us. Today, Father, we join our faith and thank you for those Healing Waters all across this globe. May many come to you this day and find rest for their weary soul we pray. Amen.

Have a blessed day, beautiful people. Time to worship the king.

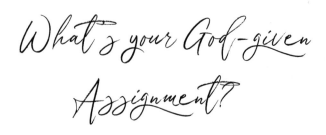

What's your God-given Assignment?

Good morning, beautiful people, good morning. Let's pray about our God-given assignments today.

See, I have this day set thee over the nations and over the kingdoms, to root out, and to pull down, and to destroy, and to throw down, to build, and to plant. (Jeremiah 1:10)

For we wrestle not against flesh and blood, but against principalities, against powers, against the rulers of the darkness of this world, against spiritual wickedness in high places. (Ephesians 6:12)

They said to me, "Those who survived the exile and are back in the province are in great trouble and disgrace. The wall of Jerusalem is broken down, and its gates have been burned with fire." (Nehemiah 1:3–4)

When I heard these things, I sat down and wept. For some days, I mourned and fasted and prayed before the God of heaven.

Father, thank you for giving each of us an assignment for our lives. Today we believe you have called us to be ambassadors to the nations, an ambassador to bring the message of the Gospel of Jesus Christ. Whatever our part is big or small you can count on us. We will do our part.

You said you would give us the words to speak before kings and rulers, and we believe your Word. Today we receive that promise.

Father, may every reader know their God-given assignment (if you don't know yours, ask him, and he will tell you). Thank you for open doors for your people all across this globe. Together we join our faith and declare open doors to the nations to bring the message of Jesus Christ. Amen.

Have a blessed day, God's beautiful people. You are on God assignment.

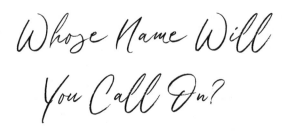

Whose Name Will You Call On?

Good morning, beautiful people, good morning. Today let's call on Jesus together.

Everyone who calls on the name of the Lord will be saved. (Romans 10:13)

To the church of God in Corinth, to those sanctified in Christ Jesus and called to be his holy people, together with all those everywhere who call on the name of our Lord Jesus Christ—their Lord and ours: Grace and peace to you from God our Father and the Lord Jesus Christ. I always thank my God for you because of his grace given you in Christ Jesus. For in him you have been enriched in every way—with all kinds of speech and with all knowledge— God thus confirming our testimony about Christ among you. (1 Corinthians 1:2–6)

Because he bends down to listen, I will pray as long as I have *breath!* (Psalm 116:2)

Father, thank you that you hear us when we call. You know our concerns before we even express them. You desire your people to call upon you. You have all the answers.

Today all across this globe, we call on Jesus. As we come to you each and every morning, your mercies are new. God, thank you that the answer is on the way. Forgive us, Lord, for when we called on others before you. Jesus, the greatest name we know. Amen.

Have a blessed day, God's beautiful people. Call on Jesus.

Are You Ready to Begin Your Journey Today?

Good morning, beautiful people. This morning let's pray for broken people. This may not be you today, but it certainly could be you tomorrow. Life's journey has a way of bringing buried hurts and pains to the forefront. We all experience sorrows on the path of life. If we put Jesus at the center of our lives, he takes the sorrow, the brokenness, the abuse, the hurt, and all the pain and removes the sting. He fills the void with his love and rebuilds our lives. Who wouldn't want to experience a life full of love, joy, and peace?

Father, we give you our heart today. We surrender all of our life to you and our life's journey. Thank you for taking the broken pieces and putting them back together. You remove all the obstacles and show us the light of Christ.

Father, as we journey life, looking through your eyes, we understand that life is a road of love, compassion, and service. Empower us to live this life through the power of the Holy Spirt. May the overflow of the abundance of love in our hearts touch the broken and bruised among us. We pray.

Our Father in heaven, hallowed be your name, your kingdom come, your will be done, on earth as it is in heaven. Give us today our daily bread. And forgive us our debts, as we also have forgiven our debtors. And lead us not into temptation, but deliver us from the evil one. For thine is the kingdom, and the power and the glory, forever. Amen. (Matthew 6:9–13)

Have a blessed day, beautiful people. Is today the day you start your journey?

We Want You Back Again

Father, our hearts are hungry to see you move on the earth like never before. We know your heartbeat, God. Your heart is that none should perish but have life. Father, we want you back again. Forgive us, God, for pushing you out of our government, schools, courts, and our daily lives. (Tell him.) Thank you for being a covenant-keeping God despite what man has done.

Father, thank you for the sending the fire. God, your people are hungry to touch the flame again all across this globe. Thank you for hearing and answering prayer as we have done as you have instructed us according to 2 Chronicles 7:14, "If my people, which are called by my name, shall humble themselves, and pray, and seek my face, and turn from their wicked ways; then will I hear from heaven, and will forgive their sin, and will heal their land." We want you back in our world again.

Thank you for pouring out your spirit according to Acts 2:17. We are ready to receive it. Thank you for healing our land. Our lives, our world is ready to receive the greatest outpouring this world has ever known. Amen.

Have a blessed day, God's beautiful people. Thank him for pouring out his spirit on your region today. Thank him for the fire. Thank him for fulfilling his promises. He loves you, yes, you!

You Were Born for Greatness

Good morning, beautiful people. You were born for greatness. Yes, you! Can you believe you were born to be a world changer? Believe it! It's really true. The world can have a different look today because you are here. You may feel insignificant today. Stop lying to both yourself and the world and declare, "I am a world changer."

Today, rise up and take that next step. This step will look different for everyone all across this globe today as we are all designed differently. Do you realize you don't have any limits? Only the ones you place on yourself? What lies are you believing? I'm not smart enough, educated enough, the right size, I'm too fat, too skinny, too tall, or too short. My hair is the wrong color, I am not attractive enough, my feet are too big, my nose isn't right, and I can't type fast enough. I don't know how, my parents didn't teach me, I have been abused, I have no money, my car is too old, and this can't be me. I just can't be a world changer. Nope not me, I am one of the unlucky ones. I don't know why. It never works for me. I am always behind the eight ball, and what would people think? Admit it, your believing a lie.

You may ask, "How do you know for sure that I am a world changer?" I'm glad you asked. I am penning these words this morning, but long before the foundations of the earth, the Lord had a plan for your life. These are your Creator's words. You don't have to believe me but choose today to believe the one who created you. He knit you together and formed you in your mother's womb. He knows you best.

The manual for daily living is the Bible. Today, bring it out, dust it off, upload it, download it, read it, and most of all, believe it. You were designed to be a world changer. You are. You are. You are.

Let's pray.

Father, we thank you for life. We thank you for designing us. Thank you for creating us to be world changers. Today wherever we find ourselves, we thank you, for you knew we'd be right where we are today long before we knew.

We break off every lie that we are believing of ourselves (name them if you can), for we are just right. We are wonderfully made, and we want to make our mark on the world today. Thank you, God, for ordering our footsteps right into destiny.

Today we declare we are world changers. We believe, we believe, we believe. We want to be all that you have created us to be. We are world changers.

Thank you for the plans you have for us, plans to prosper us, not to harm us but to give us a hope and a future (Jeremiah 29:11). Thank you for giving us our God assignments. Empower us to fulfill the purpose you have given us. Amen.

P.S. Hand knit should read your tag this morning on whatever you are wearing.

"For you created my inmost being; you knit me together in my mother's womb. I praise you because I am fearfully and wonderfully made; your works are wonderful, I know that full well" (Psalm 139:13–14).

You have greatness. Believe.

Are You Rich?

Good morning, beautiful people. We are rich. Believe. Let's pray.

Father, today we stop the busyness of the world around us and reflect on all that we have to be thankful for. Family, friends, places to live, and food to eat, we are wealthy beyond measure. To make our lives the richest it could ever be is journeying every day with Jesus. He makes all things beautiful in his time.

Today we join our faith together all across this globe for those that don't know him. We petition your throne room once again that you would draw man unto yourself. You said, O God, that it is not by might nor by power but by your spirit.

Thank you for pouring out your spirit on our world today.

Father, we pray that you would protect our borders. Expose what is being done in the dark, the schemes, and the ploys of our enemies. Keep us safe, we pray.

Today we declare your Word in Deuteronomy 28.

If you fully obey the Lord your God and carefully follow all his commands, I give you today, the Lord your God will set you high above all the nations on earth. All these blessings will come on you and accompany you if you obey the Lord your God: You will be blessed in the city and blessed in the country. The fruit of your womb will be blessed, and the crops of your land and the young of your livestock—the calves of your herds and the lambs of your flocks. Your basket and your kneading trough will be blessed. You will be blessed when you come in and blessed when you go out. The Lord will grant that the enemies who rise up against you will be defeated before you. They will come at you from one direction but flee from you in seven. The Lord will send a blessing on your barns and on everything you put your hand to. The Lord your God will bless you in the land he is giving you. The Lord will establish you as his holy people, as he promised you on oath, if you keep the commands of the Lord your God and walk in obedience to him. Then all the peoples on earth will see that you are called by the name of the Lord, and they will fear you. The Lord will grant you abundant prosperity—in the fruit of your womb, the young of your livestock and the crops of your ground—in the land he swore to your ancestors to give you. The Lord will open the heavens, the storehouse of his bounty, to send rain on your land in season and to bless all the work of your hands. You will lend to many nations but will borrow from none. The Lord will make you the head, not the tail. If you pay attention to the commands of the Lord your God that I give you this day and carefully follow them, you will always be at the top, never at the bottom. Do not turn aside from any of the commands I give you today, to the right or to the left, following other gods and serving them.

Have a blessed day, beautiful people. You are rich in him.

What Exactly Did God Say?

Good morning, beautiful people, good morning. Did you ever know something so deep in your heart, mind, body, soul, and spirit that nobody could convince you otherwise? You know because you know because you know. It's always your final answer, and nothing can make you change your mind. You know what I am talking about, right? If God said it, we believe it, and we receive it. His Word is life to our bones. Our redeemer is alive and well. Amen? Amen! Let's pray.

Father, thank you for that you created the heaven and the earth. In Genesis 1, you tell us the earth was without form and void, and darkness was upon the face of the deep. And the Spirit of God moved upon the face of the waters. And, God, you said, let there be light, and there was light. The night: you made the stars also. And, God, you set them in the firmament of the heaven to give light upon the earth and to rule over the day and over the night and to divide the light from the darkness, and you, O God, saw that it was good. And, God, you said, let us make man in our image. So, God, you created man in your own image.

Father, you knew we would need a redeemer. So in John 11:25–26, you tell us, "I am the resurrection and the life. The one who believes in me will live, even though they die; and whoever lives by believing in me will never die. Do you believe this?" Father, yes, we believe.

Father, you tell us in Luke 24:2–3 that when the stone was rolled away and when they entered, they did not find the body of the Lord Jesus. Thank you for your resurrection and your resurrection power.

Father, we believe. Amen.

Have a blessed day, God's beautiful people. Enjoy everything he has created and enjoy the fullness of your day. You are loved and created in the image of God. Believe!

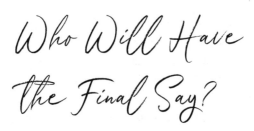

Who Will Have the Final Say?

Good morning, beautiful people, good morning. Every day we read and pray God's promises over our lives and the lives of those we love. The biggest problem I have discovered in my journey thus far is that we must stay in faith, believing. He is a covenant-keeping Jesus, and his Word is final. He never breaks a promise ever. It's a done deal, forever settled. It doesn't matter what it looks like, doesn't matter what people say. We can ask seven people their opinion and get seven different answers. God's answer; his promises are best. Stay focused on the promises of God, beautiful people.

No person/s, no devil in hell, and no scheme of the enemy can take God's promises away from us. The enemy might put up a fight, but he always loses—always. Our God made a public spectacle of him, disarmed his power and authority (Colossians 2:15). Don't you just love it? The enemy of our soul has been disarmed, totally stripped, and made a spectacle of right out in public eye for all to see. When God shows up on the scene, things change quickly, beautiful people, quickly. His timing is always best, and our position must remain in faith, believing. We need to remind ourselves of that every day. I need to remind myself of that every day. Let's pray.

Father, thank you that you are a covenant-keeping God.

In the beginning was the Word and the Word was with God, and the Word was God. Through him all things were made; without him nothing was made that has been made. In him was life, and that life was the light of all mankind. The light shines in the darkness, and the darkness has not overcome it. (John 1:1–5)

Father, your promises are standing and will continue to stand throughout our lives. Nothing has changed, nothing. Your love, your covenant promises to us that you died for is forever settled. It cost you everything, and us nothing.

Father, forgive any unbelief that has crept in (Mark 9:24). You have proven yourself faithful time and time again. As we fast, pray, meditate, declare, and believe on these Holy Scriptures, we can call forth those things that are not as if they were (Romans 4:17).

We can be fully persuaded that what you have promised will happen (Romans 4:21). It sure will. Abraham believed God, and it was accredited to him as righteousness (Genesis 15:6).

Father, we believe. We believe in you, your promises, and your Word. We put all our trust in you, for you died for us. All of our apples are in your basket, O God. Your promises stand the test of time.

Father, in Mark 11:24, you tell us if we believe, we will receive whatever we ask for in prayer. Father, today we receive according to your Word and to your will. You're the good Father. Amen.

Have a blessed day, God's beautiful people. Don't let any person or any circumstance steal the joy of your day. For this is the day, the Lord has made, and we will rejoice and be glad in it.(Psalm 118:24). Amen? Amen!

Believe God's promises... He doesn't break them. He always has the final say!

Who Is Your State's Power Source?

Good morning, beautiful people, good morning. As I awake this morning in the city of our state capital, I begin to ask the Holy Spirit to lead me how to pray for the leaders of this great state once again. Oh, how I love the beautiful state of Maine.

Today let's petition and thank God for pouring out his spirit on every state in America. Let's continue to thank him for this global awakening. Every state, every nation is full of precious people and under our God's watchful eye.

May leaders full of wisdom, courage, and integrity rise to position. Maine has been and continues to be bathed in prayer. We know that God hears and answers prayer. May every state and nation allow God to be their state's power source. Let's pray.

Father, thank you that you are over the government. Psalm 22:28 tells us, "For dominion belongs to the Lord and he rules over the nations."

Praise be to you, Lord, the God of our father Israel, from everlasting to everlasting. Yours, Lord, is the greatness and the power and the glory and the majesty and the splendor, for everything in heaven and earth is yours. Yours, Lord, is the kingdom; you are exalted as head over all. Wealth and honor come from you; you are the ruler of all things. In your hands are strength and power to exalt and give strength to all. Now, our God, we give you thanks, and praise your glorious name. (1 Chronicles 29:10–13)

Father, thank you for putting people in position. Thank you that you hold the final authority. We know that prayer is the key. We petition you today and thank you for pouring out your spirit all across this globe. Thank you for this awakening. Amen.

Have a blessed day, God's beautiful people. Be sure to pray, vote, and praise him for this awakening.

Who Owns the Earth?

Good morning, beautiful people, good morning. Let's pray together to the man in charge and owns it all. Father, thank you that you love people. You loved them so much you died for them while they were yet sinners (John 3:16). Thank you for your mercy and grace for the world. Thank you for lighting a fire on every reader today.

We surrender full control of our lives to you, O Lord. (Tell him if this is true.) You order our footsteps; you breathe on the flame, God. King of glory, show yourself strong to the nations today. You are no respecter of persons (Acts 10:34).

We declare today the king of glory owns the earth according to his Word. He is the founder.

The earth is the Lord's, and the fullness thereof; the world, and they that dwell therein. For he hath founded it upon the seas, and established it upon the floods. Who shall ascend into the hill of the Lord? or who shall stand in his holy place? he that hath clean hands, and a pure heart; who hath not lifted up his soul unto vanity, nor sworn deceitfully. He shall receive the blessing from the Lord, and righteousness from the God of his salvation. This is the generation of them that seek him, that seek thy face, O Jacob. Selah. Lift up your heads, O ye gates; and be ye lift up, ye everlasting doors; and the King of glory shall come in. Who is this King of glory? The Lord strong and mighty, the Lord mighty in battle. Lift up your heads, O ye gates; even lift them up, ye everlasting doors; and the King of glory shall come in. Who is this King of glory? The Lord of hosts, he is the King of glory! Selah. (Psalm 24)

Have a blessed day, God's beautiful people.

Who Is Your Portion?

Good morning, beautiful people, good morning. Today let's pray together Psalm 16:5–11.

Lord, you have assigned me my portion and my cup; you have made my lot secure. The boundary lines have fallen for me in pleasant places; surely, I have a delightful inheritance. I will praise the Lord, who counsels me; even at night my heart instructs me. I have set the Lord always before me. Because he is at my right hand, I will not be shaken. Therefore, my heart is glad and my tongue rejoices; my body also will rest secure, because you will not abandon me to the grave, nor will you let your Holy One see decay. You have made known to me the path of life; you will fill me with joy in your presence, with eternal pleasures at your right hand.

Father, thank you that our lives are in your hands. As we look to you each and every day, you will make our hearts glad. There is nothing and no one hidden from you. In your presence is fullness of joy.

Today all across this globe, your people thank you for the path of life. Amen.

Have a blessed day, beautiful people. Thank you for being our portion.

What Is Your Creed?

Good morning, beautiful people, good morning. Let's tell Jesus what we believe.

Father, thank you that you gave us all free will to choose to believe or not to believe. You don't force your will on anyone. However, you say in Mark 9:23, "If we can believe, all things are possible to him that believeth."

I believe in Jesus. I believe in the Holy Scriptures. I believe your Word is powerful. I believe in Hebrews 4:12, "For the Word of God is alive and active. Sharper than any double-edged sword, it penetrates even to dividing soul and spirit, joints and marrow; it judges the thoughts and attitudes of the heart."

I also believe in Hebrews 11:6, "Without faith it is impossible to please, him for he that cometh to God must believe that he is, and that he is a rewarder of them that diligently seek him."

I pray, God, for everyone who doesn't believe today but is willing to just ask you to reveal yourself to them, you will. "For God so loved the world that he gave his one and only Son, that whoever believes in him shall not perish but have eternal life" (John 3:16).

Thank you for the Holy Spirit. Lead and guide us today. Thank you for "giving your angels charge over us" (Psalm 91:11). I believe; that's my creed. Amen.

Have a blessed day, beautiful people. Don't be double-minded. Settle your creed today.

What Ville Are You Stuck In?

Good morning, beautiful people. We all have struggles; no one is exempt. The mind is truly a battlefield. Today whether you are dealing with negativeville, fearville, angerville, lonelyville, confusedville, or whatever ville you find your thoughts, there is freedom. It's called the Word of God and prayerville. Let's pray some scripture's together.

If you hold to my teaching, you are really my disciples. Then you will know the truth, and the truth will set you free. (John 8:31–32)

Therefore, there is now no condemnation for those who are in Christ Jesus. (Romans 8:1)

And we know that in all things God works for the good of those who love him, who have been called according to his purpose. (Romans 8:28)

Why, my soul, are you downcast? Why so disturbed within me? Put your hope in God, for I will yet praise him, my Savior and my God. (Psalm 42:5)

Do not be anxious about anything, but in every situation, by prayer and petition, with thanksgiving, present your requests to God. And the peace of God, which transcends all understanding, will guard your hearts and your minds in Christ Jesus. (Philippians 4:6–7)

I meditate on your precepts and consider your ways. (Psalm 119:15)

Against all hope, Abraham in hope believed and so became the father of many nations, just as it had been said to him, "So shall your offspring be. "without weakening in his faith, he faced the fact that his body was as good as dead—since he was about a hundred years old—and that Sarah's womb was also dead. Yet he did not waver through unbelief regarding the promise of God, but was strengthened in his faith and gave glory to God, being fully persuaded that God had power to do what he had promised. (Romans 4:18–21)

We demolish arguments and every pretension that sets itself up against the knowledge of God, and we take captive every thought to make it obedient to Christ. (2 Corinthians 10:5)

And without faith it is impossible to please God, because anyone who comes to him must believe that he exists and that he rewards those who earnestly seek him. (Hebrews 11:6)

Father, thank you for your Word. Today we declare it over our lives.

We do not need to stay stuck in any ville but yours. You and you alone have the final say. Your Word does not lie. You told us to cast down imaginations and every high and lofty thing that exalts itself against the true knowledge of God (2 Corinthians 10:4–5).

Today we will choose to submit our thoughts to the Word of God and replace any negative thoughts, fears, and anxieties with your Word. (Do You?)

Today we declare we are moving into Freedomville. For whom the Son sets free is free, indeed (John 8:36). No matter what thoughts come our way today, together all across this globe, we will declare the Word of God. We will speak it out loud to the enemy of our soul. Moved to Freedomville, and we are enjoying life. Amen.

Have a blessed day, beautiful people. Enjoy Freedomville.

Tell the Thief to Take a Hike

Good morning, beautiful people. I was thinking this morning about a time I would come home, and things would be missing. It was a difficult time, and I was trying to rise above it. The grill, the lawn mower, the firepit, things would just disappear, be gone. I would never know what to expect when I would return to my home. The thief had come.

The thief was trying to destroy my peace, making me feel unsafe. However, I discovered who the thief was. Once you know who the thief is, you can do something about it. I chose to let it go back then but no longer. I served notice to the thief that he will no longer steal from me.

It's the same way in our spiritual lives. The thief who came to rob, kill, steal, and destroy must be served notice. Be gone in Jesus's name, thief. You have been evicted. We serve you notice.

Although it wasn't a good time, I had to rise up. I had to determine in my mind that I would not allow the thief to destroy or steal anything else from me. I began to speak the Word of God to the thief.

Thief, your messing with God's anointed, and I wouldn't do that if I were you. God will have the final say. No weapon formed against us will ever prosper, thief (Isaiah 54:17). We belong to our Creator. Let's pray.

Father, thank you that it is a happy day. Thank you that you loved your people enough to die for them. We thank you that no matter what is happening around us, no matter what season of life we are in, we can have happy, happy days. No thief can take away what God has ordained. God hijacked the plan of the enemy of our soul, and we can declare he is defeated foe. Our God made a public spectacle of him, and he will continue to do so (Colossians 2:15).

Today may many believe God's Word and have a happy, happy day. We can enjoy life because Jesus has paid the price to give us life and life more abundantly (John 10:10). Amen? AmenIt is only the thief who comes to kill, rob, steal, and destroy. Time for him to flee. For John 3:16 states, "For God so loved the world that he gave his one and only son, that whoever believes in him shall not perish but have eternal life."

Have a blessed day, beautiful people, and tell the thief to take a hike and enjoy your day. Have a happy, happy day!

Worth More Than Gold

Good morning, beautiful people, good morning. Every morning, I like to talk with my Heavenly Father and ask the Holy Spirit to lead my day. I ask him to guide me, highlight what I need to know, and show me things that I couldn't see with my natural eyes and mind. I ask him to empower me to make a difference, to protect me as I journey the day. I ask him to make me sensitive to his spirit. That's my daily prayer, then I embark on my day. Then if there's interruptions, changes, etc., I am not so easily frustrated. I know that Jesus is in my day. I pause at times and ask Father, you order my footsteps, right? That's what his Word tells us. Let's pray.

Father, thank you that man makes their plans, but God orders our footsteps. The footsteps of the righteous are ordered of the Lord. That's what your Word tells us, and we believe.

Father, every person we meet today was created in your image. Every life has great purpose and value. No one has ever done or will ever do anything that would cause you not to love them. You died for them when they were yet sinners.

Today you are saying, "Come, come as you are to me, my son, my daughter. I paid the price. You could never be good enough on your own merit. I make you righteous through the blood I shed on the cross." You say that to every person breathing on planet earth today. That's your heart for mankind.

Thank you, God, for what you are doing on the earth today. Thank you for moving across this land. Thank you for the healing waters of Jesus Christ. Thank you for beauty for ashes. Every day is full of thanksgiving for your mercy and grace.

Together and all across this globe, we thank you for Joel 2:28, "The day of the Lord. I will pour out my Spirit on all people." We receive. Amen.

Have a blessed day, beautiful people. Ask him to lead you today by the power of his Holy Spirit. He hears you when you call (Psalm 91:15). Love much, laugh often, and live life to the fullest.

Who Brings the Increase?

Good morning, beautiful people. Today let's thank God for the increase.

Then the Lord replied: Write down the revelation and make it plain on tablets so that a herald may run with it. For the revelation awaits an appointed time; it speaks of the end and will not prove false. Though it lingers, wait for it; it will certainly come. (Habakkuk 2:2–3)

But you will receive power when the Holy Spirit comes on you; and you will be my witnesses in Jerusalem, and in all Judea and Samaria, and to the ends of the earth. (Acts 1:8)

Now to him who is able to do immeasurably more than all we ask or imagine, according to his power that is at work within us. (Ephesians 3:20)

Father, thank you for the dreams and visions you have placed in the hearts of your people. Thank you for birthing them for such a time as this. God, you said in your Word in the last days, you would pour out your spirit on all flesh. "And it shall come to pass afterward, that I will pour out my Spirit on all flesh; your sons and your daughters shall prophesy, your old men shall dream dreams, and your young men shall see visions" (Joel 2:28).

Today we join our faith together all across this globe for every dream you have placed in the heart of mankind. As Christians, we stand together and declare they are coming to pass. For you said, O God, it's not by might nor by power but by your spirit. Thank you for pouring your spirit out on our land.

Today, may the dreams you placed in the heart of every woman and every man be rekindled and set on fire. It is not man who brings the increase but to the Lord Jesus Christ himself. Thank you, Jesus, for igniting the fire. Your answer is the same for those dreams you placed within us, yes, and amen. Thank you for the increase. All across this globe today, we declare Jesus reigns. We declare increase. Amen.

Have a blessed day, beautiful people. This is the day the Lord has made, and we will rejoice and be glad in it. Give a shout for increase.

Yes, It's for You

Good morning, beautiful people, good morning. Together, let's pray these Holy Scriptures.

Thanks be to God for his indescribable gift! (2 Corinthians 9:15)

For the wages of sin is death, but the gift of God is eternal life in Christ Jesus our Lord. (Romans 6:23)

For it is by grace you have been saved, through faith—and this is not from yourselves, it is the gift of God. (Ephesians 2:8)

A man's gift makes room for him, and brings him before great men. (Proverbs 18:16)

Father, thank you for this free gift of salvation (totally unearned and undeserved). Thank you for the gift you have placed inside every person in whom was created in your image. Today we join our faith together and believe many will come to know you this day. The greatest love story... the cross.

We join our faith together all across this globe today and declare the gift you have given us will make room for us. You said you would give us the words to speak in front of kings and rulers. Together we will walk out your Word. Thank you for open doors. Amen.

Have a blessed day, beautiful people, for this is the day the Lord has made, and we will rejoice and be glad in it.

Who Holds Your Every Moment?

Good morning, beautiful people. I am blessed to meet so many wonderful people. As I listen to the many struggles people have in their lives, I know who holds their every moment. He knows the way every one of us should take. He knows the number of breaths we will breathe each and every day. He truly is our portion.

I am tender toward people who need inner healing and deliverance. Maybe because I know firsthand how it feels to be bound. Jesus is true to his word. Whatever you have need of today, Jesus is your healer. From to physical health, emotional well-being, finances, family struggles, and I am sure you have a list. Rest assured today that God himself has the answer. His eye never leaves you, and he says, "Yes, my daughter. Yes, my son, come to me and declare my Word [our answer] over the situation, for my Word does not return void but accomplishes great and mighty things."

Somebody shout the Word. Father, thank you for this day. Thank you for being our healer. Thank you that you truly are all we need. You have every answer to life's many twists and turns. We hear your voice whether we turn to the right or to the left, saying, "This is the way, walk ye in it" (Isaiah 30:21).

We believe you truly hold every moment of our lives in your hands. We believe you truly want the very best for us. Thank you. We can declare your Word over our lives. You have given us your Word to stand on. We never have to second-guess. We just need to find out what does the Word say. Declare it and believe it. That's our portion, and to that, we say, "Amen!"

Have a blessed day, God's beautiful people. Believe.

"In the beginning was the Word, and the Word was with God, and the Word was God" (John 1:1). Declare his promises over your life today! Stay blessed.

Who Is Your Walking Partner?

Today, let's pray about believing God's Word as we journey here on earth.

Walk in obedience to all that the Lord your God has commanded you, so that you may live and prosper and prolong your days in the land that you will possess. (Deuteronomy 5:33)

Your word is a lamp for my feet, a light on my path. (Psalm 119:105)

He has shown you, O mortal, what is good. And what does the Lord require of you? To act justly and to love mercy and to walk humbly with your God. (Micah 6:8)

Father, thank you for journeying with us. Today we will choose to enjoy our day as you walk us through the challenges of life. Thank you for prospering us, and may our lives be full of mercy as we walk humbly with our God.

All across this globe today, we declare this is our time. Thank you, God, for encounters and divine appointments. Amen.

Have a blessed day, beautiful people, be glad in it.

Are You Searching? Believe

Good morning, beautiful people. Are you searching today for answers to life's problems? We all walk through circumstances that are tough during our vapor of life here on earth. There is a man, Jesus, who will journey every place, even the tough places with you. He will bring you to the other side.

There is nothing that you can't talk to him about (pray). There is nothing that you have done or will ever do that can separate you from the love of God. Can you believe this? Can you receive this? It is true. Let's pray.

Father, thank you that you loved people enough to die for them. It is the best news this world has ever received. Thank you for tearing down strongholds of unbelief today. Thank you for changing mind-sets.

Today all across this globe, we join our faith and speak hope to the person who is contemplating suicide. We declare you will live and not die in Jesus's name. We speak freedom according to John 8:36, "Whom the son sets free is free indeed to the person addicted." To every alcoholic, we declare sobriety in the name of Jesus.

We speak peace to troubled minds today all across this globe. The love of Christ has come to set you free. Believe.

Father, you said we have not because we ask not. (Ask, talk to him about anything.) We have asked, and we receive. Thank you for pouring out your spirit. You are a good God. Thank you for mercy, thank you for grace.

Thank you for the abundant life. Fill our hearts to overflowing in your presence today so that the world may see that you are the answer to life's many questions. Amen.

Have a blessed day, God's beautiful people. You are loved with an everlasting love. Declare your freedom in Christ Jesus.

"Love never ends" (1 Corinthians 13:8).

You Are a Star

Good morning, beautiful people. On Saturday, I traveled north to Madawaska, Maine, (the heart of the St. John Valley) to celebrate my youngest daughter's twenty-sixth birthday. She inquired what time she was born, and isn't it funny how the details of giving birth comes rushing back to the forefront of your mind so very quickly? It hardly seems like twenty-six years ago, I checked into the local hospital to be induced for her delivery. Time does truly fly by. I guess I must admit I just cannot be twenty-nine anymore.

Brooke, now married and a mother herself, is discovering the joy of motherhood. Children don't come with instructions; it's on the job training. I went to work full time when Brooke was one year old to meet the demands of a family of five. We shared special memories yesterday of camping trips, to surviving the family flu. We chuckled at the memory of all three of my daughters and me bedding down on the living room floor, waiting for the sickness to pass. Their dad would sit on the sideline, arms and legs crossed as he kept his eyes on the situation. He always thought someone would choke to their end. Isn't it amazing what memories we have in the recesses of our minds? Being the youngest of three, her famous words were no fair.

Mr. Emmett, my third grandson, will grow up in a small town of less than three thousand people per google. I love all the crosses I see and all the yellow stars around this town. Yellow stars on homes, churches, and businesses alike. It represents the Acadian culture. The meaning of the cross will never change for me. It is the same yesterday, today, and forever. I had my picture taken on a visit once, standing in front of the Acadian Historic Cross. Shh…I never told my daughter. Oh, how I love the cross.

I was amazed at my grandson and the technology he has already learned on the family iPad. He knows how to play games, go to different apps, and go back into programs of his choosing. Mr. Emmett turned one in March. How can that be? He knows how to find his way to his father's favorite hockey team app (somehow I think it might be his too— the Montréal Canadiens). I believe it is his paternal grandfather's favorite team as well.

I couldn't help on the way home, thinking about the kingdom of God and how it has no borders. On Saturday, I penned my prayer of the day, and people across this globe prayed the prayer of Jabez with me before leaving to celebrate with Brooke, Andrew, and Mr. Emmett. Together we asked God himself to enlarge our territories. I thought about the different cultures, different styles of worship, and different ways we present the Gospel of Jesus Christ. Everyone has their own preference, their heritage, but the meaning of the cross is the very same. A man named Jesus paid a dear price for us all; may we never forget it.

I chuckled myself at some of the memories as I prayed for all the stars in my family this morning. I may not be as techy as these young grandsons of mine, but I will always be quick to lead them to the cross app (Bible) for the answers in their lives.

I now have another memory to tuck away in the recess of my mind of yesterday's celebration. To everyone across this globe, remember you are loved and valued. You are a star in your Father's eyes. No matter where you are around this world, if you are alive, you are a star. Pull it up on your iPad today. Upload it, download it, and most of all, believe it. You are the apple of your Father's eye (Zechariah 2:8–9).

Have a blessed day, God's beautiful people. You are a star.

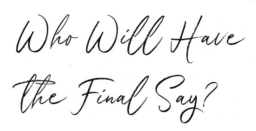
Who Will Have the Final Say?

Good morning, beautiful people, good morning. Every day we read and pray God's promises over our lives and the lives of those we love. The biggest problem I have discovered in my journey thus far is that we must stay in faith, believing. He is a covenant-keeping Jesus, and his Word is final. He never breaks a promise ever. It's a done deal, forever settled. It doesn't matter what it looks like, doesn't matter what people say. We can ask seven people their opinion and get seven different answers. God's answer, his promises are best. Stay focused on the promises of God, beautiful people.

No person's, no devil in hell, and no scheme of the enemy can take God's promises away from us. The enemy might put up a fight, but he always loses, always. Our God made a public spectacle of him, disarmed his power and authority (Colossians 2:15). Don't you just love it? The enemy of our soul has been disarmed, totally stripped, and made a spectacle of right out in public eye for all to see. When God shows up on the scene, things change quickly beautiful people, quickly. His timing is always best, and our position must remain in faith, believing. We need to remind ourselves of that every day. I need to remind myself of that every day. Let's pray.

Father, thank you that you are a covenant-keeping God.

In the beginning was the Word and the Word was with God, and the Word was God. Through him all things were made; without him nothing was made that has been made. In him was life, and that life was the light of all mankind. The light shines in the darkness, and the darkness has not overcome it. (John 1:1–5)

Father, your promises are standing and will continue to stand throughout our lives. Nothing has changed, nothing. Your love, your covenant promises to us that you died for is forever settled. It cost you everything and us nothing.

Father, forgive any unbelief that has crept in (Mark 9:24). You have proven yourself faithful time and time again. As we fast, pray, meditate, declare, and believe on these Holy Scriptures, we can call forth those things that are not as if they were (Romans 4:17).

We can be fully persuaded that what you have promised will happen (Romans 4:21). It sure will. Abraham believed God, and it was accredited to him as righteousness (Genesis 15:6).

Father, we believe. We believe in you, your promises, and your Word. We put all our trust in you, for you died for us. All of our apples are in your basket, O God. Your promises stand the rest of time.

Father, in Mark 11:24, you tell us if we believe, we will receive whatever we ask for in prayer. Father, today we receive according to your Word and to your will. You're the good Father. Amen.

Have a blessed day, God's beautiful people. Don't let any person or any circumstance steal the joy of your day. For this is the day the Lord has made, and we will rejoice and be glad in it (Psalm 118:24). Amen? Amen!

Believe God's promises… He doesn't break them. He always has the final say!

Are You a Faithful Coworker?

Good morning, beautiful people, who makes things grow? Is it us or is it God? Are you a faithful coworker in God's Kingdom?

I planted the seed, Apollo's watered it, but God has been making it grow. So, neither the one who plants nor the one who waters are anything but only God, who makes things grow. The one who plants and the one who waters have one purpose, and they will each be rewarded according to their own labor. For we are co-workers in God's service; you are God's field, God's building. Everything is God's and it's him that brings the increase. (1 Corinthians 3:6–9)

People are gems to God, precious. Today I wanted to ask you to put your whole heart in the offering. For if he has our whole heart, he has it all. There would be nothing we would hold back from our God, and he for us his people. Surely he would give us the increase according to his Word. Let's pray.

Father, there's nothing you desire more from us than our hearts. For when you have our whole heart, you have it all. There is nothing we would hold back from you if you were our passion.

Forgive us, God, when we place other things before you. We cast down our idols. In Matthew 19:29, Jesus tells us that "everyone who has left houses or brothers or sisters or father or mother or wife or children or fields for my name sake will receive a hundred times as much and will inherit eternal life."

Thank you, God, that you are the God of increase. May we be found faithful and good stewards with everything that you can trust us with for your glory alone. Amen.

Have a blessed day, God's beautiful people. He desires your whole heart. Can you surrender it today?

Have You Been Ransomed?

Good morning, beautiful people, good morning. If we were all 100 percent honest with ourselves, with others, and our God, we would have to admit we are all in need to be ransomed. What keeps us from accepting that ransom? Is it self-sufficiency, pride, arrogance, feelings of inferiority, shame, denial, and the list seems endless?

We need to begin every day with the Word of God. We need to begin our day with the man who ransomed us. He paid the price for it all. The free gift of salvation cost him everything and us nothing. Even on my best days, I fall short. His Word tells us that all have fallen short of the glory of God (Romans 3:23). All means all.

There are so many things I love about Jesus, but one thing I love is that we are all equal before him. It doesn't matter if you have a million dollars in your bank account, or it is empty. It doesn't matter what you have done or how intelligent you are. At the cross, we all come to know God in the same way. It's all through the blood of Jesus Christ. We don't earn it, deserve it, but because of his great mercy and grace, we can receive it.

I know this scripture is shared a lot, but it is so true.

For God so loved the world that he gave his one and only Son, that whoever believes in him shall not perish but have eternal life. The key word is believing. Ephesians 2:8 For it is by grace you have been saved, through faith—and this is not from yourselves, it is the gift of God. Oh, what a gift! (John 3:16)

Father, thank you for ransoming us. The free gift you have given us is priceless. Journeying every day with the man who created us is so amazing. The love you have for us makes us want to know you deeper. Strip away all our religious mind-sets, traditions of man and draw us close to you. Reveal truth to us, O God, show us things today we didn't know yesterday.

We want to know you more. We desire to walk in the full inheritance that is ours from the ransom that was paid. Holy Spirit, comforter and friend, teach us according to the Word (John 14:26). Amen.

Have a blessed day, God's beautiful people. Have you been ransomed?

Have You Found Him to Be Trustworthy?

Good morning, beautiful people, good morning. The Lord has been so faithful and trustworthy of keeping his promises to me. I love to review the many prayers he has answered. I love to read and reread them. It keeps me looking to him and knowing he is trustworthy. Today let's pray Psalms 145 together.

I will exalt you, my God the King; I will praise your name for ever and ever. Every day I will praise you and extol your name for ever and ever. Great is the Lord and most worthy of praise; his greatness no one can fathom. One generation commends your works to another; they tell of your mighty acts. They speak of the glorious splendor of your majesty—and I will meditate on your wonderful works. They tell of the power of your awesome works—and I will proclaim your great deeds. They celebrate your abundant goodness and joyfully sing of your righteousness. The Lord is gracious and compassionate, slow to anger and rich in love. The Lord is good to all; he has compassion on all he has made. All your works praise you, Lord; your faithful people extol you. They tell of the glory of your kingdom and speak of your might, so that all people may know of your mighty acts and the glorious splendor of your kingdom. Your kingdom is an everlasting kingdom, and your dominion endures through all generations. The Lord is trustworthy in all he promises and faithful in all he does. The Lord upholds all who fall and lifts up all who are bowed down. The eyes of all look to you, and you give them their food at the proper time. You open your hand and satisfy the desires of every living thing. The Lord is righteous in all his ways and faithful in all he does. The Lord is near to all who call on him, to all who call on him in truth. He fulfills the desires of those who fear him; he hears their cry and saves them. The Lord watches over all who love him, but all the wicked he will destroy. My mouth will speak in praise of the Lord. Let every creature praise his holy name for ever and ever. Amen.

Have a blessed day, beautiful people. He is trustworthy!

Have You Suffered Loss?

Good morning, beautiful people, good morning. This morning, I am reminded of some of the most painful moments I have ever lived. As I prepare for the upcoming Healing Waters Women's Conference, Time to Live Free, I revisit some of those places in my own life. I am so glad to know a man who can take the most painful, devastating places, and rebuild them. Only Jesus, our Creator, can make us whole again, only he. Praise his name.

Today, Father, we pray for the hurting. Thank you that you bind up their wounds. Thank you for the healing waters of Jesus Christ. Thank you that you bring beauty out of our ashes, the oil of joy for mourning, the garment of praise for the spirit of heaviness; that we might be called trees of righteousness, the planting of the Lord; that you might be glorified. Amen.

Read Isaiah 61 today and ask Jesus to rebuild the devastation in your life.

Have a blessed day, God's beautiful people. Talk to him about your hurts and let him heal them today.

He Brought the World Goodness and Light

Good morning, beautiful people, good morning. Isn't God good? Take a few moments today and reflect on the goodness of God. He has done so much for us, beyond what we can even comprehend. His love for us is amazing.

Father, thank you for the light of the world, Jesus, Emmanuel. All across this globe today, let's share the goodness of God. Through acts of kindness, compassion, and love, may the world be a better place because Christ reigns in us.

May every person no matter where they are, living in a nursing home to a homeless shelter, from a soup kitchen to the mansion on the hill, may the love of Christ be shared from heart to heart.

Father, as we enjoy the season of Christmas and the spirit of giving, may we remember to share our goodness with all the people who you would entrust to us. Enlarge our hearts this Christmas as you fill us fresh every morning by the power of the Holy Spirit. May the goodness of God shine brightly through each of us today and every day throughout the coming year.

O God, may hope arise in people's lives as we all work together to make the world a better place. May the joy of Christmas be extended to all. Amen.

Have a blessed day, God's beautiful people. Share some goodness and shine your light.

"For you were once darkness, but now you are light in the Lord. Live as children of light" (Ephesians 5:8).

He Don't Mind the Questions

Good morning, beautiful people. I laugh at all the questions kids ask. Some are so funny, some are just so serious and innocent as they desire to discover truth. God said to come to him as a child. I love as God's children, we can ask him anything. He makes a way for us. He loves that we trust him to make the way, even in the wilderness. He shows us the way out. He tells us the truth. Let's pray.

Father, thank you for childlike faith. You tell us to come to you as a child. You tell us to come as we are. You tell us to believe your Word. You tell us we have not because we ask not. You tell us to ask, to believe, and to receive. You tell us so much in these Holy Scriptures.

Father, lead us in all truth. You said the Holy Spirit would teach us. What is the next step? Where is the open door? How do we do this? Where is that? Our lives are full of questions, and you bring the answers as you lead us each and every day.

Thank you, Father, for the plans you have for our lives. As we journey every day with you, you lead us right into destiny. Thank you for the gifts and talents you have placed within us. May we steward them well for your glory, God. Show yourself strong through us today as we embark on a new day. Amen.

Have a blessed day, God's beautiful people. He doesn't mind you asking him the questions; he has the answers.

"Call to me and I will answer you and tell you great and unsearchable things you do not know" (Jeremiah 33:3).

What's Living on the inside of You?

Good morning, beautiful people, good morning. As we start each day, let's ask the Holy Spirit to lead and guide us. This morning, I look back in a prayer journal from 2007. I penned these words one early morning.

Oh, my beautiful daughters…

The waters are gushing; you come thirsty again. Let me refresh you. Let my Word cause you to soar once again. I am a Father to the fatherless. I am wine to the empty wineskin. I am a husband to the husbandless.

What are you in need of, my dear daughters? Come, come, I ask you to come. I have all you need.

The waters are rigid because of the rocks beneath. Let me remove your rocks so my river can flow through you once again. "For out of your belly shall flow rivers of living water" (John 7:38).

I had a dream one night around that same time. It was about some people in my life that didn't like the fountain. They were continually wanting me to put it in a black bag and hide it. I was so excited about this fountain that I wanted to tell the whole world. I didn't want to hide it, but I wanted them to accept me, but they did not. They did not like the fountain. They did not want to be led by anything other than their own desires, their flesh, and their will. Some folks wanted monetary gain, wealth more than anything. They would do anything for earthly success instead of following the plan God had laid out for them. They chose to be led each day by their own desires, denying the power (2 Timothy 3:5). Let's pray.

Father, thank you for the Holy Spirit. Lead us each and every day. We want to know you in the fullness of the Godhead. Fill us full of fresh living water. Teach us, Holy Spirit, direct our path and remove any rocks that are making the waters rigid. We choose to walk in forgiveness with those who don't like our fountain. Holy spirit, forgive us for when we were led by anything or anyone other than the truth of your Word. Holy Spirit, take full control of our lives today and every day as we yield our will to the will of our Father. Amen.

Have a blessed day, beautiful people. Let the river flow.

He Is Before All Things

Good morning, beautiful people. Today let's pray from Colossians 1:17–20.

And he is before all things, and in him all things consist. And he is the head of the body, the church, who is the beginning, the firstborn from the dead, that in all things he may have the preeminence. For it pleased the Father that in him all the fullness should dwell, and by him to reconcile all things to Himself, by Him, whether things on earth or things in heaven, having made peace through the blood of his cross.

Father, today we acknowledge that it's all about you and for your glory alone. I thank you that you will give us God assignments as you can trust us. It's all for your glory and building the kingdom of God. I thank you for reconciling mankind to yourself. May it always be all about you.

Today we join our faith all across this globe and declare that you are the one true God in which man can be saved. We thank you for showing yourself strong all across this globe this day. Amen.

Have a blessed day, God's beautiful people. Stay blessed.

He Is in Your Day

Good morning, beautiful people. Isn't the morning sky just beautiful? I love pictures captured here in Northern Maine. I am so thankful that Jesus Christ is the same yesterday, today, and forever (Hebrews 13:8). He certainly is with us as we journey every day. Oh, for eyes to see and ears to hear for Christmas. Let's pray.

Father, as we journey the day knowing you are God with us, give us eyes to see and ears to hear what the spirit is saying. Your love for mankind is amazing. Your grace, your mercy is new every morning. Great is your faithfulness. Your unfailing love makes our hearts secure as we put our trust in you, even the wind must obey your command.

Father, just as you light up the morning sky and shine down on us, may the light of Christ beam brightly across our nation/s this morning. Every day is a new beginning, a day to see you in every moment. Yesterday is gone, never to be relived. Our life is like a vapor here today and gone tomorrow. May we find you every day, in every way, and may the light within us burn the fears away.

Father, light up the sky in lives around this globe today who may be losing hope. May they see you in their day, may they know you in a deeper way, and may the love you have for them cast every fear away. Amen.

Have a blessed day, God's beautiful people. Find him in your day.

"Every good and perfect gift is from above, coming down from the Father of the heavenly lights, who does not change like shifting shadows" (James 1:17).

He Is Never Too Busy

Good morning, beautiful people, good morning. Life gets busy at times. Isn't it great to know that God is never too busy for us? We can call on his name day or night, and he is always there.

As I was getting groceries yesterday, I remembered people I hadn't called back. Oops. At times, we feel we are too busy to get everything done in a day. Excuses take the place of actions. When it comes to our God, he is never too busy. He created the heavens and earth in seven days. He can handle all that concerns us. We need to call on him. Let's pray.

Father, thank you that you are never too busy to hear what is on our hearts and minds. We do need to look for those impossible situations to become possible as we put our faith in you. Your Word tells us in Matthew 19:26, "With man this is impossible, but with God all things are possible."

Father, we love to see our God of all possibilities work among us every day. As we review the answers to our prayers, it builds our faith to believe you will answer in the best way for us. Your timing is perfect, and your answer is the same. We give you thanks.

Have a blessed day, beautiful people. Call on Jesus for whatever is concerning you. You will soon discover he is the faithful Father.

Are You Broken Inside?

Good morning, beautiful people, good morning. Although it's early morning, and daylight hasn't shown through yet, I look outside my living room window once again to try to see the daisies on my front lawn that just appeared out of nowhere. Usually I have dandelions that need mowing on my front lawn. I just can't get myself to mow down the daisies that wasn't there just a few days ago. God is so good; he is so good to us.

No matter what you are going through today, remember that the one who created you loves you beyond measure. You are the apple of his eye. He wants the very best for you. He will turn your brokenness into joy. He tells us mourning may last for a night, but joy comes in the morning. Let's pray Psalm 30 together and thank him for the joy.

I will exalt you, Lord, for you lifted me out of the depths and did not let my enemies gloat over me. Lord my God, I called to you for help, and you healed me. You, Lord, brought me up from the realm of the dead; you spared me from going down to the pit. Sing the praises of the Lord, you his faithful people; praise his holy name. For his anger lasts only a moment, but his favor lasts a lifetime; weeping may stay for the night, but rejoicing comes in the morning. When I felt secure, I said, "I will never be shaken." Lord, when you favored me, you made my royal mountain stand firm; but when you hid your face, I was dismayed. To you, Lord, I called; to the Lord I cried for mercy: "What is gained if I am silenced, if I go down to the pit? Will the dust praise you? Will it proclaim your faithfulness? Hear, Lord, and be merciful to me; Lord, be my help." You turned my wailing into dancing; you removed my sackcloth and clothed me with joy, that my heart may sing your praises and not be silent. Lord my God, I will praise you forever.

Father, thank you for healing the brokenness inside each of us. Only you can restore us and make us whole again. We join our faith together today for people who feel broken inside, not worthy, or loved. You love them beyond measure. No one is rejected by you, no, not one. We tear down every lie they are believing and pray, O God, that you would reveal yourself to them as Father Abba, lover of their soul. Thank you, Jesus, for turning wailing into dancing all across this globe today. Amen.

Have a blessed day, beautiful people... Dance!

Are You Carrying your Candle?

Is the Holy Spirit leading your life every day? Are you ready to go a little higher today? Let's pray.

Father, you said that you sent us the Holy Spirit, the advocate (John 14:26), and he will teach us all things and will remind us of everything you have said to us. Holy Spirit, lead us today. We desire a day full of encounters of God and with God.

Father, your word states man makes his plans, but you, O God, orders our footsteps. "In their hearts, humans plan their course, but the Lord establishes their steps" (Proverbs 16:9). Order out footsteps today and make our spirits to be sensitive to where we are journeying.

Open our eyes to see and our ears to hear what the spirit of the Lord is saying today. We want to see Jesus as we journey our day. Make us sensitive to the ways of your spirit, O God. We want to be like you, to reflect your glory on the earth.

Father, lead us today to the path you have ordained for us before the foundations of the earth that we may share it with another (Jeremiah 1:5). Amen.

Have a blessed day, beautiful people…carry your candle high today.

Are You Connected to the Higher Power?

Good morning, beautiful people, good morning. Let's get connected to the higher power.

It teaches us to say "No" to ungodliness and worldly passions, and to live self-controlled, upright and godly lives in this present age. (Titus 2:12)

Everything is permissible for me—but not everything is beneficial. Everything is permissible for me—but I will not be mastered by anything. (1 Corinthians 6:12)

Father, thank you today that you are our deliverer. Today anyone across this globe, who is caught in the web of addiction, they can be free.

Jesus, you are our higher power. You said not to conceal our sin but to confess it, renounce it, and find mercy.

God, you are able to lead your people out of addiction. We join our faith together for their way of escape. Set it up as they cry out to you this day.

Today may many find you as Jesus, their deliverer. You are well able to care for them. Amen.

Have a blessed day, God's beautiful people. Stay connected to your higher power, Jesus.

Are You Continuing to Pray and Believe?

Good morning, beautiful people. I wanted to share this story with you today. It helps to strengthen us to believe.

It has been some years now, but I remember this story just like it happened just yesterday. I was leading a women's prayer meeting at a local church I was attending. On this particular evening, nobody came, and it was just me. Usually I had a few or at least one other to join my faith with in prayer. By myself, I began to inquire of the Holy Spirit about what we would pray for that rainy Maine evening. I didn't have any particular agenda, just inquiring what was on the heart of the creator of the universe.

Atlanta, Georgia, came to mind, so I began to pray for Atlanta, Georgia. I knew nothing about Atlanta really, never been there, nor did I know anyone there at that time. I do know God, and he is all about people, and so am I. I began to pray for the people in Atlanta. Souls, souls, souls, I remember praying asking the Lord to draw his people unto himself.

I walked around the basement of the church, praying and declaring the Word of the Lord as I petitioned the king of kings for his people in Atlanta, Georgia.

I laughed out loud this early morning as I thought about the next event that happened. I was matching socks in my bathroom as my washer and dryer are both located there. I had a bucket we kept mismatched socks in, and they were plentiful with a family of five. Do you often wonder what happens to the other sock? I never did figure out that dilemma. After a while, I would empty the bucket in the trash and begin once again with a fresh start of socks.

This particular day, I decided to work in the mismatch-sock bucket. I found a Charisma Magazine in the mix. My brother and covenant sister had been blessing me with them. Somehow among the socks was this magazine. As I flipped the pages, I was drawn to read about the "Threshing Floor Conference" at the Dome in Atlanta, Georgia. I welled up with excitement as my heart began to leap about this conference. I mentioned it to a prayer partner that evening, and she agreed to pray I would know for sure if I was to be headed to the Atlanta Dome.

Was this really the Holy Spirit drawing me to Atlanta for this prayer conference? A few weeks went by, and my prayer partner called as she felt it was time to book the tickets, and she was going to go with me. Do you know how thankful I am when God sends someone with me? (Remind me to tell you about getting lost at the campground for over two hours, trying to make change for my three daughter's kingdom-bound experience. It amazes me how camping trailers all look-alike.)

Another praying sister from Maine decided to meet us there, and I was filled with excitement. I believe in the power of prayer. I really am convinced beyond a shadow of doubt at this form of communication with the creator of the universe. The answer to my prayer doesn't always look like what I think, but I know that God hears and answers prayer.

It was at that conference I picked up a brochure for the International School of Mentorship with Judy Jacobs. I could barely believe that would be my next step, but it was. A few weeks ago, I had Pastor Judy on my radio broadcast, Destiny Moments. She spoke about her newest book, You Are Anointed for This. As I interviewed her with my newest grandson, Emmett, in my arms, I thought about the vision statement of my life. I had asked of the Lord many years ago that I would be a woman who would leave a legacy of prayer for my three daughters. Somehow he saw my heart and heard my prayer and enlarged my territory. So today I ask of you, what can I join my faith with you for? I believe in the prayer of agreement. I believe in the one who can answer. Let's pray.

Father, I thank you for every reader today. We join our faith for every need, every situation, and every reader across this globe. God, for everyone who is joining me today in prayer, we declare the Word of the Lord over their situation. We thank you for victory in your holy name, Jesus.

Thank you for no weapon formed against them will ever prosper, and every tongue that rises up against them will be condemned. Thank you for watching over your Word to perform it. We thank you in advance for the answer, your answer to life's many issues. We give you praise. To God be all the glory. Amen.

"Pray without ceasing. In everything give thanks: for this is the will of God in Christ Jesus concerning you" (1 Thessalonians 5:17–18).

Enjoy your journey with Jesus today, wherever he leads you. Many blessings!

The Healing Has Begun

Good morning, beautiful people, good morning. Let's thank God in advance for the healing.

Father, thank you for healing. Your Word is full of scriptures to declare over our lives in regard to healing. Whether it is our nation, towns, cities, homes, or our personal lives, you are the healer.

Thank you that the healing has begun in our nation. Let it spread to the nations. You are a God who rebuilds the ancient ruins (Isaiah 61:4). You are the one true God who watches over your Word to perform it. May the people believe what your Word can accomplish and choose to believe.

We thank you today that as we believe your Word through the power of the Holy Spirit, we experience the manifestation of your Word as Christ the healer. Thank you for the healing balm of Gilead (Jeremiah 8:22).

Oh, how we love Christ the healer!

Father, thank you for grace and mercy. Thank you that the healing has begun. Thank you, God, that your healing crosses borders. Thank you for new territories.

"He sent out his Word and healed them and delivered them from their destructions" (Psalm 107:20).

Have a blessed day, beautiful people. Thank him for your healing.

The High Road...Forgiveness

Good morning, beautiful people, good morning. Today let's choose to take the high road and forgive once again.

For if you forgive men when they sin against you, your heavenly Father will also forgive you. But if you do not forgive men their sins, your Father will not forgive your sins. (Matthew 6:14–15)

Then Peter came to Jesus and asked, "Lord, how many times shall I forgive my brother or sister who sins against me? Up to seven times?" Jesus answered, "I tell you, not seven times, but seventy-seven times or seventy times seven. (Matthew 18:21–22)

So watch yourselves. If your brother or sister sins against you, rebuke them; and if they repent, forgive them. Even if they sin against you seven times in a day and seven times come back to you, saying, "I repent," you must forgive them. (Luke 17:3–4)

Get rid of all bitterness, rage and anger, brawling and slander, along with every form of malice. Be kind and compassionate to one another, forgiving each other, just as in Christ God forgave you. (Ephesians 4:31–32)

Do not be overcome by evil, but overcome evil with good. (Romans 12:21)

Father, thank you for forgiving us our sin. We have all have fallen short in our walk with you. Today we choose to let go of all hurt, past pain, memories, bitterness, false accusations, etc., and trust your Word for our lives. It is true, hurting people hurt people. Let that not be us today.

Father, you said to never repay evil with evil but overcome evil with good. May that always be so in our lives, Jesus. Even if we feel stepped on at times, I thank you that it is you, O Lord, who repays us. Snakes bring retaliation, but we are not snakes, we are lovers of God. Therefore, we choose to forgive. We choose to wait for you to show yourself strong on behalf of our obedience to you.

Today all across this globe, we choose to take the high road. We will take the high road of forgiveness. We will choose to follow in the footsteps of Jesus Christ, even when we suffer for it. Amen.

Have a blessed day, God's beautiful people. Forgive and take the high road.

The Best

Good morning, beautiful people. Life sure is a beautiful gift to enjoy. Every day is a new beginning. Yesterday is gone, just the memories of the day. Make the most of every day and choose to enjoy each and every moment. Wherever you are and whatever you are doing, choose today to follow Jesus. He will lead you each step of the way.

As my grandson would say about his baby brother, "He is the bestest in the whole world. That's what Jesus says about you. You are the best."

Father, thank you for journeying every day with mankind. No matter what the cost, may we be willing to pay it to follow you. Your mercy and grace are new every morning. Awaken the world to your presence through our daily lives. May we choose to love deeply, offer forgiveness, and be merciful to one another.

Father, 1 Corinthians 13:12–13 tells us that for now we see only a reflection as in a mirror, then we shall see face-to-face. Now I know in part, then I shall know fully, even as I am fully known. And now these three remain: faith, hope, and love. But the greatest of these is love.

Father, thank you for life. Amen.

Have a blessed day, God's beautiful people. Take up your cross and follow Jesus. It's the best way to go! You are his best. As Mason used to say: "You are the bestest in the whole world."

The Love We Don't Deserve

Good morning, beautiful people, good morning. Every day we wake up, we have so much to be thankful for. Another new beginning with a man who loved us enough to die for. His love is beyond what our limited minds can even fathom. He doesn't only just tell us how much he loves us, he shows us his love. We cannot earn his love, deserve his love, and there is nothing that can separate us from his love—nothing. Did he really say nothing?

Romans 8:31–38, let's review this once again. It's got to go deep within our soul so we never question it again.

What shall we say about such wonderful things as these? If God is for us, who can ever be against us? Since he did not spare even his own Son but gave him up for us all, won't he also give us everything else? Who dares accuse us whom God has chosen for his own? No one—for God himself has given us right standing with himself. 34 Who then will condemn us? No one—for Christ Jesus died for us and was raised to life for us, and he is sitting in the place of honor at God's right hand, pleading for us. Can anything ever separate us from Christ's love? Does it mean he no longer loves us if we have trouble or calamity, or are persecuted, or hungry, or destitute, or in danger, or threatened with death? (As the Scriptures say, "For your sake we are killed every day; we are being slaughtered like sheep." No, despite all these things, overwhelming victory is ours through Christ, who loved us. And I am convinced that nothing can ever separate us from God's love. Neither death nor life, neither angels nor demons, neither our fears for today nor our worries about tomorrow—not even the powers of hell can separate us from God's love. No power in the sky above or in the earth below—indeed, nothing in all creation will ever be able to separate us from the love of God that is revealed in Christ Jesus our Lord.

Father, thank you for your love. Embed it deep within our hearts that we will never question your love. May that love radiate from us to others today. As we walk in the fruit of the spirit, may we remember that love is the greatest of them all. The love of God sometimes is the hardest gift to receive but fills our hearts with abundant joy every day when we truly understand our days are in his hands.

Have a blessed day, God's beautiful people. Thank him for grace.

The Mighty One Has Spoken

Good morning, beautiful people, good morning. Let's pray today that the mighty one has spoken.

Father, thank you for watching over your Word. You said in Psalm 50, "The mighty one, God the Lord Has spoken and called the earth from the rising of the sun to its going down. Out of Zion, the perfection of beauty, God will shine forth. You said to gather my saints together to those who made a covenant. You said to call on you in day of trouble and you will deliver us and we shall glorify you." Yes!

You speak clearly to the wicked as they hate your instruction and cast your Words behind them. May they turn from their wickedness, we pray.

Thank you for showing yourself strong on the earth today. May God's people continue to rise up and stand for what is right. The world belongs to you and its fullness. May man never forget these words as we keep our eyes fixed upon you and your Word.

Hallelujah, he reigns!

Have a blessed day, God's beautiful people… Thank him for speaking on the earth today.

The Night the World Changed Forever

Good morning, beautiful people, good morning. Isn't it interesting how one night can change everything? The birth of Jesus changed the world forever. May the truth of the good news of Jesus permeate the earth so that all will know the best news this world has ever known.

God gave his Son, Jesus, so we could be righteous. The Bible tells us there is no one righteous, not even one; there is no one who understands, no one who seeks God. All have sinned and fall short of the glory of God (Romans 3:10, 11, 23).

Romans 10:9 tells us that if we confess with our mouth, Jesus is Lord and believe in our heart that God raised him from the dead, we will be saved.

Oh, how we love to celebrate the birth of Jesus. Let's pray.

Father, thank you for the birth of Jesus. The Holy Scriptures tells us to believe in the Lord Jesus, and we will be saved (Acts 16:31). Jesus Christ is able to save those who come to God through him (Hebrews 7:25). If we confess with our mouth, Jesus is Lord, and believe in our hearts that God raised him from the dead, we will be saved (Romans 10:9).

Father, forgive us for our sins and thank you for making our lives acceptable before our God. On our own, we could never measure up. Thank you for forgiving us and giving us eternal life. We believe! Amen.

Have a blessed day, God's beautiful people. His life and death paid for it all. Believe.

Are You Empty-handed but Alive?

Good morning, beautiful people, good morning. Are you feeling a little empty handed this morning and don't know where to turn? You can always cry out to God for help, and he will send you help from on high. He will give you a thought, send someone to help you, or speak the answer to you through his Word. One thing for sure is that he hears you when you call (Jeremiah 31:3).

I remember living in an apartment for a season and had nothing. Empty handed was certainly putting it mildly. What I did have though was a relationship with Jesus Christ, and that was more than enough. He made a way for me. I remember the green beans and new potatoes he sent me from a neighbor when I had no food. I learned to take everything to my Heavenly Father during that time in my life. I would never trade this trial as it drew me closer to the man who created me.

"Consider it pure joy, my brothers and sisters, whenever you face trials of many kinds, because you know that the testing of your faith produces perseverance. Let perseverance finish its work so that you may be mature and complete, not lacking anything" (James 1:2–4).

Father, thank you for being our God, and we your people. You take us in just as we are. You are no respecter of persons. We are all equal at the foot of the cross. Empty-handed people are the best receivers. So many depend on themselves and have no need for God to do much. They run to their provider whomever that is (mother, father, sister, and brother) and have no need of you, God. Draw them today, good Father.

Father, take empty hands all across this globe and fill them with the blessings of God. You said in Deuteronomy 28, "Blessings for obedience." Let it be so for your glory alone, Jesus. Amen.

Have a blessed day, beautiful people. Jesus loves the empty handed!

Are You Feeling a Little under the Weather?

Good morning, beautiful people, good morning. Do you have days when you don't feel just right? Maybe you ate something that didn't agree with you, or maybe just a bit too tired, or the day is not turning out as you planned. I recently had a day like that. No matter what I tried to do, it just didn't work out well. I ended up going to rest to see if things would turn around. Well, guess what? It turned around; it's a new day. It will for you too. This is your season, friend. Things are changing rapidly, and you have the victory. Let's pray.

Father, thank you that rainy days don't last forever in our lives. No matter what we are going through, it will soon pass. Things always turn around in our favor. Because we believe in Jesus and the Holy Scriptures, we can declare turnaround, even when we are under the weather. Sickness must flee, disease must go, and peace must come. Weeping may endure for a night, but joy comes in the morning. Yes, joy comes in the morning (Psalm 30:5).

When we believe what you have spoken to us and submit our lives to you and your plan, all is well. Our lives are in your hands. No weapon formed against us will ever prosper (Isaiah 54:17). The days and seasons always change in our favor as we continue to draw close to you.

Oh, how we love journeying life everyday with you. Amen.

Have a blessed day, God's most beautiful people. Your under the weather day is almost over. Believe!

Are You Guilty by Association?

And this gospel of the kingdom will be preached in the whole world as a testimony to all nations, and then the end will come.
—Matthew 24:14

He *said to them, "Go into all the world and preach the gospel to all creation."*
—Mark 16:15

Declare his glory among the nations, his marvelous deeds among all peoples.
—Psalm 96:3

Therefore go and make disciples of all nations, baptizing them in the name of the Father and of the Son and of the Holy Spirit, and teaching them to obey everything I have commanded you. And surely, I am with you always, to the very end of the age.
—Matthew 28:19–20

For I am not ashamed of the gospel, because it is the power of God that brings salvation to everyone who believes: first to the Jew, then to the Gentile.
—Roman 1:16

I pray that your partnership with us in the faith may be effective in deepening your understanding of every good thing we share for the sake of Christ.
—Philemon 1:6

Father, thank you for mercy and grace. We are not ashamed of the Gospel of Jesus Christ. Today we can declare all across this nation that you are alive and well, and your spirit does live within us.

As born-again, spirit-filled believers, we will stand for what we believe in. Your Word does not return void, and you are watching over it to perform it. From the White House to every court house and to every home all across this land...BELIEVE. Jesus is the way the truth and the life (John 14:6).

Now don't keep this good news to yourself, go tell someone. Amen.

Have a blessed day, God's beautiful people, for this is the day the Lord has made, and we will rejoice and be glad in it.

Are You Hiding Out with God?

Good morning, beautiful people, good morning. This morning, I was reading from the Holy Scriptures in Colossians 3. Paul tells us to set our minds on things that are above, not on things on earth. For we have died (to self), and our lives are hidden with Christ in God. Then Paul tells us in verse 5, there are some things we need to put down (idols). Let's tell God we lay down our idols once again today, just in case we picked any back up.

Father, thank you that our mind is set on you and you alone. Anything that exalts itself against you and your Word, we lay it down. We have given you all our heart. (Tell him.) Your heart, your will is what we desire. We made our choice, and we lay down our idols once again. We will press on toward the mark for the prize of the high calling of God in Christ Jesus (Philippians 3:14).

Father, thank you that nothing, nothing can snatch us from your hand (John 10:28). You are an amazing God, and we are your people. Thank you for hiding us in you. You alone are our passion.

Have a blessed day, God's beautiful people. Stay hidden in him.

Can God Interrupt Your Day?

Good morning, beautiful people, good morning. This morning, as I was putting together my thoughts of what I believed my day would look like, I began to pray and ask the Holy Spirit what I should pen on this beautiful but very cold morning. I must laugh right out loud as I heard him inquire if he could interrupt my day. Of course, God, I am not leaving home without your Holy Spirit leading me. You said you order our footsteps, right? Yes, but have eyes to see and ears to hear what I am saying. Hmmm…I wonder what today will bring? Let's pray.

Father, thank you for this beautiful morning. Thank you for communicating with us in so many ways. Sometimes you tell us to take another route, sometimes to share a hug, sometimes to take someone food, but you are always speaking to us.

Father, may we hear you well today. May we see your hand and be obedient to whatever you may ask of us. As we journey the day with you, may we be blessed with the opportunities to share your love, your Word, and whatever you may of ask of us.

Father, never let us get too busy nor let complacency set in that we miss the opportunities you present us each and every day. Father, yes, please interrupt our day. Thank you for the blessing to work in your kingdom. Amen.

Have a blessed day, God's beautiful people. Let God interrupt your day.

Are You His?

Good morning, beautiful people, good morning. Today let's pray together:

Let love and faithfulness never leave you; bind them around your neck, write them on the tablet of your heart. Then you will win favor and a good name in the sight of God and man. Trust in the Lord with all your heart and lean not on your own understanding; in all your ways submit to him, *and he will make your paths straight.* (Proverbs 3:3–6)

And the Lord said to Moses, "I will do the very thing you have asked, because I am pleased with you and I know you by name." Then Moses said, "Now show me your glory." *And the* Lord *said, "I will cause all my goodness to pass in front of you, and I will proclaim my name, the* Lord, *in your presence. I will have mercy on whom I will have mercy, and I will have compassion on whom I will have compassion.* (Exodus 33:17–19)

For the Lord God is a sun and shield; the Lord bestows favor and honor; no good thing does he withhold from those whose walk is blameless. (Psalm 84:11)

Father, thank you for your faithfulness. Together all across this globe, we join our faith for our destiny. We are so sure we belong to you (if you are not sure, then today's the day to get that straightened out—talk with him). We thank you that our righteousness is in you. You know everything about us, and by your amazing grace, you still say they belong to me.

Father, thank you for favor, thank you for ordering our footsteps, and may our walk be pleasing in your sight, O God. Show us your glory. Amen.

Have a blessed day, beautiful people. Shout I belong to Jesus.

Are You Hurting?

Good morning, beautiful people, good morning. Today let's pray for people who are hurting.

I believe I will see the goodness of the Lord in the land of the living. Wait on the Lord; be strong, and may your heart be stout; wait on the Lord. (Psalm 27:13–14)

Do not fear, for I am with you; do not be dismayed, for I am your God. I will strengthen you, I will help you, yes, I will uphold you with My righteous right hand. (Isaiah 41:10)

I have told you these things so that in Me you may have peace. In the world you will have tribulation, but be of good cheer, I have overcome the world. (John 16:33)

Father, today we pray for your people who are hurting emotionally, spiritually, mentally, or physically. God, you know their every need. Your Word states, "He *causes his sun to rise on the evil and the good, and sends rain on the righteous and the unrighteous*" (Matthew 5:45). Together all across this globe, we join our faith for wholeness for your people. May their strength be renewed as they meditate on your Word. You are faithful. Amen.

Have a blessed day, God's beautiful people. Thank him for your healing.

You Just Gotta Love Christmas in July

Good morning, beautiful people. I have been praying and preparing for a party I am helping a friend with Christmas in July. I love Christmas. I love to live in the spirit of Christmas all year long. Oh, how the birth of Jesus changed everything. My prayer is that you know him, and he changes everything for you.

Today let's thank God that Jesus was born. Today I don't know what each of you is struggling with. We all have struggles. Some with addictions, anxiety, fear, misunderstandings, broken relationships, health, and so many other issues. Your help is in the Word of God. You can take Jesus at his word. He is not a man that he should lie.

Today whatever your struggle is, find a scripture in the Bible that addresses it and begin to pray the scripture and believe that God himself will get involved. Believe me, he will get involved. The greatest man that ever walked this earth wants to journey life with you. Can you believe?

To the anxious and fearful, Jesus says, "Do not be anxious about anything, but in every situation, by prayer and petition, with thanksgiving, present your requests to God" (Philippians 4:6). "Cast all your anxiety on me [Jesus] because I care for you" (1 Peter 5:7).

To the fearful, declare today, "For God hath not given us the spirit of fear; but of power, and of love, and of a sound mind" (2 Timothy 1:7).

To the people struggling when evil seems to prevail, declare, "Do not be overcome by evil, but overcome evil with good" (Romans 12:21).

To the people struggling with sickness and disease, declare, "He sent his Word, and healed me, and delivered me from my destructions" (Psalm 107:20). "He was wounded for my transgressions, he was bruised for my iniquities. The chastisement of our peace was upon Him, and with his stripes, we are healed" (Isaiah 53:5).

He is the man with the answer for everything. You just gotta know him.

Father, thank you for the birth of Jesus, our Savior and King. Thank you for getting involved in our daily lives. No matter what the situation, you are greater. You have a plan, and you have given us promises in your

Word that you will work it all out for good in all our lives.

Today all across this globe, we join our faith together that many will believe and touch the hem of your garment. May hope arise today, and our enemies be scattered. We pray the blinders that have veiled the eyes of your people be removed today as the God of this world (enemy) has blinded them. "May truth reign in their hearts as they begin to declare and believe your Word over their lives" (2 Corinthians 4:4).

Today may good overcome evil all across this world. May the light in your people shine brightly today as we all stand strong in your Word. "Faith comes from hearing the message, and the message is heard through the Word about Christ" (Romans 10:17).

Thank you for being our God. We are blessed to be your people.

Have a blessed day, beautiful people. Enjoy Christmas in July and thank God that a baby has changed everything.

Are You in the Storm? Stay Focused

Good morning, beautiful people, good morning. Yesterday, as I was driving, and the snow and freezing rain was hitting my windshield, I couldn't stop thinking how quickly storms hit our lives. One day, it almost seems like springtime has arrived, and then another storm hits. It is so comforting to know that no matter what is going on in our lives, we can hold on to every promise that is ours through the hope we have in Christ Jesus. He truly is the anchor of our soul.

As I traveled slowly but confidently down the steep hills and winding turns, I kept focused on the road ahead of me. I finally reached my destination, my home. As I put my vehicle in the garage, the ice began to melt and fall away immediately. The storm was now behind me. This early morning, I listen to the winds as they blow profusely outside my window. It was so comforting to know whether today there will be another storm, or the sun will shine, we don't face it alone. God's Word tells us, "He will never leave us nor forsake us" (Hebrews 13:5). Let's pray.

Father, thank you for your Word. Thank you that all things work together for good for those who are in Christ Jesus (Romans 8:28). Whether we are in the eye of the storm, or we are smoothly sailing across the sea of life, you are journeying with us. Nothing can separate us from your love, nothing.

Father, Romans 8:35–39 tell us, "Who shall separate us from the love of Christ? Shall trouble or hardship or persecution or famine or nakedness or danger or sword? As it is written: 'For your sake we face death all day long; we are considered as sheep to be slaughtered. No, in all these things we are more than conquerors through him who loved us. For I am convinced that neither death nor life, neither angels nor demons, neither the present nor the future, nor any powers, neither height nor depth, nor anything else in all creation, will be able to separate us from the love of God that is in Christ Jesus our Lord.'"

Thank you for your love. You bring every person who will journey life with you to the other side of the storm. The sun will shine once again in their lives. You are the same God who tells the winds to blow, the snow to fall, and the sun to shine, and you have your eye on us today. God, may we never forget it no matter what part of the winding road or steep hill we are on. Amen.

Have a blessed day, beautiful people. Stay focused on the promises of God. He will bring you through.

The Results Are In, He Is Still in Control

Good morning, people, good morning. Isn't it good to have the freedom of choice and we can exercise our right to vote accordingly, and changes are made? However, one thing never changes, his Word and his promises still stand throughout our changing times. You can tally it up anyway you desire. The end result will always be the same. He will always have the final say. Our God reigns. Let's pray.

Father, thank you that today is just as bright as it was yesterday. As times change, government changes; one thing remains the same. You are the same yesterday, today, and forever (Hebrews 13:8).

Father, as we prepare to begin a new season, we can rest assured that we can continue to put all our trust and our faith in you. Your watchful eye is over us. Psalm 91:9–11 tells us that the Lord is our refuge, and if we make you our dwelling place, no harm will overtake us, no disaster will come near our tent. For you will command your angels concerning us to guard us in all our ways.

Father, as we begin our day today, we continue to worship you in spirit and in truth. For the results are in, and you are still in control. You are watching over your Word to perform it (Jeremiah 1:12). Some things never change; it was settled long ago. "The earth is the Lord's, and everything in it, the world, and all who live in it; for he founded it on the seas and established it on the waters" (Psalm 24:1–2). To that, we say amen.

Have a blessed day, God's beautiful people. Believe God's Word.

He Knows the Way You Should Take

Good morning, beautiful people, good morning. On Monday morning of this week, I was on my morning walk, doing what I do every morning—praying. As I came down Industrial Park here in my city, a little boy's sandal caught my attention. Right in the path before me was this little blue-and-orange sandal. I stood there for a few moments as I looked at it before me. So many thoughts ran through my head as I remembered the little boy's dedication I attended just a few weeks prior. My heart skipped a few beats.

I remember that Sunday morning very clearly. I felt impressed to attend church in another town. As they announced this baby's dedication, I leaned over to my sister and said, "Now I know why I am here." Mom sang this beautiful song, and I must admit, I have played it every day since. When I saw this picture that Mom posted, I just had to ask permission to use it. I would say this baby is thanking his mom today for dedicating him to the Lord. Can you imagine having the creator of the universe, the person who formed you in your mother's womb, watching over you? I would say that would make for a happy baby.

I was giving a friend a ride to work later that morning. I told her I had to go back and pick up the sandal that was in my path earlier. She said, "Oh, I know who lost it." This morning, as I gave her a ride once again, she said the boy's mom was grateful to have both sandals once again. I love how God knows the way we should take. I love that he knows the number of hairs on our heads. I love how he orders our footsteps.

If you haven't dedicated your child to the Lord, there is no time like the present. A child is never too old to be dedicated or christened. Talk to God about it today. He has the master plan for all our lives. He knows the way we should take.

Father, you said children are a gift from you, O Lord (Psalm 127:3). Just as we cannot understand the path of the wind or the mystery of a tiny baby growing in its mother's womb, so we cannot understand the activity of God, who does all things (Ecclesiastes 11:5). You always amaze us,

God.

Thank you for the blessing of children. May many moms and dads across this globe today choose to dedicate their children to you. Even if there is only one parent present, you know the way they should take.

We pray you strengthen parents today. May they choose to train their children up in the ways of the Lord, and when they are old, they will not depart from it (Proverbs 22:6).

Thank you for watching over your Word to perform it (Jeremiah 1:12). Amen.

Have a blessed day, beautiful people. It's a little chilly here in Maine as the season is changing. I am blessed once again this morning as I look down at my sweatshirt to prepare for my morning walk. It reads, Speak hope, speak love, speak life (Transformations Ministries). Powerful words. Thank you, God, for knowing the way we should take.

Have a blessed day, God's beautiful people.

Are You Flourishing?

Good morning, beautiful people, good morning. Today let's pray together about flourishing. Let's pray.

It is good to praise the Lord and make music to your name, O Most High, proclaiming your love in the morning and your faithfulness at night, to the music of the ten-stringed lyre and the melody of the harp. For you make me glad by your deeds, Lord; I sing for joy at what your hands have done. *The righteous will flourish like a palm tree, they will grow like a cedar of Lebanon; planted in the house of the Lord, they will flourish in the courts of our God. They will still bear fruit in old age, they will stay fresh and green, proclaiming, the Lord is upright; he is my rock, and there is no wickedness in him.* (Psalm 92:1–4 and 12–15)

1. In his days may the righteous flourish and prosperity abound till the moon is no more. (Psalm 72:7)

Father, thank you for flourishing your people. It is your will that we bear fruitful lives for your glory. Today may someone be drawn to the light that lives in each of us because we are Christians.

Today all across this globe, we declare we need more of you and less of us. We surrender all. Do you? Amen.

Have a blessed day (flourishing day), for this is the day the Lord has made, and we will rejoice and be glad in it.

Are You Free?

Good morning, beautiful people. This morning, I reflect on a Bible study I wrote for a friend dealing with shame. Shame is not my portion, and neither is it yours, my friend, if you are a born-again believer in Jesus Christ. The Bible is very clear on this. Today let's take a closer look at this subject.

Romans 3:23–24 states, "For ALL have sinned and fallen short of the glory of God and all are justified freely by his grace through the redemption that came by Christ Jesus." The question really is do you believe this, and can you receive it?

Ephesians 2:8–9 states, "For it is by grace you have been saved, through faith-and this not from yourselves, it is the gift of God, not by works, so that no one can boast." Have you received this free gift, truly received it?

We know from his Word that he paid a dear price for our sins, and we are a new creation when we receive him. Second Corinthians 5:17–21 states, "Therefore, if anyone is in Christ, he is a new creation; the old has gone, the new has come! All this is from God, who reconciled us to himself through Christ and gave us the ministry of reconciliation that God was reconciling the world to himself in Christ, not counting men's sins against them. And he has committed to us the message of reconciliation. We are therefore Christ's ambassadors, as though God were making his appeal through us. We implore you on Christ's behalf: Be reconciled to God. God made him who had no sin to be sin for us, so that in him we might become the righteousness of God."

This verse brings a chuckle every time I read it. I became a Christian when my children were young. I would watch Joyce Meyer on television, and she would teach on righteousness. I so needed to believe this. I would walk around my house and repeat out loud, "I am the righteous of God through the blood of Jesus Christ." I needed to believe this. I would always tell my children they were the seed of the righteous as my children. I tried to teach them this early in life. One day, a daughter of mine got mad at my other daughter, and they were having an all-out disagreement, and one said to the other one, Don't say that to me, I am the seed of the righteous. I think of that memory with a smile.

Oh, the righteousness of God through the blood of Jesus, I received it, and so should you. Titus 3:5 states, "He saved us, not because of righteous things we had done, but because of his mercy. He saved us through the washing of rebirth and renewal by the Holy Spirit."

"But God, who is rich in mercy, for his great love wherewith he loved us, Even when we were dead in sins, hath quickened us together with Christ, by grace ye are saved" (Ephesians 2:4–5). Can you believe this?

I have received the freedom of guilt from my past, and today you can too. Hebrews 8:12 states, "For I will I forgive their wickedness and will remember their sins no more." First John 1:9 states, "If we confess our sins, he is faithful and just and will forgive us our sins and purify us from all unrighteousness."

Have a talk with your Heavenly Father today (pray). My heart leaps as I type out the final verse to a short version of this study. "So if the Son sets you free, you will be free indeed" (John 8:36). Do you believe this? You are free.

Let's take a moment and together pray this prayer.

Father, I thank you for dying on the cross for my sins. Holy Spirit, teach me and lead me in all truth. I realize even on my best days, I could never earn my salvation. It is a gift freely given to me by my Heavenly Father. Today I am reassured of my salvation, and I believe Jesus bore my sins on that cross. Today I receive freedom from guilt and shame. I am not perfect, and when I sin, I have an advocate with the Father. I will enjoy my journey with Jesus as he changes me from glory to glory according to his Word. My desire is to be more like him. Today I choose to believe the Word (my Bible) that he has forgotten my sins as far as the east is from the west. I now have a new beginning. I believe he will never leave me nor forsake me. I will not allow shame to be put on me by others for my past sins nor will they be my focus. I have given them to Christ. I receive my new beginning. Shame is not my portion. I am free.

Can you receive your new beginning? "So if the Son sets you free, you will be free indeed" (John 8:36).

Reflection

What does that freedom look like for each of us? I compare it to prison doors being opened and people walking out free. What are you going to do with your new-found freedom? My prayer is you will help others get free. You are free!

Have a blessed day, beautiful people. Stand firm and do not be burdened again by a yoke of slavery (Galatians 5:1).

He Said What?

Good morning, beautiful people, good morning. Jesus told us in John 19:30, "It Is finished." It's a done deal, paid for, it's complete. Man cannot give you this. You can't buy it, earn it, and none of us deserve it. The finished work of the cross is mine and yours if you will ask and receive.

As a young girl growing up in church, I thought that if I was good enough, I possibly could make it to heaven. It didn't take me long to figure out I just couldn't obtain such a status on my own.

As an adult, I realized we are all sinners, but it was all paid for by the blood of Jesus Christ. There would be nothing in my past, present, or my future that could ever separate me from Jesus Christ and his love for me. His blood was enough. No perfection status I could ever obtain on my own could surpass the work of the cross. That sure makes this girl want to shout it is finished this morning. Let's pray.

Father, thank you for the gift of salvation. John 3:16 tells us, "For God so loved the world that he gave his one and only Son, that whoever believes in him shall not perish but have eternal life." In John 14:6, Jesus tells us that "I am the way, the truth, and the life. No one can come to the Father except through me." Thank you. There is no social status, race, color, or creed that can stop us from receiving the greatest gift ever given to mankind.

Father, today may many hearts be opened to receive the good news of the Gospel of Jesus Christ. Draw them by your spirit, we pray. Your heart is that none should perish (2 Peter 3:9), and your heart is our heart. Thank you for the finished work of the cross. Amen.

Have a blessed day, beautiful people. Shout it is finished!

Heal Every Heartache

Good morning, beautiful people. We are a group of diverse people journeying life together. Some people are so sweet, kind, loving, and some are just plain mean, nasty, and challenging. For the mean folks, I try to take a step back to see if I can discover where their life was broken. I pray that God himself would bind up their wounds. I have discovered some of the meanest people are just full of fear, hurt, and buried pain. Some of the nicest people have just buried their pain deep and in need of love as well.

We can't ignore the mean, bruised people in our path. We as Christians must reach out with the love of Christ and show them compassion. Let's pray that we can share the love of Christ with someone today.

Father, thank you for your love. You are all love and compassion, full of mercy and grace. Your love is so amazing. Today for broken people across this globe, we bring them to the healing waters of Jesus Christ. You have come to bind up their wounds and set them free.

Father, every hurt, every failure, every time we were wounded, you saw it all. You say come, come to me, my son, my daughter, and let me heal those places and make you whole again. I am your good Father.

There is no brokenness you can't heal, and no pain you can't take away. Father, give us the strength and willingness to reach out to people that are hurting today. Amen.

Have a blessed day, beautiful people. Come into his presence today and let him heal those deep broken places in your life.

"The Spirit of the Lord is on me, because he has anointed me to proclaim good news to the poor. He has sent me to proclaim freedom for the prisoners and recovery of sight for the blind, to set the oppressed free" (Luke 4:18).

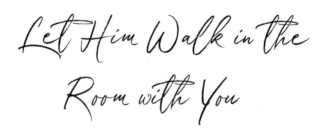

Let Him Walk in the Room with You

Good morning, beautiful people, good morning. This morning, I was thinking how I really disliked doing things alone. I avoided places where I had to go by myself. After my divorce, I knew that was an area that I would need to work on. I began to pray that God would strengthen me. Guess what? I started getting invitations to go places where I had to go alone. God showed me every time I was not alone, he was there. There was no place I would journey on this side of heaven again that God himself would not be with me. What a promise, what a victory. Let's pray.

Father, thank you that you never leave us nor forsake us. Your mercy is new every morning. Great is your faithfulness. No matter where we journey, whether we are with a crowd or we go alone, your presence is with us.

Father, for everyone going through a dark place today, we lift them up to you. There is nothing that can separate them from your love. Strengthen them today, we pray. Divorce, abortion, trauma, death of a loved one, addiction, and brokenness, you have to hold on, God's people. We have the victory.

Father, you said to draw close to you, and you would draw close to us (James 4:8). Strengthen your people today, and may we all walk confidently in your promises, knowing we are not alone. Amen.

Have a blessed day, God's most beautiful people, let him walk in the room with you today. I am.

Let It Calm Your Soul

Good morning, beautiful people, good morning. Let's allow God's Word to calm our soul.

For the word of God is quick, and powerful, and sharper than any two-edged sword, piercing even to the dividing asunder of soul and spirit, and of the joints and marrow, and is a discerner of the thoughts and intents of the heart. (Hebrews 4:12)

Father, thank you for speaking to us through your Holy Scriptures. Your Word speaks to us every day. Yes, yes, yes, it does. You communicate with mankind in so many ways. Your written Word (Bible) is a powerful tool in which we can read, we can believe, and, with great expectation, look for you to reveal every answer we need. You are truly the answer for every need mankind has today. We keep our eyes fixed on you and your Word.

Father, use these words to encourage us, mold us, shape us, comfort us, and change us to be more like you. You speak rest to the weary soul. You speak peace to the anxious mind. You speak love to the brokenhearted. You speak healing to the sick and afflicted, and whatever the situation is in our lives, you have it covered with your Word.

It's always best to have everything in writing (a written contract), and we have it. Father, you gave us your Word. You don't erase it, change it, or take it back. It is forever settled. Thank you for these Holy Scriptures. They truly are life to our bones.

The Bible with our contract (his covenant) is our instruction for daily living. Jesus, you truly are the answer. Since you created us in your image and gave us our manual for daily living, we are excited to meet with you every day to know what you have to say to us. Holy Spirit, lead us today in the Holy Scriptures.

Have a blessed day, beautiful people. Journey with Jesus every day and thank him for speaking to you through his Word. He is the man with all the answers and solution to every problem you have.

Let the Future Begin

Good morning, beautiful people. Let's thank God today for our futures.

Father, thank you for victory. Thank you for your Word that sustains us. How do we ever thank you? By giving you all the glory, by taking you at your Word, and by believing these Holy Scriptures. You said, God, in Deuteronomy 20:4, "For the Lord your God is the one who goes with you to fight for you against your enemies to give you victory."

Father, in John 16:33, you said, "*I have told you these things, so that in me you may have peace. In this world you will have trouble. But take heart! I have overcome the world.*" Don't these verses make you want to do a little dance?

O God, let the healing begin in our lives, in our nation, and to the nations. Thank you for hearing when we call. You are a faithful, faithful God. Amen.

Have a blessed day, God's beautiful people. He loves you! (John 3:16).

Let the Rescue Begin

Good morning, beautiful people, good morning. Today I wanted us to join our faith for the prodigals. So many people I have met have been hurt by Christians. I am sure most people don't even realize how they come across. I know I don't at times. For the most part, I have found people are good. They would never intentionally hurt a person. However, it is true, hurting people hurt people. Church is no different. A group of imperfect people coming together to grow more into the image of Christ. So today let's ask God himself to show us someone that has left the fold that we could reach out too. Let the rescue begin.

Father, you left the ninety-nine and went after the one (Luke 15:4). Today we call back the prodigals. Give us the words to say and the open doors to them. May their hearts be open to receive the love you have for them through us. Where there has been hurt, thank you for healing them. Where there has been offense, we pray that forgiveness will flow. It's time for the prodigals to come home, and we want to do our part. Set it up, O God.

Together all across this globe, let's declare the prodigals are on their way home. Amen.

Have a blessed day, beautiful people. Keep your eyes open and do your part.

"Suppose one of you has a hundred sheep and loses one of them. Doesn't he leave the ninety-nine in the open country and go after the lost sheep until he finds it?" (Luke 15:4).

Let the River Flow

Good morning, beautiful people, good morning. Today let's pray a few scriptures on hardening of the heart.

Whoever conceals their sins does not prosper, but the one who confesses and renounces them finds mercy. Blessed is the one who always trembles before God, *but whoever hardens their heart falls into trouble.* (Proverbs 28:13–14)

They are darkened in their understanding and separated from the life of God because of the ignorance that is in them due to the hardening of their hearts. (Ephesians 4:18)

Father, today we come before you and give you permission to examine our hearts. We love you, Jesus, and we want to make sure there is a flow of your spirit in our lives. We give you permission to show us anything that has hardened our hearts. We will obey whatever you tell us to do. Make it clear to us, O God, for some of the rocks (wounds) have made our hearts stony.

Rain down on us today, O Lord, and cleanse us. Break up the rocks (hardness), the ice (coldness), and let the love of God flow once again in us and through us. Make our lives a river of life to others that are losing hope today all across this globe. For your glory alone, Jesus, you are so worthy.

Have a blessed day, beautiful people. Let the river of life flow through you today.

Let Your Heart Spill the Beans

Good morning, beautiful people, good morning. Today is my middle daughter's birthday. My granddaughter went with her dad to purchase a cake to celebrate yesterday. She was supposed to keep it a secret. Her mom texted me to say as Maisie ran in the house, this precious two-year-old kept repeating, "Mommy cake, Mommy, cake." She had spilled the beans. Her love for her mother was so overwhelming than to keep the secret of the cake.

It makes me ponder how people can be so in love with Jesus and not spill the beans. Let's pray.

Father, your Word tells us in Ephesians 3:17–19 (Paul), "That Christ may dwell in our hearts through faith. And pray that we, being rooted and established in love, that we may be able to comprehend with all the saints what is the breadth and length and height and depth, and to know the love of Christ which surpasses knowledge, that we may be filled up to all the fullness of God. Thank you for filling our hearts with your love." Thank you for the opportunity today to spill the beans from the abundance of our heart.

Father, don't let us miss the opportunity to see the person losing hope, knowing we have the answer. Give us the courage to share our faith with a hurting world. (The great commission.) "Go therefore and make disciples of all nations, baptizing them into the name of the Father, Son and the Holy Spirit" (Matthew 28:19). Amen.

Have a blessed day, God's beautiful people, spill the beans and tell others about Jesus!

"For out of the abundance of the heart, the mouth speaketh" (Matthew 12:34).

Let's Keep Asking

Good morning, beautiful people, good morning. Today let's thank the Lord for his spirit moving across our nation like never before.

Truly, truly, I say to you, unless one is born again, he cannot see the kingdom of God. Nicodemus said to him: How can a man be born again when he is old? Can he enter a second time into his mother's womb and be born? Jesus answered, Truly, Truly, I say to you, unless one is born of water and the spirit, he cannot enter the kingdom of God. That which is born of the flesh is flesh, and that which is born of the spirit is spirit. Do not marvel that I said to you, you must be born again. The winds blow where it wishes, and you hear its sound, but you do not know where it comes from or where it goes. So, it is with everyone who is born of the Spirit. (John 3:3–8)

The person without the Spirit does not accept the things that come from the Spirit of God but considers them foolishness, and cannot understand them because they are discerned only through the Spirit. (1 Corinthians 2:14)

Father, thank you for breathing on our nation once again. Spirit of God, move all across this land, we pray. We join our faith together and declare your mighty winds of revival are blowing.

Father, let your fire blaze higher today all across this land, we pray.

Thank you for pouring out your spirit. We are continuing to declare Joel 2:28 and Zechariah 4:6.

Father, thank you for all your blessings. We are a blessed people. All across this globe today, we are declaring the winds are blowing. The spirit of the Lord is moving. Thank you for breathing down on us. Amen.

Have a blessed day, beautiful people. Keep asking, believing, and receiving.

Let's Say Yes

Good morning, beautiful people, good morning. Today let's pray that we will be obedient followers of Jesus Christ. Let's say yes.

Then Jesus told his disciples, If anyone would come after me, let him deny himself and take up his cross and follow me. (Matthew 16:24)

We know that we have come to know him if we keep his commands. Whoever says, "I know him," but does not do what he commands is a liar, and the truth is not in that person. (1 John 2:3–4)

As Jesus was walking beside the Sea of Galilee, he saw two brothers, Simon called Peter and his brother Andrew. They were casting a net into the lake, for they were fishermen. "Come, follow me," Jesus said, "and I will send you out to fish for people." At once they left their nets and followed him. As obedient children, do not conform to the evil desires you had when you lived in ignorance. But just as he who called you is holy, so be holy in all you do; for it is written Be holy, because I am holy. (Matthew 4:18–20)

My sheep hear my voice, and I know them, and they follow me. *(John 10:27)*

Then spake Jesus again unto them, saying, I am the light of the world: he that followeth me shall not walk in darkness, but shall have the light of life. (John 8:12)

And he said to all, "If anyone would come after me, let him deny himself and take up his cross daily and follow me. (Luke 9:23)

Father, today we say yes to following you. Where you lead us, we will follow. We thank you for leading us beside still waters as you speak to us as only you can. Sometimes you ask us to step out into the unknown; other times the path is made very clear. Either way, we say yes to being fishers of men. Where you lead us, we will follow. No turning back, absolutely no turning back.

Today all across this globe, we declare our *yes* means *yes*, *we* will follow you. Are you ready to totally surrender and follow him? If you are, tell him so.

On the mountaintops of our lives, we will shout *yes*, and down in the valley, we still will say *yes*.

We declare we are totally surrendered to your will and to your way. We declare today, we are followers of Jesus. We say yes.

Have a blessed day, God's beautiful people. Say yes to whatever he may ask of you.

Letting Go, Putting the Past in the Past

Good morning, beautiful people. Let's choose to let go and put our past in our past. We are women of great value and of great worth. It's time for us to live like it. Let's ask the Holy Spirit to show us anything that may be lingering in any crevices of our heart. Are there any lies left? Anything hidden that hasn't come to light yet? Is there anything more we need to address and say goodbye too. Once and for all, we are putting the past in the past.

We desire to live free as the butterfly. We want our wings to fly, to soar right into our destiny. The plan that God has for our life, we desire to fulfill it, and he desires for us to fulfill it as well. Let's pray and ask the Holy Spirit to show us if there's more and prepare us to release it.

Father, show us what's in our hearts today. Repressed memories, buried hurts, pain, anguish, show us what's left. Remove any residue of woundedness that needs to be healed.

Father, we thank you in advance for what you are doing. Amen.

We have identified, and we have processed the pain, the hurt. We now have a choice, and we choose to release it. There is not enough alcohol, drugs, pain medication on this planet to take care of the anguish some have gone through. We have given them to the Lord Jesus Christ. We will never take them back. Ever. As we go through this list, do you have any other bondages, lies, and torment that comes to your mind? If so, write it down. We are taking it all to our Father tonight. His love for us covers it all. He will rebuild the ancient ruins of our lives according to Isaiah 61.

He tells us he loves us unconditionally. First John 4:16 tells us, "And so we know and rely on the love God has for us. God is love. Whoever lives in love lives in God, and God in them."

There is no fear in love. But perfect love drives out fear, because fear has to do with punishment. The one who fears is not made perfect in love. (1 John 4:18)

I have loved you with an everlasting love; I have drawn you with unfailing kindness. (Jeremiah 31:3)

See what great love the Father has lavished on us, that we should be called children of God! And that is what we are! The reason the world does not know us is that it did not know him. (1 John 3:1)

For all have sinned and fall short of the glory of God. (Romans 3:23)

And hope does not put us to shame, because God's love has been poured out into our hearts through the Holy Spirit, who has been given to us. (Romans 5:5)

Who shall separate us from the love of Christ? Shall trouble or hardship or persecution or famine or nakedness or danger or sword? As it is written: "For your sake we face death all day long; we are considered as sheep to be slaughtered." No, in all these things we are more than conquerors through him who loved us. For I am convinced that neither death nor life, neither angels nor demons, neither the present nor the future, nor any powers, neither height nor depth, nor anything else in all creation, will be able to separate us from the love of God that is in Christ Jesus our Lord. (Romans 8:35–39)

Now, isn't that just sweet! It's like honey to our lips!

I have hearts that represent the heart of your Heavenly Father. His heart is full of love for you. Nothing but plain old love. Girlfriends, you don't need to be jealous of each other. You don't need to compare yourself to each other. You just need to be you. You were created in the image of God. You are a precious gem! All the pain you have endured, the hardships, and the sadness, he wants to take it all. He will take it all. He will restore you. Do you really believe this? "Go up to Gilead and get balm, Virgin Daughter Egypt. But you try many medicines in vain; there is no healing for you" (Jeremiah 46:11).

Sometimes medicine is not the answer. I believe in medicine, and God does use it. But I believe the best medicine you can take is the word of God. You can read it, chew on it, talk to your Heavenly Father about it and ask the Holy Spirit to bring revelatory knowledge.

Every day we need to take three pills.

The life pill. We need to choose to live and declare John 10:10 over our lives. If any other voice speaks to us and tells us contrary to the Word of God, we must silence the voice. Say Jesus, the blood. Jesus came to give us life and life more abundantly.

We need to choose to love, even the mean, nasty folks. How many know some mean sisters? "A new command I give you: Love one another. As I have loved you, so you must love one another" (John 13:34).

Laugh every day. A merry heart doeth good like a medicine, but a broken spirit drieth the bones. Laugh. Try to laugh at least three times a day. We eat three meals a day, right? That feeds our body. Laughter feeds our soul. It's good medicine.

Miracles Are for Today

Good morning, beautiful people. Let's pray miracle scriptures.

Jesus performed many other signs in the presence of his disciples, which are not recorded in this book. *But these are written that you may believe, that Jesus is the Messiah, the Son of God, and that by believing you may have life in his name.* (John 20:30–31)

Very *truly I tell you, whoever believes in me will do the works I have been doing, and they will do even greater things than these, because I am going to the Father.* (John 14:12)

Then the disciples went out and preached everywhere, and the Lord worked with them and confirmed his word by the signs that accompanied it. (Mark 16:20)

Father, thank you for miracles. Today we join our faith together all across this land for every person who needs a miracle. You said it is not by might nor by power but by your spirit. We thank you for the miracle-working power of Jesus Christ. Today we pray obedience for your people.

May we all do as you instruct by the power of your Holy Spirit. Let us see the miracle-working power of Jesus Christ this day. Amen.

Have a blessed day, beautiful people. Believe in miracles.

God, Thank You for the Morning

Good morning, beautiful people, good morning. I love to wake up every morning and spend time in the presence of God. I choose to forgive everyone who thinks I am too radical because, yes, yes, I am. Radical it is. When you have been to the pit like Joseph, and God brought you out, you can't wait to wake up every morning to see what is going to happen next. He will always have the final say on writing our story if we will believe. His love is just amazing. Today let's worship him and believe his love letter to us. These Holy Scriptures are life to even the driest bones. Let's pray.

Father, thank you for the morning. Every sunrise shows your love and brings forth your glory in our lives. We thank you that you paint beautiful pictures not only in the sky but in lives of people who can believe on the name of Jesus Christ.

There is no mountain too high and no valley to low that your hand can't reach down and show the beauty and the resurrection power of Jesus Christ. Father, your agape love cannot be equaled or surpassed by anyone or any earthly thing. Thank you that it is available to all and given freely by you every day.

Father, we pray for people all across this globe to return to their first love. If they have never experienced your love, we pray today is their day. Nobody loves us like you do. Amen.

Have a blessed day, God's beautiful people. Thank him for the morning. He loves us.

"Whoever does not love does not know God, because God is love. This is how God showed his love among us: he sent his one and only Son into the world that we might live through him. This is love: not that we loved God, but that he loved us and sent his Son as an atoning sacrifice for our sins" (1 John 4:8–10).

Miracles Happen Every Day

Good morning, beautiful people. Today let's pray about miracles.

Simon himself believed and was baptized. And he followed Philip everywhere, astonished by the great signs and miracles he saw. (Acts 8:13)

God did extraordinary miracles through Paul. (Acts 19:11)

To one there is given through the Spirit a message of wisdom, to another a message of knowledge by means of the same Spirit, to another faith by the same Spirit, to another gifts of healing by that one Spirit, to another miraculous powers, to another prophecy, to another distinguishing between spirits, to another speaking in different kinds of tongues and to still another the interpretation of tongues1 (Corinthians 12:8–10)

And God has placed in the church first of all apostles, second prophets, third teachers, then miracles, then gifts of healing, of helping, of guidance, and of different kinds of tongues. (Corinthians 12:28–29)

God also testified to it by signs, wonders and various miracles, and by gifts of the Holy Spirit distributed according to his will. (Hebrews 2:4)

Father, thank you for being a miracle-working God. It is a blessing journeying everyday with the one what created us. You always answer when we call (Psalm 4:1).

Today we join our faith together all across this globe for anyone needing a miracle. We thank you, Lord, for sending your answer. You answer in ways we never could think or imagine. Your answers are always the best.

Use the body of Christ today to be that miracle for each other. Thank you for an assignment today bigger than ourselves. We will stand, believe, and take action. Fulfill your Word in all our lives. Whatever miracle needed for everyone praying this prayer today, we stand in faith to receive your answer.

Miracle-making God, have your way in our lives today.

We declare miracles are coming down. We declare miracles happen every day.

Have a blessed day, God's beautiful people. This is the day the Lord has made, and we will rejoice and be glad in it. Believe.

Life Is for Living

Good morning, beautiful people, good morning. Every day we can choose happiness, or we can choose to live the mundane. We make the choices for our lives with the help of the Holy Spirit. Today let's declare we will fulfill our God given destiny. Amen? Amen! Let's pray.

Father, thank you that you have given us life and life more abundantly (John 10:10). Empower us to make the choices of how we will live each day according to the plan you have predestined for each of our lives. Your plan is our personal journey. There is absolutely nothing better than journeying every day with Jesus Christ.

Today we can choose to let no person nor circumstance dictate our happiness. The journey will have many twists and turns, but ultimately we will arrive right on time to the course God has chosen for us.

Father, healing waters, yes, we do believe. Setting us free, that's our heart's desire. Healing, wholeness completing the deep work in us. Yes, that's what we so desire. You, O Lord, you are the one. The only one who can complete the deep work in us. Strongholds destroyed by the power of your name. Thank you for turning our darkness into light.

Oh, how we love to praise your name!

Have a blessed day, God's beautiful people. Decide today to enjoy life, love deeply, and journey every day with Jesus.

"I perceived that there is nothing better for them than to be joyful and to do good as long as they live; also, that everyone should eat and drink and take pleasure in all his toil—this is God's gift to man" (Ecclesiastes 3:12–13).

Listen and Obey

Good morning, beautiful people. This morning, I was reviewing my journal once again. After a time of prayer and fasting, I penned these thoughts one early morning. The time is now. Go, go, go. I want to use you as forerunners trailblazers. Go ahead and light the way. Many will come, and many will ask how you have done this. Your answer will be, "It's Jesus. It's Jesus, just listen and obey. There is no other way than to listen as you pray."

If you have experienced a season of trials, and you have endured them, then this word is for you.

I have seen your heart, and I have seen your pain. You have endured much. I have heard your many cries. I have tried you and found you trustworthy and faithful. I will open doors for you that no man could ever close. I will do exploits through you because you listen and obey. Do as I instruct. Keep your ears sharp for what the spirit is saying. Love is the greatest gift. What I have freely given you, go give it away.

Father, the greatest gift we have ever received was Jesus. Oh, how we love you, Jesus. Today we join our faith all across this globe for an explosion of the Gospel of Jesus Christ. Father, you said we have not because we ask not God (James 4:2). We want the world to know Jesus.

Father, you said it is not by might nor by power but by your spirit. Thank you, spirit of God, for drawing souls unto yourself. Thank you for signs, wonders, and miracles as we obey your voice (Mark 16:17).

Thank you for the blessings that will come upon us and overtake us according to your Word in Deuteronomy 28 if we obey the voice of the Lord our God. Give us sensitive ears to hear what the spirit of the Lord is saying and the courage to step out and be obedient. We give you all the glory for everything you do in us and through us.

Oh, how we love you, Jesus. Amen.

Have a blessed day, beautiful people. Listen as you pray and then obey. Share your faith.

Living a Destiny Moments Life

Good morning, beautiful people. I have had several destiny moments with people in the last few days. There is no way I could make any of this happen. It's Jesus. It's all about Jesus.

I was in a restaurant with a friend, celebrating her birthday. The lady at the next table had lost her keys, had been looking for several hours, and had now called the tow truck. The dealership, where she had purchased the vehicle, would begin the process to make her a new key. This was the day she had planned out just for herself, and it wasn't going so well.

As I overheard her conversation and felt for her, I inquired if I could pray with her. I prayed the prayer of agreement from Matthew 18:19, "Again, truly I tell you that if two of you on earth agree about anything they ask for, it will be done for them by my Father in heaven." Together we thanked God for revealing where the keys were. I then told her to call the three stores she was in. First store no keys, second store no keys. "Oh, hold on they are being turned in right now," the lady said.

This dear woman jumped up gave me a high five, and I went to retrieve the keys for her. Isn't that the God we serve? Our paths may never cross again, but as long as she remembers, it's all about Jesus, and he cares about every detail of her life. I'm good. Let's pray.

Father, thank you for destiny moments. Thank you that every detail of our lives, you care about. Thank you for the promise of the prayer of agreement.

As we journey our lives today, may we all remember that it's all about Jesus. "He is the way, the truth, and the life" (John 14:6).

Father, give us all the opportunity to have those destiny moments with others today. You are always watching over your Word to perform it. Amen.

Have a blessed day, beautiful people. Live your life looking for your destiny moments.

Mercy, Mercy, and More Mercy

Good morning, beautiful people. Today let's thank the Lord for mercy.

Praise be to the God and Father of our Lord Jesus Christ! In his great mercy he has given us new birth into a living hope through the resurrection of Jesus Christ from the dead. (1 Peter 1:3)

David said to Gad, "I am in deep distress. Let us fall into the hands of the Lord, for his mercy is great; but do not let me fall into human hands." (2 Samuel 24:14)

Hear my cry for mercy as I call to you for help, as I lift up my hands toward your Most Holy Place. (Psalm 28:2)

You, Lord, are forgiving and good, abounding in love to all who call to you. (Psalm 86:5)

The Lord is good to all; he has compassion on all he has made. (Psalm 145:9)

Be merciful, just as your Father is merciful. (Luke 6:36)

But because of his great love for us, God, who is rich in mercy. (Ephesians 2:4)

He saved us, not because of righteous things we had done, but because of his mercy. He saved us through the washing of rebirth and renewal by the Holy Spirit. (Titus 3:5)

Let us then approach the throne of grace with confidence, so that we may receive mercy and find grace to help us in our time of need. (Hebrews 4:16)

Blessed are the merciful, for they will be shown mercy. (Matthew 5:7)

Father, thank you for mercy. We do not receive what we deserve because of the mercy you have given us. Today we thank you for strengthening us. May we always choose to be merciful. Lord, you were good to all, and that is our heart's desire. You didn't give us what we deserved; you showed us mercy while we were yet sinners. Let us extend it to a hurting world.

O God, the greatest gift we can give away is to show mercy and to love one another. Even in hardship, you showed mercy. You said, "Blessed is the merciful for they will be shown mercy" (Matthew 5:7).

All across this globe today, we declare mercy reigns. Have a blessed day, God's beautiful people. Be merciful!

Miracles Are Breaking Loose! Believe

Good morning, beautiful people. I have had the privilege to witness miracles. I have interviewed people who have received miracles on my radio broadcast. I have been part of prayer assignments in which God performed a miracle. Today I will speak with people right here in Aroostook County, Maine, that have received miracles. I speak with Facebook message, etc., with ordinary people who God has used to perform miracles every day.

On my birthday this past July, I received a book, True Stories of the Miracles of Azusa Street and Beyond. The subtitle, Re-live one of the Greatest Outpourings in History that is Breaking Loose Once Again… Doesn't that make you want to give a shout? That was a great gift.

God's Word says Jesus Christ is the same yesterday, today, and forever (Hebrews 13:8).

In John 14:12, it says, "Very truly I tell you, whoever believes in me will do the works I have been doing, and they will do even greater things than these, because I am going to the Father." He tells us in Mark 16:20, "Then the disciples went out and preached everywhere, and the Lord worked with them and confirmed his Word by the signs that accompanied it."

Whatever you need today, ask him. Jesus already paid the price. Jesus is alive and well. Read these Holy Scriptures and believe them. He says in Jeremiah 32:27, "Behold, I am the Lord, the God of all flesh. Is there anything too hard for Me?" Let's pray.

Father, for everyone needing a miracle today, we join faith together all across this globe. Yes, we declare you are alive and well, and your spirit is moving across this land. God of miracles, we believe in you. Yes, we do!

Thank you for this great outpouring that is breaking loose. We receive it. Amen.

Have a blessed day, God's beautiful people. Believe…

Miracles, Can You Believe and Receive?

Good morning, beautiful people, good morning. Miracles happen every day. I was in services recently that many, many people received their miracle. Hundreds of people were healed. Whatever you have need of, let's join faith and ask the miracle-maker, Jesus Christ.

Father, you tell us in James that we have not because we ask not God. So today we ask you and thank you for our miracle. Today we are asking, believing, and receiving.

Doctors do what they can do, but they don't have the final say. You do the impossible. I have witnessed too many miracles in my lifetime to not believe. You ask us every day. "Can you believe?" Father, forgive our unbelief. I have seen you move mightily in miracles. Thank you that you are the same God yesterday, today, and forever. Jesus, thank you that you show up right on time every time. Faith arise in your people across this globe today.

For that person that you healed yesterday, they are rejoicing today. For the people you will heal today, we give you thanks. We thank you ahead of time. Thank you for being a healing Jesus. You said by your stripes, we are healed. You already paid the price.

"He sent his Word and Healeth thee. We receive the Word of The Lord, for it never changes" (Psalm 107:20).

Declare today and every day, beautiful people, that healing is your portion. Thank him ahead of time for divine health. Now that's faith.

Together we pray our Father's prayer.

Our Father in heaven, hallowed be your name, your kingdom come, your will be done, on earth as it is in heaven. Give us today our daily bread. And forgive us our debts, as we also have forgiven our debtors. And lead us not into temptation but deliver us from the evil one. For thine is the kingdom, and the power, and the glory, for ever and ever. Creative miracles, reversal of symptoms, whatever is needed in every believer's life today, we receive. Amen.

Have a blessed day, God's beautiful people. He loves you. Be healed in Jesus's name!

Mission Kindness

Good morning, beautiful people. It's a little frosty this morning here in northern Maine. However, the warmth from the fire of God in our hearts makes the day so warm and inviting.

As I was glancing through my journal and saw some notes from a mission trip to Los Angles from several years ago, I thought about the blanket that God himself provided for a woman in need. Sometimes the mission is more for us than the people who receive. My heart was so full of joy that I was able to be a part of something so precious. Causing people who are losing hope to find it in God once again is priceless. There is nothing we will ever give to people more valuable than the Word of God and to show them his love and kindness.

Today let's sprinkle kindness everywhere we go. Let's bring hope to someone who may be losing it. Where are they, you may ask? Let's ask God himself.

Father, thank you for divine appointments today. Show us someone, God, who needs a little kindness. Show us someone who needs a little hope. Use us today, Father, to be your hands extended. Thank you for bringing us together.

Thank you, God, for giving us eyes to see you at work in the world around us. Thank you for ears; we pray to hear what you are saying. May we be obedient to the call to be more like you. Let our lives show the love of Christ and kindness everywhere we journey. Amen.

Have a blessed day, beautiful day, you are loved!

"Therefore, as God's chosen people, holy and dearly loved, clothe yourselves with compassion, kindness, humility, gentleness and patience" (Colossians 3:12).

Mouth Speak Good Words

Good morning, beautiful people, let's pray about our speech today.

Let the words of my mouth and the meditation of my heart be acceptable in your sight, O Lord, my rock and my redeemer. (Psalm 19:14)

The tongue has the power of life and death, and those who love it will eat its fruit. (Proverbs 18:21)

For as a man thinketh in his heart, so is he. (Proverbs 23:7)

Father, help us to speak life everywhere we go. Holy Spirit, convict us of any negative words spoken against ourselves or others. Purify our words, O God. May we meditate on your Word both day and night. Help us to think the best of everyone we meet. They too were created in your image.

Father, may the world see you in us through the words we speak and the things we do. Help us, God, to be a good witness. May we be bold as a lion and gentle as a dove. Amen.

Have a blessed day, beautiful people, for this is the day the Lord has made, and we will rejoice and be glad in it. Thank him for purifying our mouths.

Narrow or Wide? You Choose

Good morning, beautiful people. Today let's pray Matthew 7:21–27 together.

Not everyone who says to me, "Lord, Lord," will enter the kingdom of heaven, but only the one who does the will of my Father who is in heaven. Many will say to me on that day, "Lord, Lord, did we not prophesy in your name and in your name drive out demons and, in your name, perform many miracles?" Then I will tell them plainly, "I never knew you. Away from me, you evildoers!" "Therefore, everyone who hears these words of mine and puts them into practice is like a wise man who built his house on the rock. The rain came down, the streams rose, and the winds blew and beat against that house; yet it did not fall, because it had its foundation on the rock. But everyone who hears these words of mine and does not put them into practice is like a foolish man who built his house on sand. The rain came down, the streams rose, and the winds blew and beat against that house, and it fell with a great crash."

Father, thank you for your Word. Today we ask you to fortify the walls of our lives. When the enemy comes in like a flood, you, O God raise up a standard. Going to church and doing good deeds doesn't cut it with you. You are looking for people who are sold out to do the will of their Father. You said to enter through the narrow gate. "For wide is the gate and broad is the road that leads to destruction, and many enter through it. But small is the gate and narrow the road that leads to life, and only a few find it" (Matthew 7:13–14). Today we declare we are on the narrow road that leads to life. Make any adjustments to our lives, Lord, that keeps us on the narrow road. Amen.

Have a blessed day, God's beautiful people. Stay on the narrow road.

Need a Dose of Happiness?

Good morning, beautiful people, let's meditate on being happy.

When he arrived and say what the grace of God had done, he was glad and encouraged them all to remain true to the Lord with all their hearts. (Acts 11:23)

Whoever gives heed to instruction prospers and blessed is the one who trusts in the Lord. (Proverbs 16:20)

For you make me glad by your deeds, Lord; I sing for joy at what your hands have done. (Psalm 92:4)

He has told you, O man, what is good; and what does the Lord require of you but to do justice, and to love kindness and to walk humbly with your God? (Micah 6:8)

Rejoice in the Lord always; again, I will say, rejoice (Philippians 4:4).

Father, oh, what a happy day. Our days are filled with joy as we meditate on your Word. It is so very true; your Words are life to our very bones. We thank you that the joy of the Lord is our strength (Nehemiah 8:10). It is an amazing journey as we walk with you each and every day.

Today all across this globe, we pray for a happy day. We encourage ourselves with the Word of the Lord and declare it is a happy day. Amen.

Have a blessed day, God's beautiful people. Enjoy your happy day!

Need a Fresh Start?

Good morning, beautiful people. I was driving to Washburn, Maine, a week or so ago, and this church sign caught my attention.

Today let's thank Jesus for all he has done for us. If you haven't begun to walk with him, today is your day. Start you journey with the man who is rich in love and full of mercy.

But God, being rich in mercy, because of the great love with which he loved us, even when we were dead in our trespasses, made us alive together with Christ— by grace you have been saved—and raised us up with him and seated us with him in the heavenly places in Christ Jesus, so that in the coming ages he might show the immeasurable riches of his grace in kindness toward us in Christ Jesus. For by grace you have been saved through faith. And this is not your own doing; it is the gift of God, not a result of works, so that no one may boast. (Ephesians 2:4–9)

Father, thank you for the gift of salvation. This free gift we didn't earn, couldn't earn if we tried, but given by your grace alone. From Washburn, Maine, all across this globe today, we pray many will read this sign and respond to your call. You are no respecter of persons, and your love for mankind is just amazing.

Father, you have the power to break addictions, to meet needs, and change hearts and circumstances.

All across this globe today, we declare the king of glory wants to journey life with us.

Together let's pray we will all experience the amazing love he has for us in a deeper way this year. He wants to be involved in our daily lives, and we need him to be. We can talk with him about anything today! There is no secret formula. He's waiting to hear from us. Amen.

Have a blessed day, God's beautiful people. Every day we have a new fresh start.

Need Hope?

Good morning, beautiful people. Today let's pray about hope.

Now the God of hope fill you with all joy and peace in believing, that ye may abound in hope, through the power of the Holy Ghost. (Romans 15:13)

For we are saved by hope: but hope that is seen is not hope: for what a man seeth, why doth he yet hope for? (Romans 8:24)

For I know the thoughts that I think toward you, saith the Lord, thoughts of peace, and not of evil, to give you an expected end. (Jeremiah 29:11)

Be joyful in hope, patient in affliction, faithful in prayer (Romans 12:12)

Father, thank you for the birth of Jesus. Today for anyone losing hope, you, O God, are their hope. Your Word says that the God of hope will fill us with all joy and peace in believing. Thank you for bringing hope to this world through your son, Jesus.

All across this globe today, we declare and decree that the God of all hope will strengthen is. We believe in the Word of the Lord, and we are filled with hope today. Amen.

Have a blessed day, God's beautiful people. Share your hope.

Need Repair?

Good morning, beautiful people. Today let's thank God for putting our lives back together again.

The Lord *is close to the brokenhearted* and saves those who are crushed in spirit. (Psalm 34:18)

He *heals the brokenhearted and binds up their wounds.* (Psalm 147:3)

1. Peace I leave with you; my peace I give you. I do not give to you as the world gives. Do not let your hearts be troubled and do not be afraid. (John 14:27)

Father, thank you today that many broken lives will receive healing. I pray churches all across this globe will turn into a hospital for your people. Lord, we bring them to the healing waters of Jesus Christ. Jesus, thank you for making your people whole again. Life isn't always easy, and the trials sometimes almost takes their hope away. You, O God, are our hope, our healer, and our friend.

Father, we join our faith for one another that you will put the pieces of shattered lives back together again. We give you all the glory.

All across this globe today, we declare Jesus is our healer. We declare the healing waters are flowing. Amen.

Have a blessed day, God's beautiful people. Thank him for rebuilding the broken places in your life.

Need Some Fire? Ask and Receive

Good morning, beautiful people. Today let's ask for a fresh infilling of his Holy Spirit. Let's pray together.

And *I will ask the Father, and he will give you another advocate to help you and be with you forever—the Spirit of truth. The world cannot accept him, because it neither sees him nor knows him. But you know him, for he lives with you and will be in you. I will not leave you as orphans; I will come to you. Before long, the world will not see me anymore, but you will see me. Because I live, you also will live. On that day you will realize that I am in my Father, and you are in me, and I am in you.* (John 14:16–20)

I baptize you with water for repentance. But after me comes one who is more powerful than I, whose sandals I am not worthy to carry. He will baptize you with the Holy Spirit and fire. (Matthew 3:11)

Father, thank you for the power of your Holy Spirit. We ask you to fill us today with a fresh infilling so that we may walk in your anointing. We desire to bring your presence to our atmosphere all across this globe today.

Father, we give you permission to empty us of anything that is not of you. Baptize us with the Holy Spirit and fire. Holy Spirit, take full and complete control of our lives. Order our footsteps according to your Word, we pray.

We receive our fresh infilling of your Holy Spirit because we asked. For You said in John 14:12–14, "*Very truly I tell you, whoever believes in me will do the works I have been doing, and they will do even greater things than these, because I am going to the Father. And I will do whatever you ask in my name, so that the Father may be glorified in the Son. You may ask me for anything in my name, and I will do it.*" Use us for your glory today, O God. Yes, we will go. Amen.

Have a blessed day, beautiful people, let the Holy Spirit lead and guide you today and every day. Fire!

No Jealousy Allowed in His Kingdom, World Changers

Good morning, beautiful people, good morning. Today I wanted to write about a work of the flesh called jealously. God's Word tells us to rejoice with those that rejoice and weep with those that weep (Romans 12:15). It sounds pretty easy, right?

Then we see other people's lives being blessed, an increase in anointing on another man or woman's ministry, other folk's prayers being answered while we remain in faith believing. Oh, how the flesh wants to rise up. We see brother so and so or sister so and so that God chose (admit it, you wouldn't have choose them), and they are flourishing. It's challenging to your flesh, isn't it? You might as well admit it; God sees the heart. Then we meet up with the whippersnapper that came out of nowhere, and they are dripping with the anointing of God on their life. They never stepped a foot in Bible College, but their hearts are full of the Word of God. You know them, right?

Recently, I was in a service where just that happened. The older well-trained preacher asked the whippersnapper to pray for him. Ironically enough, I heard the prophetic word over Mr. Whippersnapper and had been believing with him for the ministry God called him too. Since it's God's kingdom, he can do whatever he wants, choose whomever he wants, and use anybody he desires. Let's pray he finds us fit for his use.

Father, thank you for allowing us to work in the kingdom. Father, we will rejoice with those who are prospering. We will weep with those who are weeping. We will trust you have our lives in the palm of your hands. We will put all our trust in you, and we will lean not on our own understanding.

Father, purify our hearts, purify our motives, and make us useable. Destroy the works of the flesh in us, we pray. We desire to be valuable vessels for your kingdom, we pray. We will give you all the honor, God, we give you all the glory.

Today we for ask for forgiveness for works of our flesh. Thank you for the blood of Jesus and his grace that gives us a new beginning every day.

Father, all across this globe, we declare your people are coming up higher and following after the spirit of the Lord and denying the works of the flesh. Amen.

Have a blessed day, beautiful people. Declare jealousy, be gone.

No Competitiveness in the Kingdom

Good morning, beautiful people. Let's pray about competitiveness in the body of Christ.

Father, thank you for hearing the years of intercession that has gone up before you. You said if we prayed and believed, you would move on the earth, and you are. We know your heartbeat, God. Your heart is that none should perish but have life.

Father, we thank you for your presence on the earth today. Thank you for coming back in our nation again in power and might. Thank you for coming in our personal lives with more revelation as we seek you. We desire you in a greater way. Thank you for life, the book of life (Bible), and journeying every day with us. Forgive us, God, for when we didn't speak up for you when they were pushing you out of our government, schools, courts, and our daily lives. Thank you for being a covenant-keeping God, despite what man has done. You are a true covenant keeper and igniter of the flame. Fan the flame today, we pray across your land. Blaze, Spirit, blaze.

Father, thank you for the flames that have ignited across this globe. People are hungry to touch the flame. Thank you for hearing and answering prayer as we have done and will continue to do as you have instructed us according to 2 Chronicles 7:14, "If my people, which are called by my name, shall humble themselves, and pray, and seek my face, and turn from their wicked ways; then will I hear from heaven, and will forgive their sin, and will heal their land." (Pray.)

Thank you for pouring out your spirit according to Acts 2:17. We receive you back again in a greater way. Thank you for the open heaven. We are receiving it. This flame will never die. Thank you for healing our land. Thank you for lasting fruit. Thank you for the greatest outpouring this world has ever known. To the seven continents of the world, we receive. Amen.

Have a blessed day, God's beautiful people. Thank him for pouring out his spirit on your region today. Thank him for the fire. Thank him for fulfilling his promises. Fire! Now go ignite others for his glory alone. As Christians, we are working in the same kingdom. There is no competitiveness, just completeness.

"In the last days, God says, I will pour out my spirit on all people" (Acts 2:17).

Hope, Healing, Happiness

Good morning, beautiful people, good morning. Holidays can be painful for some families. Brokenness, loss of a loved one, financial hardship, and many wounds we never may never know or see. However, we know that Jesus cares. He will walk through life with us, renew our hope, heal the hurts, and bring joy back in our lives. Because Jesus lives, we can face every tomorrow. Amen? Amen!

Father, thank you for filling lonely hearts, healing broken lives, and restoring the hope in people losing it today. You are their hope. All the world needs are in you. No matter how low someone feels today, you will reach down and lift them up. You will send them help from on high. You meet needs; you heal lives in every way. You are our God, and we are your people.

Father, today may we hear your voice and be that hope as we share the good news of the Gospel of Jesus Christ. A kind act, a smile, a handshake, or meeting the needs for people among us, everybody has something they can give.

Father, may the heart of Christ rise on the earth like never before. The good Father, Emmanuel, Elohim, Abba, Yeshua, Messiah, your name is mighty and great. Thank you for pouring out your spirit. Because you live, every person can face tomorrow. Amen.

Have a blessed day, God's beautiful people. Be full of hope, be healed, and choose to be happy because Jesus lives.

"But now, Lord, what do I look for? My hope is in you" (Psalm 39:7).

No Limits on Your Design

Good morning, beautiful people. This morning, I was thinking about the limits we put on ourselves. I do it at times and don't even recognize it. I love to dream, and I love to help other people dream as well. I like to take the limitations off as I recognize them and take steps toward fulfillment of my life's purpose. I love to help others do the same. I tell people daily they were born to be world changers. I tell myself that. I tell my children and grandchildren that. I tell people I meet every day that. Let's revisit this today.

You were born to be world changers. Can you believe it? Off with the lies and on with the truth. The world can have a different look today because you are here. You may feel insignificant today. Stop lying to both yourself and the world and declare, I am a world changer.

Today, rise up and take that next step. This step will look different for everyone all across this globe as we are all designed differently. Do you realize you don't have any limits? Only the ones you place on yourself? What lies are you believing? I'm not smart enough, educated enough, not in the right size. I'm too fat, too skinny, too tall, or too short. My hair is the wrong color. I am not attractive enough. My feet are too big; my nose isn't right; and I can't type fast enough. I don't know how; my parents didn't teach me. I have been abused. I have no money. My car is too old. This can't be me. I just can't be a world changer. No, not me, I am one of the unlucky ones. I don't know why, it never works for me. I am always behind the eight ball, and what would people think? Admit it, your believing lies.

You may ask, how do you know for sure that I am a world changer? I'm glad you asked. I am penning these words this morning, but long before the foundations of the earth, the Lord had a plan for your life. These are your Creator's words. You don't have to believe me but choose today to believe the one who created you. He knit you together and formed you in your mother's womb, and he knows you best. The manual for daily living is the Bible. Today bring it out, dust it off, upload it, download it, read it, and, most of all, believe it. You were designed to be a world changer. You are…you are…you are…

Let's pray this prayer once again today. Father, thank you for our lives. Thank you for designing us. Thank you for creating us to be world changers. Today wherever we find ourselves, we thank you, for you knew we would be right where we are long before we knew. Thank you for ordering our footsteps. Thank you for the providential plan of God in our lives.

Father, break off every lie that we are believing of ourselves (name them if you can), for we are just right. We are wonderfully made, and we want to leave our mark on the world today. Thank you, God, for ordering our footsteps right into destiny.

We are world changers. We believe, we believe, we believe. We want to be all that you have created us to be, and we want to help others do the same. (Do you?) Thank you for lighting our paths today as we believe your Word. Thank you for increase, thank you for enlarging our territories. Amen.

Have a blessed day, beautiful people. Make an impact wherever your journey takes you today.

"Your word is a lamp for my feet, a light on my path" (Psalm 119:105).

"For you created my inmost being; you knit me together in my mother's womb. I praise you because I am fearfully and wonderfully made; your works are wonderful, I know that full well" (Psalm 139:13–14).

Do You Believe Job 22:28?

Good morning, beautiful people, good morning. I have been cleaning out a little deeper in my home, preparing it to sell. I need it to be ready for when the buyer shows up. Well, I am a paper-a-holic. I have way too many papers. I got so excited about this one paper I rediscovered; I carried it with me for a few days. When I read it, I get so excited I can barely stand it. I so have to share it with you all. This is the first part.

Maine Land of Refreshing (June 18, 2010) Jacobs Root 52 Torch Pass (Cindy Jacobs)

Maine can make the main thing, the Maine thing. The Son will rise with healings in his wings-decree that a healing movement will come out of Maine.

The Lord would say, "I am going to cause many miracles to come out of Maine. I see this gate, this ladder in the heavens in Maine." And the Lord says, "Don't you know the angels are ascending and descending, and they are coming, and there are going to be many visitations?" says the Lord. And the Lord says, "Even as I visited and sent visitations into the Middle East amongst the Muslim people, I am going to visit the Muslim people who are within Maine. There will be a great moving of the Holy Spirit that will affect the whole nation even into Dearborn out of Maine," the Lord says.

And the Lord says, "Even if you re-dig the righteous roots of the Republican Party that came with abolitionism," the Lord says, "You are going to be able to abolish abortion." And God says, "I am going to begin to shift even the Republican Party in Maine from a moderate stand with Olympia Snowe, but I will bring my people into the state." And the Lord says, "I have a grass roots movement that is forming that will shift things in a way that you will almost not be able to believe." For the Lord says, "Maine will shift from the middle to a righteous stand and marry righteousness and justice."

What a timely word, what a timely time to rediscover this prophetic word over Maine. Cindy Jacobs, you are an amazing woman of God. Can't you hear me shouting, "Go Maine?"

As I drove by Whited Bible Camp the last few days in Bridgewater, Maine, and see the rebuilding of the foundation on the Tabernacle, I got so excited. Rebuilding the foundation in the natural represents the spiritual as well. Shout! Shout!

I have sensed that healing rain over Maine for some time. I have sensed the shift; I have sensed an outpouring. Let's thank God for the healing rain over Maine and ask for your state as well.

Father, thank you for the healing rain over Maine. Thank you that Maine will take a righteous stand and marry righteousness and justice. Thank you for the angels that are ascending and descending over Maine. Thank you for this great moving of the Holy Spirit that will affect the whole nation.

Thank you that you are neither Democrat or Republican, but you are a lover of people. Thank you for healing our state and your people. We receive the healing rain. Amen.

Have a beautiful day, beautiful people. Yes, decree a thing, and it will be established. Believe in Job 22:28. As Mr. Emmett would say (my grandson), I sure do!

Hold on, World, We Are on the Way

Good morning, beautiful people, good morning. Today let's get full of the Holy Ghost and be on our way. Amen? Amen!

Father, your Word says that when Peter was filled with power at Pentecost, he declared the message of Christ, and three thousand people were added to the church in one day (Acts 2:41).

Father, fill us to overflowing with the power of Pentecost. Saturate us with fresh oil. One of my favorite scriptures: "Silver and Gold have I none; but such as I have I give unto thee: In the name of Jesus Christ of Nazareth rise up and walk" (Acts 3:6).

Holy Spirit, lead us today, use us today, may we truly be a witness for you. Do a deeper work in us, O God, so the world can see you and experience the miracle-working power of Jesus Christ through us, we pray. Thank you for adding to our churches daily. We believe they are on their way. Amen.

Have a blessed day, beautiful people. Thank him for the power of Pentecost. Now be on your way to share the good news.

Holy Spirit infilling…ask and receive.

Have a blessed day, God's beautiful people. Go out and make a difference.

Need Some Fire?
Ask and Receive

Today let's ask for a fresh infilling of his Holy Spirit. Let's pray together.

And I will ask the Father, and he will give you another advocate to help you and be with you forever— the Spirit of truth. The world cannot accept him, because it neither sees him nor knows him. But you know him, for he lives with you and will be in you. I will not leave you as orphans; I will come to you. Before long, the world will not see me anymore, but you will see me. Because I live, you also will live. On that day you will realize that I am in my Father, and you are in me, and I am in you. (John 14:16–20)

I baptize you with water for repentance. But after me comes one who is more powerful than I, whose sandals I am not worthy to carry. He will baptize you with the Holy Spirit and fire. (Matthew 3:11)

Father, thank you for the power of your Holy Spirit. We ask you to fill us today with a fresh infilling so that we may walk in your anointing. We desire to bring your presence to our atmosphere all across this globe today.

We give you permission, Lord, to empty us of anything that is not of you (tell him if you are). Baptize us with the Holy Spirit and fire. Holy Spirit, take full and complete control of our lives. Order our footsteps according to your Word, we pray.

We receive our fresh infilling of your Holy Spirit because we asked. For You said in John 14:12–14, "Very truly I tell you, whoever believes in me will do the works I have been doing, and they will do even greater things than these, because I am going to the Father. And I will do whatever you ask in my name, so that the Father may be glorified in the Son. You may ask me for anything in my name, and I will do it."

Use us for your glory today, O God. Yes, we will go. (Will you?) Amen.

Have a blessed day, God's beautiful people, let the Holy Spirit lead and guide you today and every day.

Fire!

How Bad Do You Want It?

Good morning, beautiful people, good morning. Yesterday, it was taking the next step day as I walk out the sermon a friend gave at church on Sunday. She delivered a message that was simple but so profound. How bad do you want it? Those words have been ringing in my ears since they left her mouth Sunday morning. I am so full of dreams, vision, and a love for Jesus Christ. I want the world to experience the richness of journeying life everyday with Jesus. We will never get where we are going if we don't take the next step. It certainly was a word in season and the beginning of a new journey for me. I want to see the plan of God fulfilled in my life badly, and I also want to see the plan of God fulfilled in your life as well. Let's pray.

Father, thank you that you are our God, and we are your people. There is nothing that is impossible with you, O God. For your Word tells us all things are possible to those that believe (Matthew 19:26). You tell us to ask (pray), believe, and we shall receive (Mark 11:24).

Father, thank you for journeying each step as we walk out the road before us. Ashes no more! Amen.

Ashes No More
Jesus, lover of my soul
Creator of my image
Lifter of my head
My name is beautiful
Woman, pure, holy, undefiled.
Sanctified, set apart journeying with Jesus.
A path, narrow and straight
Ashes no more.
Trusting her master, her maker, the lover of her soul.
Skipping on the journey with childlike faith
Believing her father knows what's best.
The morning dew, the night's crisp air
Reminds her of the kisses from above.
Jesus, the ultimate man, the lover of her soul.
Beautiful, a receiver of his glory.
Ashes no more.

Have a blessed day, beautiful people. How bad do you want it? Take a step today!

God, How Big Are You? Show Us Once Again

Good morning, beautiful people. I celebrate every day, and I hope you do too. My prayer is that we will finish this year, seeing strongholds over our nation torn down. Always stand for what you believe in, beautiful people, even if it's not popular. Finish your year well. It truly is harvest time.

I wondered what I would pen today being New Year's day. Most days, I surprise myself, challenge myself as I begin to pray and write. Today is no different. I enjoyed my evening last night, playing with my granddaughter. Oh, she is such a delight. As she slept last night, she whined a bit throughout the night. Teething isn't fun, her gums hurt, she just wasn't feeling up to par. As I rubbed her back and watched her sleep with her occasional whining, I began to think about an article I recently read.

The words on the paper tried to convince me about what a long way America has to go to reverse Roe v. Wade. I talked back to the paper that day. Sir, are these your speculations? How did you come up with this conclusion? I found myself challenging the writer of this newspaper article as if he was sitting right in front of me. I continued to ask him who he had been speaking with. Who are you speaking on behalf of… I continued to spout out.

Have you any idea how big our God is, sir? Have you consulted with the God, Most High? What about the guy that walked on the water, Jesus? I continued to argue it out with him. What's he saying about your article? See, sir, there is power in the name of Jesus.

So it being January 1, let's start with the issue beginning with A, Abortion. I can't imagine the intense pain a child feels going through such a procedure. I just can't say any more here right now, I just can't.

I know many of you are writing out your yearly goals, your strategy, and action plans for 2017. I am as well. Will you pray with me about this issue? I am passionate about this. God is passionate about this. Thank you for doing your part.

Father, we join faith across this globe today for the United States of America. I thank you, Lord, your Word trumps it all. Together we join our faith about the an issue…abortion. We declare Roe v. Wade will be overturned. Nothing is too difficult for you. You said to ask, and we have. We give you thanks.

Father, give our leaders wisdom from your throne room, we pray. God, thank you for getting the right people in the right offices at the right place at the right time. You do order our footsteps. Thank you for supernaturally moving on behalf of these children's lives. We won't be silent anymore.

Father, for every woman who bought the lie, we ask you to heal them. We bring them to the healing waters of Jesus Christ. God, you are bigger than, mightier than, and stronger than abortion. Tear this stronghold down and all its tentacles in the name of Jesus, we pray.

We heard the Esther call, and we say yes. (Tell him.) Amen.

Have a blessed day, beautiful people. Bless a child.

"All things are possible, if you believe" (Mark 9:23).

How Far Can Grace Reach?

Good morning, beautiful people, good morning. I love the opportunity to meet new people. On Saturday, a friend and I went door to door, inviting people to come to church the next morning. We had the privilege to pray with several people and saw new faces for the very first time. Some homes we cried, some we laughed, and some we just left the invitation. As we journeyed the road, I was assured there was no one we would meet that was beyond God's grace.

I know the grace I received was his free gift to me. I didn't earn it; I don't deserve it; and I would never be worthy enough on my own. I just can't help myself from desiring every living person to receive it.

As I looked at people through the eyes of Jesus as they opened the door, I so prayed they would come. I was confident that God's Word would touch their lives and change the spiritual atmosphere in their life. His grace is enough. Amen? Amen! Let's pray.

Father, thank you for grace. There is no one who is beyond your reach. The free gift of redemption for mankind is available to all. Thank you for paying the price. Your love is just downright amazing.

Father, draw us all closer to yourself today. Amen.

Have a blessed day, God's beautiful people. His grace is sufficient for both you and me.

"For it is by grace you have been saved, through faith-and this is not from yourselves, it is the gift of God, not by works, so that no one can boast" (Ephesians 2:8–9).

Inner Hurts and Outward Expressions

Good morning, beautiful people. I recently had an activity time with some youth. We spoke about words that hurt and cause people to bleed inside (inner hurts). Sometimes the expression on another person's face is from the results from words that were spoken. Many times, it is easier to have the broken arm, the bruised body than to carry around the pain of inner hurts.

Today we can bring the painful words, the hurts, even the scars left behind and be made whole again. It can change the expression on our faces. Let's pray.

Father, thank you a bruised reed you will not break, and a smoldering wick you will not snuff out. In faithfulness, you will bring forth justice (Isaiah 42:3).

Father, thank you for the grace to forgive the words that were spoken that brought us pain. Thank you that today we can choose to forgive the people who brought the hurt. Ephesians 4:32 tells us to be kind and compassionate to one another, forgiving each other, just as in Christ God forgave us.

Father, please empower others to forgive us for when we have spoken words that brought pain to them intentionally or unintentionally. Nothing escapes your watchful eye, and you hear every word spoken.

Father, help our words to be kind and gentle as Proverbs 15:1 tells us, "A gentle answer turns away wrath, but a harsh word stirs up anger."

Together all across this globe, we release the power of forgiveness for inner hurts, and we receive the healing balm of Gilead. Amen.

Have a blessed day, beautiful people. Live your life happy and free.

Is He Your First Love?

Good morning, beautiful people, good morning. What a great time to be alive. As I review my prayers this morning from 2003–2005, I asked God to forgive me for leaving my first love according to Revelation 2:4. On 4/29/2005, I penned, "O God, forgive me for I haven't and I don't keep you in your rightful place, my first love." On 4/30/2005: "Holy Spirit, I'm here. Please direct me. I desire the double anointing. Teach me about the Elisha Generation, I pray. Holy Spirit leads and guides. Your heart is my heart, O God. You are my heart's desire."

Let's pray together 1 John 14:16, 19, "And so we know and rely on the love God has for us. God is love. Whoever lives in love lives in God, and God in them. We love because he first loved us."

"So these three things continue forever: faith, hope, and love. And the greatest of these is love" (1 Corinthians 13:13).

"For I am convinced that neither death nor life, neither angels nor demons, neither the present nor the future, nor any powers, neither height nor depth, nor anything else in all creation, will be able to separate us from the love of God that is in Christ Jesus our Lord" (Romans 8:38–39).

Father, thank you for your love for your people; so undeserving of the goodness and blessings you bestow on us each and every day. Thank you that nothing can separate us from your love, no, nothing. Today no matter what comes our way, we know we are loved. May we never leave our first love, Jesus Christ.

All across this globe today, we declare the love of God. Share his love with someone today, beautiful people. You have been called for such a time as this.

Have a blessed day, God's beautiful people.

Is It Really Whom You Know?

Good morning, beautiful people. It really is who you know.

Father, I thank you that you are God. You desire your people to do great things in this world for your glory. Getting out of the boat is not easy, nor it is comfortable, but it can be done. We keep turning over the stones and walking through the open doors to discover our steps. One step at a time, all for your glory, God, as we walk out our destiny.

Faith says we can; fear says we can't. We have so many social clubs, but what we need is to see the manifested power of Jesus Christ according to your Word. Peter walked on the water, and, Jesus, we want to walk on the water too. You are no respecter of persons (Acts 10:34). Do great and mighty things through us, we pray.

Father, thank you for doors of opportunity. All across this globe today, God's beautiful people, turn over a stone, look for the door of (opportunity), and see where you find him. Step out and walk on the water. It's time. Amen.

Have a blessed day, beautiful people. He holds your every tomorrow.

Shortly before dawn Jesus went out to them, walking on the lake. When the disciples saw him walking on the lake, they were terrified. "It's a ghost," they said, and cried out in fear. But Jesus immediately said to them: "Take courage! It is I. Don't be afraid." "Lord, if it's you," Peter replied, "tell me to come to you on the water." "Come," he said. Then Peter got down out of the boat, walked on the water and came toward Jesus. But when he saw the wind, he was afraid and, beginning to sink, cried out, "Lord, save me!" Immediately Jesus reached out his hand and caught him. "You of little faith," he said, "why did you doubt?" And when they climbed into the boat, the wind died down. Then those who were in the boat worshiped him, saying, "Truly you are the Son of God." (Matthew 14:25–33)

Is It Too Late for Your Breakthrough?

Good morning, beautiful people. Sometimes I am running late; I just am. I try to fit a lot in one day, because when this day is over, I can't get it back. One thing about Jesus, he is never late. He is always right on time. He knows what we need just when we need it, and he will always come through.

Also, it is never too late to accept Jesus into our lives. If you know him, it is never too late to draw closer. It is an amazing journey. Come away today even for fifteen minutes and get into his presence. It will be the best break you will ever know, and you are on your way to your breakthrough. Amen? Amen! Let's pray!

Father, you tell us to draw close to you, and you will draw close to us. (James 4:8) Father, we want to know you better today, better than we knew you yesterday. You are our heart's desire. As we enter your presence with thanksgiving in our hearts and a strong desire to journey every day with you, you fulfill our lives with such joy.

Father, for every reader who is going through a difficult time, reveal yourself to them as Jesus, lover of their soul. They are not alone, for your Word says you will never leave us nor forsake us (Hebrews 13:5). You are the friend that sticks closer than a brother (Proverbs 18:24). May they feel your peace today, the peace that transcends all understanding (Philippian's 4:7). Amen.

Have a blessed day, God's beautiful people. Enjoy your day, for your day will never look like today again. You are just passing through.

Is Your Life in his Hands?

Good morning, beautiful people, good morning. I pondered a lot this early morning the word surrender. God doesn't force us to follow him; he has given us free will and free choice. He doesn't demand, he gently guides. His love is beyond imaginable. It's a love that transcends beyond our limited minds. Don't you think it's time to review where you are in life? I am.

Recently I taped a last-minute interview with some friends about a conference I was involved in. As we were praying prior to the taping, I had a vision, and I saw three clocks, and they were spinning fast.

Last Saturday, I traveled downstate for a prayer meeting for persecuted Christians. I stopped at a store for a friend to purchase some items. A wristwatch caught my eye and attention. It had three little wheel clocks inside the face of this larger sized woman's watch. It quickened something inside of me. I didn't purchase the watch as I have a working watch and didn't need it. However, I couldn't get that watch off my mind. It brought back the memory of the last-minute radio taping a few weeks earlier and the vision I had while praying. The three clocks spinning will be forever etched in my mind. As we traveled further south, we discussed the watch and the vision I had while praying. I happened to look at the license plate of the car in front of me at some point, and it read "outoftme." To me, it was saying out of time. Let's pray.

Father, we don't know the time or hour that you will return. Since I was a young girl, I was afraid you would return, and I wouldn't be ready. I thought you were a Father who was looking to punish me for every wrong doing. I didn't have revelation of your love. I remember as a teenager thinking what the heck, I will never make it anyway and just gave up. Oh, what lies sometimes gets embedded in our lives. Father, thank you for deeper revelation of your love. You created the heavens and the earth, and you were pleased. Your love and mercy for mankind, we don't deserve, but you freely give it. Oh, the grace of our God.

Father, you willingly gave your Son so that mankind could be redeemed and have eternal life with you. Thank you for your love and sacrifice. Amen.

Have a blessed day, beautiful people. Have you surrendered your life to Jesus? Time is running out.

It's Called Life—Live It, Love It!

Good morning, beautiful people. This morning, I was thinking about the greatness of our Creator. Life was his idea; love was his idea; and living it to the fullness was his idea.

As we all face challenges in this life, the answer is always found in him. He will never leave us nor forsake us (Hebrews 13:5).

The plan he has for our life is always good, always on a path to walk closer with him. Today no matter what mountain is in your way, speak the Word of the Lord to it and command it to come down (Mark 11:23). Let's pray.

Father, thank you that your Word is life to our very being. In the beginning was the Word and the Word was with God and the Word is God (John 1:1). Oh, how we love journeying every day with you and your Word.

Thank you that we are called oaks of righteousness, that you have planted for your glory (Isaiah 61:3).

May the world know and see you today as you touch lives all across this globe. Do a deeper work in all of us today, we pray. Amen.

Have a blessed day, God's beautiful people. Live your life, love your life. It is all God's idea.

It's All in the Precious Blood

Good morning, beautiful people. Isn't it great all our hope is in Jesus? I wish I could say I do everything just right, and I never mess up, even as a Christian, but I wouldn't be telling you the truth. I am so thankful for Jesus, my advocate who paid the price. I can be hard on myself because of my less than perfection status. I know my weaknesses; I see my own need of a Savior. I love that I can come back to him and let him cleanse me and wash me white as snow. If we were all truthful this morning, we would have to admit we are all in need of his continued mercy and grace. Let's pray.

Father, thank you for the blood of Jesus Christ. The blood that washes our sins as white as snow. Father, thank you that we can come back to the river as often as we need to. Your love for us is beyond what we could ever imagine. May we never take for granted the price, the precious blood, you shed so we could walk in total victory. Oh, the power that is in that blood.

Father, empower us to make the right choices. However, if we do mess it up, we can come to you, and our advocate, Jesus, has marked it paid in full.

Father, Ephesians 1:7 tells us in him, we have redemption through his blood, the forgiveness of our trespasses according to the riches of his grace. As Christians, we are the richest people alive because of the price of the precious blood. Amen.

Have blessed day, beautiful people. Put your past under the blood.

It's Almost Time, Another World Changer

Good morning, beautiful people. My granddaughter and I are getting ready to go to the hospital so we can meet her new baby brother who will be born this morning. The world will change once again from the arrival of this precious new life. Oh, what a day to celebrate!

I love that God knew us before he formed us in our mother's womb (Jeremiah 1:4). Life is, has always been, and will continue to be God's idea. Let's pray.

Father, thank you for children and grandchildren; they are such a blessing from you. Thank you that today new life will enter the world, my family, another world changer. May he leave his mark on the world and not let the world leave its mark on him, we pray.

Father, thank you that children was your idea long before they were formed in their mother's womb. Thank you that you know the plans you have for every life. These plans are to prosper them, not to harm them, and give them a hope and a future (Jeremiah 29:11). To that, we say amen. Your Word will always be our final answer.

Have a blessed day, beautiful people. Celebrate life! Celebrate your day every day, for God himself is watching over you and wants you to believe his Word. He has the master plan for your life. Talk with him today (pray).

For you created my inmost being; you knit me together in my mother's womb. I praise you because I am fearfully and wonderfully made; your works are wonderful, know that full well. My frame was not hidden from you when I was made in the secret place, when I was woven together in the depths of the earth. Your eyes saw my unformed body; all the days ordained for me were written in your book before one of them came to be. (Psalm 139:13–16)

It's for the Living and the Dying

"If we live, we live for the Lord; and if we die, we die for the Lord. So, whether we live or die, we belong to the Lord" (Romans 14:18).

Father, thank you for salvation. You paid the price that we would have life. As we live our lives in you and through you, you make every crooked way straight. Even in death, we have no fear. For you are always with us.

Father, every day is a joy as we live out the journey you predestined for our lives. Because of your glory, we have the assurance of life and life more abundantly here on earth (John 10:10), knowing someday we will spend eternity with you.

Father, today we celebrate once again all the promises you have given us. Your Word is forever settled and will not return void. It is truth, it is life, and it is glorious. As we journey today, thank you for the opportunities to share the goodness of God. The good news of his resurrection power permeates the earth today, we pray. Open the door to share the love and compassion of our living Savior, Jesus Christ. Empower the body of Christ and add to the numbers daily (Acts 2:47). Amen.

Have a blessed day, God's beautiful people. Have a glorious day!

Jeremiah's Voice, Breaking Chains

Good morning, beautiful people. The hidden scars of abortion and its aftermath are devastating to a woman, her self-esteem, and her everyday health. Physically, mentally, emotionally, and spiritually, she has changed forever. As I have shared some of my journey with you in the first two parts of these posts, I hope it brings you to a new awareness of how abortion hurts women. Can God forgive a person for such a choice? Yes, yes, he can. He forgave me. Can a woman be made whole in every area of her life? Yes, yes, she can. Can a woman have children after an abortion? Yes, many do, including me. However, the enemy of your soul will whisper in your most vulnerable times that you cannot and will not have a fruitful womb. You will have thoughts that forgiveness just could not be for a woman like you. That is a lie. Many women today are still suffering in shame and hopelessness, believing those horrific lies.

The aftermath of an abortion has its own effects on women. To this very day, which is many years after my abortion, I dislike the sound of a vacuum because it reminds me of the procedure and the equipment that was used. I know women across this globe may have aftermath issues unique to their situation and how their loss affected them.

Today I want to end my post praying for women who have suffered the loss of a child through death, miscarriage, or abortion. Today I desire the creator of the universe to touch your heart like never before. Today I want to break the chains; I want to break the silence; I want to expose the lies; and I want Jesus to touch you right where you hurt. Let's pray.

Father, I thank you for new beginnings. I thank you every day is a new beginning. Today, O God, I come in the name of Jesus, the name above all names, to ask you to break the chains off women across this globe. Today I pray for courage. I pray for strength. I pray women will move from guilt and pain to freedom. Lord, you said whom the Son sets free is free indeed. That's our inheritance in Christ Jesus.

Father, I pray for every woman that is in need of healing today. God, give them strength to deal with the grief, the loss, and help them to love themselves for whom you created them to be. They do not need to compare themselves or their circumstances to anyone else's. You created them and have the ultimate plan for their life. God, set in place everything needed to bring the healing as only you can. You paid the price for our wholeness, and today we take the limits off and ask you to touch a hurting world and every hurting woman. I thank you for freedom.

Thank you that you are our judge and jury, and you say be free. You say FORGIVEN. I pray women all across this globe today receive this prayer for whatever circumstance they find themselves in. Draw them close to you, and may they be blessed beyond what they could ever think or imagine. Thank you for breaking the chains, breaking the silence, and breaking through to a hurting world with your love Message (Bible) and your healing balm of Gilead. Thank you, Jesus. Amen.

Be free… "So if the Son sets you free, you will be free indeed" (John 8:36).

Have a blessed day, God's beautiful people.

Kick Out Any Unbelief

Good morning, beautiful people. This morning, I am excited to go meet with my ACTS sisters. They hold the most incredible ACTS Catholic weekends that are life changing.

I look through my boxes in my packed-up house to review the book, Beatrice Tails (Tales), that Sister Mary Kelley penned to raise scholarship money for these retreats. Oh, how that amazing nun (sister) impacted my life.

Together as friends, we learned the love of Christ for each other as we shared our differences in faith and asked the Holy Spirit to teach us truth. A journey I will always love, learning the Word of God.

I penned these words after fasting and praying for a Protestant meeting I attended several years ago. I challenged us all with these words, I have given you a taste of my river. I will not tolerate gossip, backbiting and devouring one another. All of my people are important to me, all of my people. I do not love you anymore than I love them. Come together, lay down agendas, lay down pretense. Do you want the river to continue or do you want the spring to stop? What I am asking of you is to lay it all down. If you have fought against anyone, make it right to the best of your ability. There is no room for offense in my river. There is only room for servant hood. If you desire to be a part of what I desire to do through you, you must not think of yourselves as more important than your brother or sister. I died for them too; I died for them while they were yet sinners. Can you love like I have commanded you? Can you come together and serve from a willingness to please me? Not for recognition, not from your own fleshly desires, but because I have asked of you?

Can you imagine how much could be accomplished for the kingdom of God if we all worked together? Can you imagine what could be done on our jobs, in our families, and in our communities if we all allowed the Holy Spirit to teach us and believed our God together. Acts 4:12 tells us, "Salvation is found in no one else, for there is no other name under heaven given to mankind by which we must be saved." That's the bottom line, final answer.

Have a blessed day, beautiful people. So as Christians, let's believe and be unified today.

Laugh Right Out Loud

Good morning, beautiful people. Isn't it funny how things move smoothly and then oops a bump in the road? You just got to learn to laugh and keep going. The scripture in Psalm 126:2 says, "Our mouths were filled with laughter, our tongues with songs of joy." Then it was said among the nations, the Lord has done great things for them.

In Proverbs 17:22, "A cheerful heart is good medicine, but a crushed spirit dries up the bones."

So today let's fill our lives with some laughter.

Father, thank you for joy. The joy of the Lord is our strength. Thank you that your Word is life to our bones. All across this globe today, we declare joy. May many choose to worship you today and sing songs of praise unto the Lord our God, Most High. Amen.

Have a blessed day, beautiful people. Even if there's a bump in the road, laugh right out loud.

Leave Your Mark on This Day

Good morning, beautiful people. Life is busy, it surely is. Even in northern Maine, life seems to be a bit fast. According to the Word of God, communication with our Heavenly Father is vital to sustain us. Everyone has something they need an answer to. Have you spoken with him today? Take a few moments to thank him for your life and ask him to help you see his hand working on your behalf and the lives of others around you. Once you ask, keep your eyes and ears open, for he answers prayer.

Let's be sensitive to impressions we may have in our mind, heart, or both. Maybe that person you keep accidentally running into, could it be for a reason? Let's be vessels that God could use each and every day.

Every life counts; no one is a mistake here on planet earth according to Psalm 139. Everyone has something to offer this world, something good. What will our contribution be today?

Let's step out once again and move beyond our comfort zones, and together let's leave our mark on the world today. Sometimes the world seems cold, but because you have walked in with the light in our hearts, it changes things. Atmospheres change everywhere because of God's people.

Today let's make life better for someone else. Let's leave our mark on the day. You will soon discover your life has improved as well. You were born to be blessed and be a blessing. You will reap what you sow. God has a way of bringing what you give out back to you. He returns in ways you never even dreamed possible. I am not just writing about financial means but in every way beyond human comprehension. Isn't it an amazing journey walking and talking every day to the person who created us? When you look at people today, see them through the eyes of Jesus.

Let's pray this prayer together this morning.

Father, this is the day you have made, and we will rejoice and be glad in it. We want to live extraordinary lives, not just focusing on everyday tasks. We were created for destiny and the purpose you, O God, have for our lives. We want to fulfill it.

Father, lead us today, order our footsteps. Let the world be a better place because we have made our contribution. We want to leave our mark on this day.

God, you gave your only Son that we may have life and have life more abundantly. We want to give out of the abundance of our hearts today. Help us to be sensitive to everything and everyone around us.

We pray for the needs of all the people on the earth today. You see them all and know them. We join our faith together, God, and we offer ourselves as vessels for you to flow through. Empower us, God, and may our hearts be sensitive to your heart, we pray. As we journey life with you, may you trust us with much. You pour in our lives, God, we pour out. Fill us afresh today with the power of your Holy Spirit, we pray.

We join our faith together for folks who don't know you. Draw them, God, we pray. Jesus, lover of man's soul, thank you for pouring out your spirit on our land. A wonderful loving Father that's what you are. Today thank you for letting the world know your love once again that cost you everything and us nothing. Freely we received it; freely help us to give it away for your glory, Lord, your glory alone. Amen.

Have a blessed day, beautiful people. Enjoy your journey with Jesus.

"This is the day the Lord has made. Let us rejoice and be glad in it" (Psalm 118:24). Yes!

Let All Creation Testify

Good morning, beautiful people. Last evening, I attended a prayer meeting in Mars Hill, Maine, joining faith together for this outpouring of God's Spirit on our land. For days now, my mind keeps going back to the prayer I penned on Easter Sunday, 2017, when I returned home from a sunrise service held at Mars Hill Mountain. I just remember declaring, *"From Mars Hill Mountain to every corner of the earth, hear the Word of the Lord. Jesus lives, and he reins. Praise him today. He is so worthy."*

I sense it is like Christmas in July. It is the beginning of the harvest. Souls saved, lives restored, supernatural healings, deliverance, signs, wonders, and miracles. Somebody shout harvest! Yippee! Yippee! Yay!

Jesus tells us in Matthew 28:18–19, *"Go therefore and make disciples of all the nations, baptizing them in the name of the Father and of the Son and of the Holy Spirit."*

Father, yes, we will go. Send us to the ends of the earth from sea to sea to spread the good news of the gospel. May voices arise today all across this globe for your glory, God. Show yourself mighty in our midst today.

Oh, what joy just serving our king! Amen.

Have a blessed day, beautiful people. Share the good news.

Do You Have Room in Your Life for a Savior?

Good morning, beautiful people. Today I've made it very simple. Can you believe?

Jesus answered, I am the way and the truth and the life. No one comes to the Father except through me. (John 14:6)

And Mary said: My soul exalts the Lord, and my spirit has rejoiced in God my Savior. (Luke 1:46–47)

But for our sake also, to whom it will be credited, as those who believe in him who raised Jesus our Lord from the dead, he who was delivered over because of our transgressions, and was raised because of our justification. (Romans 4:24, 25)

For whoever wants to save his life will lose it, but whoever loses his life for me will save it. What good is it for a man to gain the whole world, and yet lose or forfeit his very self? (Luke 9:24–25)

For God so loved the world that he gave his one and only Son, that whoever believes in him shall not perish but have eternal life. (John 3:16)

Do you believe and can you follow? Let's pray.

Father, you said to let our yes be yes and our no be no. In you, there is no maybe. We either belong to the kingdom of darkness, or we belong to the kingdom of light. You don't force people to believe, you gave us all a free will.

The gospel message is very simple. Your great love for mankind cost you everything and cost us nothing. However, there is a cost to taking up our cross and following Jesus.

Together all across this globe, we join our faith today that many will believe on the name of the Lord Jesus Christ and be saved. That they will choose to pick up their cross and be faithful followers of Jesus Christ. Amen.

Have a blessed day, God's beautiful people. May Jesus reign in your hearts today.

Do You Know This Powerful Man?

Good morning, beautiful people. I love to see God perform his Word in people's lives. I am forever asking him the many questions. Why this? Why that? Tell me this, tell me that. Why not now? And how much longer? If you read my posts, you know I have many questions, and I believe he is the man with all my answers. Let's thank God today for Jesus. He has the answer for us all today. Yes, Jesus is the answer, however, you must believe when you call on his name.

Father, thank you for Jesus. Take us up higher today, God. Take us (take me) to a new level in our journey with you. For you said, O Father, you made a public spectacle of our enemy. Our enemy is anything or anybody that exalts itself against the knowledge of God. Father, you triumphed over every principality, and you tore down every stronghold and every high and lofty thing that exalts itself against the knowledge of God.

Father, draw souls to yourself, we pray (John 6:44). No one can come to Jesus unless you first draw them, and they believe. You will raise them up on the last day.

Today we are thanking you for being our power source. You are our healer, deliverer, comforter, friend, and our Father. May many decide to journey with you today and plug in to the one true God in whom man can be saved and set free.

There is power, power in the blood of Jesus and power in the name of Jesus. Believe.

All across this globe today, get plugged in to the right power source and let him set you free. His Word is life to your bones if you will only believe. Amen.

Have a blessed day, beautiful people. Spend some time with the most important man you will ever know, the man who created you. Believe in Jesus and the power of his Word.

"Yet to all who did receive him, to those who believed in his name, he gave the right to become children of God" (John 1:12).

Do You Need a Hug from Jesus?

Good morning, beautiful people. This early morning, I prayed with a friend who needs a God intervention. The problem is big. The trial is great, but it is not bigger than God. I wish she lived closer so I could give her a hug and reassure her it will all be okay. Why and how do I know for sure you may ask that it will all work out? It's because I know my God. It isn't when things are all peachy, we grow. We grow through the trials of life. Don't ever give up, beautiful people, and don't ever let go. God himself will see you through. We all just need to ask him for help. He is a friend who sticketh closer than a brother. He will send you help from on high. He loves you!

One time, during a very difficult time in my life, I cried out to God. I couldn't even lift my head to heaven. It seemed everywhere I turned, I was hard-pressed on every side. I went out on my front porch to just get some fresh air, and there was a gift bag with a teddy bear. The card read, "Here's a hug from Jesus." Let's pray.

Father, thank you for keeping us through the trials of life. Your love is amazing, and your care for your people is never ending. You even send hugs in ways we can't fathom. You never leave us alone, you never forsake us. God, you keep us through the storms of life.

Today for anyone struggling, they just need to call on your name and ask for your intervention and your plan for their life. God, you will never let them go. You have the master plan.

Have a blessed day, God's beautiful people.

Do You Need to Sit with Him Awhile?

Good morning, beautiful people, good morning. Every day we need to find time to be in the presence of God. No matter what our day is looking like, this time is vital. It is necessary to the growth of our walk with Jesus. Nobody can touch our lives like Jesus. Let's pray.

Father, as we sit in your presence today and commune with you, thank you for healing the wounded areas of our lives. You, O God, bind up the brokenhearted and set the captives free. Thank you for the healing balm of Gilead.

For the tired and weary, you are our strength. Nehemiah 8 :10 tells us that the joy of the Lord is our strength. For the wounded, you tell us you sent your Word and healed us (Psalm 107:20).

As we sit with you, you fill every void, wipe away every tear, rebuilt the ancient ruins of our lives, and the list is endless what is accomplished in your presence.

Thank you for being our God, and we your people. We believe!

Have a blessed day, God's beautiful people. May the God of hope fill you with all joy and peace as you trust in him so that you may overflow with hope by the power of the Holy Spirit (Romans 15:13).

Do You Want More of God?

Good morning, beautiful people, good morning. Life is a vapor, here today and gone tomorrow. No time to be woe is me, time to rise up and be the ambassadors we are called to be. Today let's thank the Lord for more of him in our lives. Let's thank him for more of the fire.

Whatever you are going through in your life today, get in his presence and stay there until he fills you with his fire. Let today be the day the power of God transforms your life so you can be the world changer you were created to be. (Yes, you!) If you can't do it alone, call another fire starter in the body of Christ. Don't find someone who will be pitiful with you, find someone who will pray with you until you get the fire.

Let's thank him for his Holy Ghost power and fire today. Somebody shout fire!

Father, thank you that you said we can call on you, and you will answer (Jeremiah 33:3). Today we join our faith for every person around this globe who needs fresh fire, who needs direction, who needs vision, who has a need of any kind. We bring them to you today.

Father, thank you for pouring out your spirit. Thank you for Holy Ghost fire today. Fill us all once again. We all need more of you in our lives, and we are ready to receive it. Amen.

Have a blessed day, beautiful people. Stay in his presence until you receive what you need.

Now look in the mirror, point your finger, and say, "Watch out, world… here comes fire!"

John answered and said to them all, "As for me, I baptize you with water; but One is coming who is mightier than I, and I am not fit to untie the thong of his sandals; he will baptize you with the Holy Spirit and fire. "His winnowing fork is in his hand to thoroughly clear his threshing floor, and to gather the wheat into his barn; but he will burn up the chaff with unquenchable fire." (Luke 3:16–17)

And there appeared to them tongues as of fire distributing themselves, and they rested on each one of them. And they were all filled with the Holy Spirit and began to speak with other tongues, as the Spirit was giving them utterance. (Acts 2:3–4)

Have a blessed day, God's beautiful people. Time to spread the good news like wildfire.

Does God Really Heal Us?

Good morning, beautiful people, good morning. As we prepare for the upcoming Healing Waters Women's Conference, I am so full of excitement. It is with great anticipation our team prepares to share the Word of God who heals people. His Word is powerful, and we can hold him to it. In his presence, so many things happen. Our team loves to believe God for things bigger than anything we could do on our own. Then when it happens, we know it is nothing we could ever accomplish. It's all for his glory. We are just vessels he chooses to use.

Father, thank you for being the God who heals us. No matter what we have going on in our lives, you are greater. You are more powerful than what our limited minds can comprehend. We just need to take you at your Word and believe. All things are possible with God (Matthew 19:26). All things? Yes!

Father, you said to write the vision and make it plain (Habakkuk 2:2). You said to have great expectation (Psalm 39:7). You can do whatever you want, whenever you want; you are God. You are just looking for a place to manifest the power of your spirit. A place where your glory dwells, and the presence of God is welcome with people who believe.

Thank you for being the God who heals (Psalm 107:20). Thank you for being the God who sets people free (John 8:36).

Cancer, diabetes, mental health issues, and every other sickness and disease, you bow to the mighty name of Jesus Christ. You are powerless over us. We are BELIEVERS!

Have a blessed day, God's beautiful people. Stay in faith believing in the Word of Jesus Christ.

"We no longer believe just because of what you said; now we have heard for ourselves, and we know that this man really is the Savior of the world" (John 4:42).

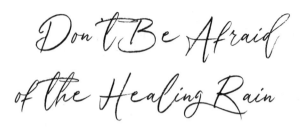

Don't Be Afraid of the Healing Rain

Good morning, beautiful people, good morning. It's a new day, a new season. Don't be afraid to ask Jesus to heal you. The healing rain is falling down. Yes, yes, it is! It's closer to you than you know.

I know people are going through some very difficult circumstances. Some are sick in body, mind, soul, and spirit. They have trials, sickness, disease, loss of loved ones, or just plain broken.

It's like our cars; they break down; and we need to take them to our mechanic. Sometimes things need to be reset to the manufacturer's specifications. Just like us, life has a way of bringing pain and disappointments, and we need to go back to our Creator and ask him to rebuild the ruins, the devastation that has come to our lives. He never turns anyone away, ever. He always says to us to bring it to him, and he will restore to us the years the locusts have eaten. Somebody shout healing rain!

Jesus is the way, the truth, and the life. Journey with him today and let the healing balm of Jesus Christ wash over you. Amen.

Have a blessed day, beautiful people. Embrace the healing rain. Jesus loves you!

Father, thank you for the healing rain. Rain down on us today. We need you more today than we needed you yesterday. Your Word tells us that nothing can separate us from your love (Romans 8:38). It also tells us that "you are the God who healeth thee" (Psalm 107:20).

We believe, and therefore, we receive. Amen? Amen!

Have a blessed day, God's beautiful people.

"If you believe, you will receive whatever you ask for in prayer" (Matthew 21:22).

Don't Be Bamboozled, You Have an Advocate

Good morning, beautiful people, good morning. This morning, I was thinking of all the different opinions, different voices we hear every day. These words all may sound good. They may be good intentions, but what does Jesus say? As we stay committed to the truth of God's Word, he will lead us to stay on the straight and narrow path. Let's commit to the voice of truth.

Father, thank you for your Word. It is a lamp unto our path (Psalm 119:105). Holy Spirit, thank you that you teach us and guide us. John 14:26 tells us, "But the Advocate, the Holy Spirit, whom the Father will send in my name, will teach you all things and will remind you of everything I have said to you."

Thank you for bringing back words of truth as we study to show ourselves approved (2 Timothy 2:15).

Father, keep us from being bamboozled. Empower us to get out of the boat and walk on the water to do great and mighty things for your kingdom. Lead us and teach us today and every day, Holy Spirit, we pray. May the opinions, the voices of man grow dim in the light of your Word. Direct our paths and order our footsteps according to your plan, O God.

Have a blessed day, God's beautiful people. Stay in God's Word and let him lead and guide you. You have a destiny to fulfill. No time to be bamboozled.

Don't Forget

Good morning, beautiful people, good morning. The season has begun, and Christmas lights and trees are appearing all over. 'Tis the season. Our lives become quite busy with shopping, Christmas programs, and festivities. Such a beautiful time of year. Oh, the joy of Christmas. Let's make sure every day we keep Christ at the forefront no matter how busy the days become. He is the reason for this season, and may we never forget it. Let's pray.

Father, thank you for this beautiful time of year. This Christmas season, may we take time every day to close ourselves in with the man who has the master plan for our lives. No matter how busy the days become, may you always have your place first.

Father, as we open our hearts to you, lead us step by step. Show us everything that is ours as Christians. The gift you freely gave us, show us what is in it. The fullness of the Godhead. Holy Spirit, show us everything that is ours in the atonement. Help us unwrap the most beautiful gift ever given to mankind. Show us what is traditions of man, religion, and what is truth as we walk close to you every day in relationship.

Father, thank you for the price you paid for our salvation. There is so much more wrapped inside the gift you gave the world. Peace, joy, love, destiny, healing, eternal life, and so much more all wrapped in the beautiful gift to the world, Jesus, Emmanuel, he is with us.

Have a blessed Christmas season, beautiful people. Don't forget to come away with him and be strengthened in his presence.

"The Word became flesh and made his dwelling among us. We have seen his glory, the glory of the one and only Son, who came from the Father, full of grace and truth" (John 1:14).

Don't Get Caught in the Web

Good morning, beautiful people. It is till dark outside here in Maine this morning, but the light that shines within beams brightly for every circumstance in our lives. All because of one man, Jesus Christ. I pray his light is shining in you. We have all believed lies from time to time as the enemy of our soul plants them in our mind.

For sure, you are worthy. Your sins will be forgiven, and he can use your life for his glory.

"I will rescue you from your own people and from the Gentiles. I am sending you to them to open their eyes and turn them from darkness to light, and from the power of Satan to God, so that they may receive forgiveness of sins and a place among those who are sanctified by faith in me" (Acts 26:17–19).

Father, thank you that we are accepted because Jesus paid the price for our sins. There is only one path, and it is narrow. Jesus Christ is the way, the truth, and the life. "No man comes to the Father but through him" (John 14:6).

Father, thank you that there is no day here on earth that is so dark that your light cannot shine through. We can celebrate every day because of Jesus Christ. We don't have to celebrate like the world does, we can celebrate life from the abundance of joy given to us by our Creator. It sure makes for a good day.

Father, tear down the lies of unbelief, lies of self-worth, and lies of wrong thinking and mind-sets. Highlight any area in our lives that we need the light of Christ to shine truth on. Amen.

Have a blessed day, God's beautiful people. Don't stay stuck in the web.

Don't Walk on By

Good morning, beautiful people, good morning. This morning, I am so excited to go meet my ACTS sisters as we prepare for the upcoming retreat. These ladies are the kindest women, full of God's love. Let's look at what kindness is.

Kindness is opening the door for someone who may be struggling. Kindness is the meal you pay for, even not knowing who they are. Kindness is a smile that brightens someone's day. Kindness is telling someone that Jesus loves them, and you care. Kindness is like wildfire; it spreads.

Today let's light the world on fire with kindness. Why? Just because we can, because we want to be like Jesus. Let's pray.

Father, the fruit of the Spirit is love, joy, peace, forbearance, kindness, goodness, faithfulness, gentleness, and self-control. Against such things, there is no law (Galatians 5:22–23). Thank you for the good shepherd who watches over his flock. His gentle care and his kind ways moves his heart of mercy and compassion to go after the lost, the hurting and bring them back to his house.

Father, give us divine appointments with people who have needs that we don't even know yet. Give us the compassion and kindness to make a difference in their lives. We want to reflect you, O God.

Father, use us today to spread the wildfire of kindness to everyone we meet. Your love is agape, your heart is to die for, your mercy is everlasting, and kindness for all mankind is ever flowing. Oh, how I love the healing waters of Jesus Christ. Amen.

Have a blessed day, God's beautiful people…Spread the kindness. Don't walk on by! Somebody shout wildfire.

Double, Double, He's Back, Put Your Running Shoes On!

Good morning, beautiful people, good morning. I get so excited over the moving of God's Spirit. I am just like a kid at the candy store when I am in a meeting where the spirit of God is moving. Everything happens at these types of meetings, everything. People are healed; they dedicate their lives to Jesus Christ and choose to follow him; and others speak in languages that makes me hungry to understand.

Last night, here in the beautiful state of Maine, Evangelist Sam Austin has hit the ground running. He and his beautiful wife have arrived at Whited Bible Camp, and he is praying his luggage would catch up. I laughed as he preached amongst preachers with their suits fit for a king in his running shoes.

I lay in my bed late last night, pondering his message on the Holy Spirit and the altar. I am up early this morning and pulled a prayer journal from 2003 and a few books that were on the top of a packed box a friend packed up for me. Listen to this line up of books, Such A Vision of The Street: Mother Teresa-The Spirit and the Work (Eileen Egan), Dream Again: Miracles Happen Everyday! (Tommy Barnett), The Power of a Praying Woman (Stormie Omaritian), Access to The Anointing, Steps into The Supernatural (Michelle Corral), and Prayer Rain (Dr. D. K. Olukoya). I must admit I am addicted to my Bible and books.

I review my prayer journal from September 2003. Double, double, speak it, decree it (Job 22:27), and call those things which be not as though they were (Romans 4:17). Put everything on the altar and have faith, Angel. I penned that day. Your place of pain will be double rain, and God will restore as he did for Job. I go on to journal and pray for my children, family, coworkers, and the youth of this nation. I tell Jesus how much I love him. I thank him for my protection, the trial, and remind him of his Word in Deuteronomy 28:7, "The Lord will grant that the enemies who rise up against me will be defeated before me. They will come at me from one direction but flee from me in seven. Somebody shout seven." Oh, the joy of communicating (prayer) with our Creator. Let's pray.

Father, thank you for the greatest outpouring of your spirit this world has ever known. Thank you for double, double. Thank you for filling our youth with fresh fire. Blaze, Spirit, blaze all across this globe, we pray. Restore to us the years the locusts have eaten according to your Word, O God.

Thank you for double, double. Double for the trouble. Jesus, be glorified in our lives. Our eyes are fixed on you. We see the need of the people on the streets, who need to dream again. You, O God, are their living hope. We thank you for pouring out your Holy Spirit in their lives. Rain down healing rain, rain down.

Thank you for hearing and answering our prayers, Mighty God. We have our running shoes on. Amen.

Have a blessed day, God's beautiful people.

Even in Darkness, He Is There

Good morning, beautiful people. This morning, I thank him once again that he is the God who sees and hears it all. There is nothing hidden from him. He looks right into our heart and examines it accordingly. Every heart motive, every thought, and every whisper in secret conversations, he hears and sees it all. There is nothing that escapes his watchful eye. All from a love of a Heavenly Father.

Mother Theresa said it this way, "People are often unreasonable irrational and self-centered. Forgive them anyway. If you are kind, people may accuse you of selfish ulterior motives. Be kind anyway. If you are successful, you win some unfaithful friends and some genuine enemies. Succeed anyway." Let's pray.

Father, thank you that you know the way we should take. Before we speak a word, you know it from afar. Examine our lives today and purge from us the things that are displeasing to you. Without you, we are like lost sheep gone to the slaughter. With you, we are sealed securely in the heart of our Heavenly Father.

Jesus, light of the world, thank you for journeying every day with us. Holy Spirit, lead us beside still waters today. We pray Psalm 123, "The Lord is my shepherd, I shall not want. He leadeth me beside still waters. He restoreth my soul."

Have a blessed day, God's beautiful people. Allow him once again to examine our heart and see if there is any darkness that he needs to bring to the light.

Don't Run on an Empty Tank

Good morning, beautiful people. Every morning, before we start our day, we must spend time in prayer and worship with our Heavenly Father. He fills our lives with his power, his Word, and his truth. Then whatever we face each and every day, we can face it head on, full of his power.

In life, you are moving forward or backward; there is no coasting. With our journey with God, we must continually fill up in his presence and move forward, not looking back. Let's declare in 2019, we will fill up every day and journey our lives led by the power of his Holy Spirit. Let's pray.

Father, thank you for filling us full to overflowing with the power of your Holy Spirit. Thank you for fresh fire and fresh anointing. Thank you for empowering us with your love so that we may empower others.

Father, today we set our face like flint and run the race confidently, knowing you will not let us fail. You are our God (Isaiah 50:7).

Father, you said you left us the Advocate, the Holy Spirit, and he will teach us all things and will remind us of everything you have said to us (John 14:26). Thank you for filling us with that Pentecostal power that we read about in the book of Acts. Amen!

Have a blessed day, God's beautiful people. Keep yourself full of the Holy Spirit by spending time with him today. Somebody shout power!

Nothing Can Hold Us Down

Good morning, beautiful people, good morning. Let's make up our minds today that nobody, no circumstance, and absolutely nothing is going to hold us back from what God has for us. He holds our destinies, and we won't stop short. Fear, shame, doubt, unbelief, and any and all forces that fight against us must come down from their high place. Nothing is going to stop the plan of God—nothing. Amen? Amen! Let's pray.

Father, thank you that even death could not hold you down. You tell us to speak to the mountains, and they must move. You give us power and authority and tell us we can do all things through you (Philippians 4:13). Jesus is the way, the truth, and the life (John 14:6).

Father, thank you for cleansing our minds and removing any lies from the enemy that we are not worthy, we messed up too badly, or there is no hope. We speak to the enemy of our soul today and declare the victory.

Father, thank you that everything is possible for the one who believes (Mark 9:23). We cast aside all doubt and run the race fast and furious in 2019. Nothing, no nothing is going to hold us back because we believe God and his Word. You said it was finished, and it is finished (John 19:30). We will make it to the finish line. Amen.

Have a blessed day, God's beautiful people. Don't let nothing hold you down!

Sing and Believe

Good morning, beautiful people. This morning, I was thinking about the journey of faith. We know that without faith, it is impossible to please God (Hebrews 11:6). Each and every day, we can choose to stay in faith believing God's promises, or we can choose to let doubt creep in. Today let's give doubt a kick out the door and sing our praises even before the answer comes. God delights when we trust him even when circumstances are difficult.

Today no matter what your enemy looks like, face it head on and declare, "I believe God, and he is working it all out for my good" (Romans 8:28). Sing today like you have never sung before. He loves to hear your praise. Amen?

Father, we do sing hallelujah today. You are so worthy. Take delight in our praises, O God. In Psalm 60:12, David tells us, "Through God we shall do valiantly for he it is that shall tread down our enemies."

Father, thank you that no matter what our enemies looks like, you have triumphed over them all. Defeated is their destiny. You made a public spectacle of our enemies, triumphing over them by the cross (Colossians 2:15).

Father, as we sing our praises and put our trust in you, we can journey the day with great expectation. You gave us the victory. "For the Lord our God is the one who goes with us to fight for us against our enemies to give us victory" (Deuteronomy 20:4). Amen!

Have a blessed day, God's beautiful people. Sing hallelujah, I have the victory!

Did You Know God Favors You?

Good morning, beautiful people, good morning. Have you ever just stopped in your tracks and say, "Wow, I don't deserve this. How does this happen to me? This is too good to be true, but it really is?"

Knowing God, loving God, and journeying with Jesus, you begin a life of God's favor. What is God's favor? His unquestionable love, never being alone again, an advocate in all circumstances of our lives, to name just a few. His mercy and grace sustains us through every challenge of life. Oh, what a life living in God's favor. Let's pray.

Father, thank you for your favor. Thank you for your gift of Jesus Christ. We don't deserve all that you have done for us. Your love is never ending and has no boundaries. There is nothing that can separate us from the love of God (Romans 8:35–39). Your favor is beyond what our limited minds can comprehend. Thank you for your favor.

Father, as we journey the day, we can lay down all our anxieties, fears, stress, and sorrow. We can put our faith in you and know that all things work together for good for those that love and serve the Lord and are called according to your purpose (Romans 8:28). Since your heart is that none should perish (2 Peter 3:9), you are calling us all to live a life in Christ. Living our lives every day in Christ and through Christ is where we want to be. Amen? Amen.

Have a blessed day, God's beautiful people… Declare today, I am favored of the Lord, he favors me.

"For his anger lasts only a moment, but his favor lasts a lifetime; weeping may stay for the night, but rejoicing comes in the morning" (Psalm 30:5).

Celebrate Veterans' Day

Good morning, beautiful people, good morning. Today let's pray for our veterans. People are important to God. He knows everything about us, and he knows the sacrifices people have made for others. On this day, we honor and celebrate those who were in the armed forces. They paid a service to our country, and sometimes it has cost them their very life. Only God himself could repay such a person.

Father, thank you for freedom. Today we pray a special prayer for all those that have served our country and paid the price for our freedom here in the United States of America.

Father, may we never take for granted the price they paid and the sacrifice made by their families. Today as we journey the day, may we take a moment to personally thank them for their service.

Father, we ask you to bring healing today for every veteran who has been wounded while serving our country. Only you, O God, can restore the years the locusts have eaten (Joel 2:25). We bring them to the healing waters of Jesus Christ and ask you to make them whole once again.

Father, only you can make sure every need is met on their behalf. You know every detail from the day they were the born until today. We ask you, Father, that you would heal their spirits and bless their lives according to the Word of God. Amen.

Have a blessed day, God's beautiful people. Celebrate a veteran today!

A Real Pioneer

Good morning, beautiful people. Let us run with perseverance the race marked out for us.

Fixing our eyes on Jesus, the and perfecter of faith. For the joy set before him he endured the cross, scorning its shame, and sat down at the right hand of the throne of God. Consider him who endured such opposition from sinners, so that you will not grow weary and lose heart. (Hebrews 12:2–3)

Father, thank you for this Word. You said to run (not walk) with the race that you have marked out for our lives. You said, God, to keep our eyes fixed on Jesus. You said not to grow weary and lose heart.

Today may many all across this globe pick up their pace and begin to run again with what is before them. Jesus the Pioneer, the Perfecter of our faith, continue to strengthen us and order our footsteps as we run the race. Help us shake off all distractions as you have already gone before us and made the way. There is no stopping what God is doing.

Have a blessed day, beautiful people. Run with Jesus the pioneer.

The Clarion Call

Good morning, beautiful people, good morning. As I was preparing for a meeting last week, I kept hearing the words clarion call in my spirit. Since these are words I don't usually use, I began to look up its meaning. I believe God is saying it is time. The time to move beyond complacency. It is time to step out to and be fruitful for his kingdom. Your vision is meaningless, beautiful people, unless you have an action plan. Get in God's presence today and ask him for strategies, ask him to download the plan and how you are to get it accomplished.

At this meeting, I invited people who I knew needed something from God. Some needed healing, some deliverance, some to be strengthened for their journey, some direction, but all needed something from God. Let's be honest, beautiful people, folks all around us are losing hope. Isn't it time to step out of our comfort zones and make a difference in our communities, states, and in our nation? I believe Jesus is saying so. We don't need to agree on everything, but we need to be about our Father's work.

I am reminded about a word I penned in September 2005. I have given you a taste of my river. I will not tolerate gossip, backbiting, and devouring one another. All of my people are important to me, all of my people. I do not love you any more than I love them. Come together, lay down agendas, your pretense. Do you want the river to continue? Or do you want the spring to stop? What I am asking of you is to lay it all down. If you have ought against anyone, make it right to the best of your ability. There is no room for offense in my river. There is only room for servanthood. If you desire to be a part of what I desire to do through you, you must not think of yourself as more important than your brother or sister. I died for them too. I died for them when they were yet sinners. Can you love like I have commanded you? Can you come together and serve from a willingness to please me? Not for recognition, not from your own fleshly desires, but because I have asked of you? Let's pray.

Father, thank you for your amazing love. May our lives be empty of ourselves and be full of courage, strength, and love to fulfill the vision you have entrusted to us. Today may people all across this world hear the call to action. The time is now. The clarion call has gone out, and it is time to respond.

Have a blessed day, God's beautiful people. Somebody shout action.

Leader or Follower? We Get to Choose

Good morning, beautiful people, good morning. As we finish this month out, let's finish it well. Let's allow Jesus, by the power of his Holy Spirit, to lead us. I have heard people say recently, "I am going to do this. I am going to follow this pattern." They never asked Jesus how he would like it done or if he wanted anything different. It sort of makes me sad.

It brought back to memory a time when I was holding a Christmas tea for a community outreach. The day before I went over everything and checked it twice, I laid it all out on my dining room table and began to pray. Jesus, is there anything else you want done? Jesus, did I forget anything? Jesus, do you want anything changed? All I heard was toothpicks. I had forgotten the toothpicks for the fruit.

Another time, I was at a meeting, and I asked the Holy Spirit if he wanted me to say anything or do anything. He said to take a birthday cake to an elderly lady in the next town. That seemed odd, but after the meeting, I left to purchase a birthday cake and went to the woman's apartment. I must admit, I was sweating it a bit. She opened the door, and I gave her the birthday cake. A big smile came on her face as it was her birthday. Her daughter wasn't going to be able to spend time with her that day due to illness, so God sent me. He wanted her to have a birthday cake.

Over the years, I have developed a relationship tender to the Holy Spirt. I try hard to listen and obey. I have made mistakes; I have gotten it wrong. One thing I know for sure, God is not mad at us for learning to listen and obey him. He is the proud Father, always spurring us on. Let's pray.

Father, thank you for the Holy Spirit, our leader and guide. Where you lead us, we will follow. Speak to our hearts today, and we will be obedient to what you say. When we haven't gotten it quite right, you still say that's my child in whom I am well pleased.

Father, thank you for God assignments today. May the world be a better place because we obeyed the voice of our Father through the power of his Holy Spirit. Amen.

Have a blessed day, God's beautiful people. Listen and obey, follow your assignment today.

It's All in What You Believe

Good morning, beautiful people, good morning. As we journey with Jesus this year, let's believe his Word 100 percent. Let's take him at his Word and believe together for great and mighty things. Let's believe for miracles. Let's believe for our destinies, our loved ones, and thank him for the answers to our many prayers. He longs for us to believe him. I love to dream big, and he loves to show me that he is a big God.

Today let's get focused on what we are believing for in 2019. "Let's write the vision and make it plain, that we may run with it" (Habakkuk 2:2). I like to do vision boards as I can look at them, and it helps me to stay focused. Do whatever works for you to keep focused and run the race and win. Jesus is with you, strengthening you, saying, "Go, go, you got this! Run! Win the race!"

"Do you not know that in a race all the runners run, but only one gets the prize? Run in such a way as to get the prize" (1Corinthians 9:24). If you hear a voice that says you can't do it, laugh right out loud. It's the wrong voice. God's voice says all things are possible to them who believe (Mark 9:23). He did say all things, right? Let's pray.

Father, thank you that we believe in you. Thank you that you are running the race with us. We are removing any and all limitations, and we are going for the gold. In the book of James, it tells us we have not because we don't ask God. Today we are asking you to strengthen our belief and forgive any unbelief. "We can do all this through him who gives us strength" (Philippians 4:13).

Father, keep us focused as we keep our eyes steadfast on you and your Word, knowing you are the author and finisher of our faith (Hebrews 12:2). Amen.

Have a blessed day, God's beautiful people. It's all in what you believe. Believe in Jesus Christ (Acts 16:31).

Far Reaching, Believe

Good morning, beautiful people. God's love is far-reaching. His mercies are new every morning, and great is his faithfulness. His blood was enough. His love for us is so amazing. Let's pray.

Father, thank you for the blood that was shed for us. You paid the ultimate sacrifice that we may walk in victory from your birth to your death, and then the resurrection took care of it all. Nothing can pluck us out of your hands. John 10:28–30 tells us that you give unto us eternal life, and we will never perish, neither shall any man pluck us out of your hand. Thank you that nothing can separate us from your love. The joy of the Lord is our strength.

Father, Ephesians 1:7 tells us we have redemption through Christ's blood, the forgiveness of sins in accordance with the riches of God's grace. Thank you for mercy and grace. Thank you for drawing souls unto yourself. May many come to know Jesus Christ, the lover of man's soul this Christmas season. "No one comes to Jesus unless he is first drawn by the Father" (John 6:44).

Have a blessed day, God's beautiful people. He knows right where you are at, and he says his blood was enough. Draw close to him.

Expect the Unexpected

Good morning, beautiful people. On Saturday, I had an unexpected God intervention. I worked diligently with everything I had in the natural on something that needed repair but to no avail. This item hadn't been working right for months. That evening, I sat at my dining room table and prayed a simple, quick prayer asking God himself for help. Within a short time (half hour), the situation was all taken care of. The item worked fine and has worked fine ever since. I had done nothing. With God, we should expect the unexpected.

Yesterday, being Sunday during our worship service at church, I felt so strong in my spirit to tell the people that we need to expect the unexpected. We need to lay down our own thoughts and trust God with all that we are and all that we have. Let's pray.

Father, thank you that you are the God of the unexpected. "Ah, Sovereign Lord, you have made the heavens and the earth by your great power and outstretched arm. Nothing is too hard for you" (Jeremiah 32:17).

Father, we receive the unexpected because we believe you are the God of all possibilities. Father, help us put aside natural reasonings and doubts and believe.

"Jesus said to him, if you can believe, all things are possible to him who believes" (Mark 9:23).

We believe! Amen? Amen!

Have a blessed day, God's beautiful people. Expect the unexpected.

Is John 14:6 Supernatural?

Good morning, beautiful people, good morning. What are you believing? Yesterday, I drove to pray at Whited Bible Camp, where we will hold our third annual Healing Waters Women's Conference. I looked at the many homes on the journey south and wondered what they believed. Oh, how I prayed they would believe in the supernatural, eternal, infallible, living Word of God. Jesus Christ, "He is the way, the truth, and the life. No one comes to the Father but through him" (John 14:6).

I never argue or debate the Holy Scriptures, but always ask the Holy Spirit to reveal truth. There are man-made rules in every church. Those man-made rules are not supernatural. It may be a good idea, it may help the organization, but if it's not in the Holy Scriptures, it is not the supernatural Word of God.

When you journey with Jesus every day and believe, you will receive (Mark 11:24). James 4:2 says, "We have not because we ask not God." If you need healing of mind, body, soul, or spirit, let him touch you today. He is the God who healeth thee.

Father, thank you for revealing truth. As we journey the day, may we meet people who we can share the love of Christ with. May these words Jesus loves you and his blood is enough radiate in their hearts, and may they believe.

Father, continue to reveal truth to us through the Holy Scriptures and prayer. Amen? Amen!

Stay blessed, beautiful people. Shout I believe!

A Thankful Heart Sings

Good morning, beautiful people. Today let's praise the Holy One together.

Sing to the Lord a new song; sing to the Lord, all the earth. Sing to the Lord, praise his name; proclaim his salvation day after day. (Psalm 96:1–2)

But let all who take refuge in you be glad; let them ever sing for joy. Spread your protection over them, that those who love your name may rejoice in you. (Psalm 5:11)

Sing the praises of the Lord, enthroned in Zion; proclaim among the nations what he has done. (Psalm 9:11)

Sing the praises of the Lord, you his faithful people; praise his holy name. (Psalm 30:4)

Come, let us sing for joy to the Lord; let us shout aloud to the Rock of our salvation. (Psalm 95:1)

Praise the Lord, all you nations; extol him, all you peoples. For great is his love toward us, and the faithfulness of the Lord endures forever. (Psalm 117:1)

Awake, my soul! Awake, harp and lyre! I will awaken the dawn. I will praise you, Lord, among the nations; I will sing of you among the peoples. (Psalm 57:8–9)

Father, thank you, thank you, thank you for your Word. How can we not meditate on it day and night? It makes our heart full of joy. You turn our mourning into dancing and our sorrows into joy. We just want to praise your Holy Name. Today for people all across this globe, circumstances don't need to dictate the joy in their lives. The Word of God (the Lord's promises) will bring hope into the darkest situations. Together we can choose to praise you while we are waiting for you to fulfill them. You are not a God who you should lie. Your promise is a promise.

Today we declare in Jesus, there is fullness of joy. Today we will sing a new song, a song of praise.

All across this globe today, let the fires of praise rise up. Spirit, blow all across this land, we pray. Amen.

Have a blessed day, beautiful people. Sing a new song today.

A Treasure on an Island

Good morning, beautiful people. I love the blessings of God every day. He always puts the wind back in our sails. No matter how battered the ship becomes, he takes our lives and puts us on his course once again.

I recently had the privilege to visit an island and found some deep treasures there. Peace, tranquility, and the presence of God's spirit was evident on my short visit. The treasures were priceless as I look upon my mementos this morning. A small chest and a memory book for my grandchild was some of my great finds, along with a few hours in a place where peace abides, and God's presence was so evident.

Today, know that you are God's treasure. If you are his, he has you etched in the palm of his hand (Isaiah 49:16). If you don't know him, today is your day. His love abounds throughout the universe, and he desires to journey life with you. Just find a moment to talk with him today. He longs to commune with you. You truly are the apple of his eye, and he will hide you under the shadow of his wings (Psalm 17:8).

Father, thank you for the peace that transcends all understanding. Your watchful eye keeps our ships sailing in the right direction. You light the path every day with your Word. Thank you for your presence that dwells in us and around us.

As we journey today, may we be a vessel that you use to bring hope and healing to a battered life as we lead them to the light of Jesus Christ. Amen.

Have a blessed day, beautiful people. He loves you with an everlasting love (Jeremiah 31:3).

But you are a chosen people, a royal priesthood, a holy nation, God's special possession, that you may declare the praises of him who called you out of darkness into his wonderful light. Once you were not a people, but now you are the people of God; once you had not received mercy, but now you have received mercy. (1 Peter 2:9–10)

The Prayer of Jabez

Good morning, beautiful people, good morning. Together let's pray the prayer that Jabez cried out to the God of Israel. God, granted his request.

"Oh, that you would bless me indeed and enlarge my territory. That your hand would be with me, and that You would keep me from evil, and that I might not cause pain" (1 Chronicles 4:10).

Father, thank you that you are no respecter of persons. God, just as you granted Jabez his request, you, O God, will grant ours. Today we thank you for enlarging our territories. Lord, thank you that your hand is with us. Continue to protect us from evil, and may we not cause anyone pain, we pray.

Today all across this globe, we declare we are blessed. We declare you, O God, are giving us opportunities to expand our territory, and your hand will protect us. The time is now, and we will step out. Amen.

Have a blessed day, God's beautiful people. For this is the day the Lord has made, and we will rejoice and be glad in it.

The Results Are In, He Is Still in Control

Good morning people, good morning. Isn't it good to have the freedom of choice, and we can exercise our right to vote accordingly, and changes are made? However, one thing never changes, his Word and his promises still stand throughout our changing times. You can tally it up anyway you desire. The end result will always be the same. He will always have the final say. Our God reigns. Let's pray.

Father, thank you that today is just as bright as it was yesterday. As times change, government changes, one thing remains the same. You are the same yesterday, today, and forever (Hebrews 13:8).

Father, as we prepare to begin a new season, we can rest assured that we can continue to put all our trust and our faith in you. Your watchful eye is over us. Psalm 91:9–11 tells us that the Lord is our refuge, and if we make you our dwelling place, no harm will overtake us, no disaster will come near our tent. For you will command your angels concerning us to guard us in all our ways.

Father, as we begin our day today, we continue to worship you in spirit and in truth. For the results are in, and you are still in control. You are watching over your Word to perform it (Jeremiah 1:12). Some things never change; it was settled long ago. "The earth is the Lord's, and everything in it, the world, and all who live in it; for he founded it on the seas and established it on the waters" (Psalm 24:1–2). To that, we say amen.

Have a blessed day, God's beautiful people. Believe God's Word.

The Road to a Free and Better Life

Good morning, beautiful people, good morning. Let's thank God for freedom. Let's thank him for his Word and how he puts us on the road to freedom.

"For whom the son sets free is free indeed" (John 8:36).

Father, thank you for Jesus. Thank you, God, that you are the all-powerful, all-sufficient one. There is no God like our God. Thank you for being the chain breaker. Thank you for the freedom you paid for your people. Thank you for bestowing on us a crown of beauty instead of ashes, the oil of joy instead of mourning, and a garment of praise instead of a spirit of despair. Thank you for righteousness, a planting of the Lord for the display of your splendor. Thank you for rebuilding the ancient ruins and restoring the places long devastated, for renewing the ruined cities that have been devastated for generations.

Thank you for rebuilding lives. Thank you for setting the captives free. Thank you for being a God of justice. Thank you for a double portion. Thank you for being a covenant-keeping God. Thank you for the Holy Scriptures. Thank you that this is the year—the year of God's favor. Thank you for the anointing that breaks yokes. Thank you for being a chain-breaking God (Isaiah 61). Thank you for setting us free and using us today to set others free. Amen.

Have a blessed day God's beautiful people… Enjoy your freedom in Christ.

The Solution

Good morning, beautiful people, good morning. Let's pray together and ask God to lead us every day through the Holy Scriptures.

Father, thank you for speaking to us through your Holy Scriptures. Your Word speaks to us every day. Yes, yes, yes, it does.

You communicate with mankind in so many ways. Your written Word (Bible) is a powerful tool in which we can read, we can believe, and, with great expectation, we can look for you to reveal every answer we need. You are truly the answer for every need mankind has today. We keep our eyes fixed on you.

Father, you use these words to encourage us, mold us, shape us, comfort us, and change us to be more like you.

You speak rest to the weary soul, you speak peace to the anxious mind, you speak love to the brokenhearted. You speak healing to the sick and afflicted, and whatever the situation is in our lives, you have it covered.

It's always best to have everything in writing (a written contract), and we have it. Father, you gave us your Word. You don't erase it, change it, and take it back. It is forever settled. Thank you for these Holy Scriptures. They truly are life to our bones.

The Bible with our contract (his covenant) is our instruction for daily living. Jesus, you truly are the answer.

Since you created us in your image and gave us our manual for daily living, we are excited to meet with you every day to know what you have to say to us. Holy Spirit, lead us today in the Word.

Have a blessed day, beautiful people. Journey with Jesus every day and thank him for speaking to you through his Word. He is the solution to every problem you have.

Scriptures from Psalm 46

God is our refuge and strength, an ever-present help in trouble. Therefore, we will not fear, though the earth give way and the mountains fall into the heart of the sea, though its waters roar and foam and the mountains quake with their surging. "Selah." Nations are in uproar, kingdoms fall; he lifts his voice, the earth melts. The Lord Almighty is with us; the God of Jacob is our fortress. "Selah." I will be exalted among the nations, I will be exalted in the earth." The Lord Almighty is with us. "Selah."

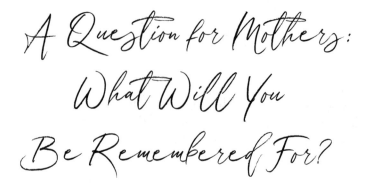

A Question for Mothers: What Will You Be Remembered For?

Good morning, beautiful people. Life is short like a vapor really. Today I thought of the different mothers I know. Some are young and some are old. Some have a few children and some have many. Then I remembered the question, the one that really challenged my life years ago. What legacy will you be remembered for? I pondered that same question again today.

Some mothers found it rewarding to meet their children at bars, clubs, and places the world would say is cool. Some mothers chose to allow parties that would include underage drinking, sex, and anything goes at their home to win the approval of children. Some mothers worked outside the home and worked diligently at balancing the demands of motherhood. Some moms I know stay at home and care for their children and go without the extra things, struggling to meet their monthly bills. Some mothers I know are single, raising a child on benefits provided by the government. Some mothers I know have lost their children because of neglect, abuse, death, divorce, waywardness, and the list goes on. There are so many women reading this today that Mother's Day is a challenge.

One thing I am certain of someday, your mother will leave this earth. Someday you will have memories stored in the recesses of your mind of theme parks, birthday parties, good times, bad times, and all the experiences the vapor of life has given you. I don't believe you will remember the great wealth you accumulated or went without. I don't believe the final hours will be that at all. I believe you will sense the people you hold dear in your heart surrounding you as the choices you made about eternity here on earth takes you to your next step in destiny.

Today I challenge you to seek your Creator, invite Jesus into your life, and ask for forgiveness of the choices as a mother you have made that were against his ways. One more thing to your all-ready list of motherhood. No matter what category as a mother you are in, don't forget the power of a mother's prayer. Take time today to pray for your child. No matter how bleak the situation looks, the creator of the universe has it all under control. Nothing surprises him—nothing. It's pretty simple really—you believe the Bible or you don't. Like I heard a friend say when the rubber meets the road, what is it? Can you whisper a prayer? Let's pray.

Father, we join faith with every mother across this globe today. We pray, creator of the universe who sees it all, Creator of all mankind, bless each and every mother. The wayward child, we join our faith today, and we call you home. The issues of life in every relationship, O God, you have the answer, and today we petition your throne room and thank you in advance for it.

Father, today we pray for our child (call out their names), and we join our faith for everything they have need of, O God. Whatever choices they make, Lord, here on their journey, may the choice of knowing you be one. Thank you for drawing them unto yourself, O God. Thank you for creating motherhood, and we pray a strengthening for every mother across this globe today. Stand strong, hold tight to the Word of the Lord; it will not return void (that's his promise according to Isaiah 55:11).

Have a blessed day, God's beautiful people. Bless a mother.

"For you created my inmost being; you knit me together in my mother's womb" (Psalm 139:13).

Embrace This Season of Life

Good morning, beautiful people. I love fall, the changing of the leaves, the coolness of the air, and pumpkins everywhere. Different seasons require change. We change the type of clothes we wear from short sleeve to long sleeve. Some folks grow their hair longer for the colder season. We pack away our flip-flops and begin to look at our boots once again here in Maine. Another season has passed our life, and we will never relive the days gone by. Today let's ask the Holy Spirit to lead us, to renew us, to heal us and to anoint our next season and make our hearts more like his.

Father, thank you for this season of our life. Yesterday is now gone, and the summer days are now just a memory. The changes you have made in us through the power of your Holy Spirit will lead us into the next season of our life.

Make our hearts pliable, Father, as you change us to reflect your glory. As we embrace this season of our life, show us your glory, we pray. We want to know you better than we did last season. We want to recognize your voice faster, quicker, and be more obedient than the previous days of our life. O God, never let our heart grow cool to the things of you, we pray. Burn within us, fire of God. Burn, Spirit, burn. Amen.

Have a blessed day, God's beautiful people. Embrace this season of your life as he changes us to reflect his glory.

"Teach me your way, Lord, that I may rely on your faithfulness; give me an undivided heart, that I may fear your name" (Psalm 86:11).

Enlarge your Vision, Beautiful People

Good morning, beautiful people, good morning. Isn't God so very good? I was a volunteer last evening for World Vision at a MercyMe Concert. As I prayed over these dear children from around the world, my heart was enlarged for countries I have never even heard of. While passing out the card with these sweet little faces, my heart was moved with compassion. Hearing stories of kids dying from starvation, lack of clean water, and disease, enlarged my heart to tragedies around the world, including the United States. O God, enlarge our hearts and open our minds to what is going on around this world. Let's pray.

Father, thank you for enlarging our vision. Forgive our complacency and open our hearts today to make a difference, not only here but globally. Father, thank you for assignments that are so much bigger than ourselves. Your Word tells us in Isaiah 9:6–7,

And the government will be on his shoulders. And he will be called Wonderful Counselor, Mighty God, Everlasting Father, Prince of Peace. Of the greatness of his government and peace there will be no end. He will reign on David's throne and over his kingdom, establishing and upholding it with justice and righteousness from that time on and forever.

Father, we are your ambassadors here on earth. Thank you for using us in your kingdom. Thank you for taking us to new dimensions. O God, thank you for your mercy, your grace that we are so undeserving. Tear down our religious mind-sets and bring the truth of your Word to us, we pray. Father, thank you for sending these children help from on high. Amen.

Have a blessed day, beautiful people. We have so much to be thankful for so very much.

The Tree of Life

Good morning, beautiful people. Together let's pray from Proverbs 11. The Lord detests dishonest scales, but accurate weights find favor with him. When pride comes, then comes disgrace, but with humility comes wisdom. The integrity of the upright guides them, but the unfaithful are destroyed by their duplicity. Wealth is worthless in the day of wrath, but righteousness delivers from death. The righteousness of the blameless makes their paths straight, but the wicked are brought down by their own wickedness. The righteousness of the upright delivers them, but the unfaithful are trapped by evil desires. Hopes placed in mortals die with them; all the promise of their power comes to nothing. The righteous person is rescued from trouble, and it falls on the wicked instead. With their mouths the godless destroy their neighbors, but through knowledge the righteous escape. When the righteous prosper, the city rejoices; when the wicked perish, there are shouts of joy. Through the blessing of the upright a city is exalted, but by the mouth of the wicked it is destroyed. Whoever derides their neighbor has no sense, but the one who has understanding holds their tongue. A gossip betrays a confidence, but a trustworthy person keeps a secret. For lack of guidance a nation falls, but victory is won through many advisers. Whoever puts up security for a stranger will surely suffer, but whoever refuses to shake hands in pledge is safe. A kindhearted woman gains honor, but ruthless men gain only wealth. Those who are kind benefit themselves, but the cruel bring ruin on themselves. A wicked person earns deceptive wages, but the one who sows righteousness reaps a sure reward. Truly the righteous attain life, but whoever pursues evil finds death. The Lord detests those whose hearts are perverse, but he delights in those whose ways are blameless. Be sure of this: The wicked will not go unpunished, but those who are righteous will go free. Like a gold ring in a pig's snout is a beautiful woman who shows no discretion. The desire of the righteous ends only in good, but the hope of the wicked only in wrath. One person gives freely, yet gains even more; another withholds unduly, but comes to poverty. A generous person will prosper; whoever refreshes others will be refreshed. People curse the one who hoards grain, but they pray God's blessing on the one who is willing to sell. Whoever seeks good finds favor, but evil comes to one who searches for it. Those who trust in their riches will fall, but the righteous will thrive like a green leaf. Whoever brings ruin on their family will inherit only wind, and the fool will be servant to the wise. The fruit of the righteous is a tree of life, and the one who is wise saves lives. If the righteous receive their due on earth, how much more the ungodly and the sinner!

Father, thank you for your favor. Together your people all across this globe put our trust in you. We thank you, Lord, that the righteous man or woman finds favor, and you will open doors for them than no man could ever open. We thank you today, Lord, you are watching over your Word and will perform it. We thank you that our righteousness is in you, and it produces life and not evil. We thank you our worth is not in riches and earthly possessions, for they will fail, but our worth is found in you. We pray many will find gold today. May they come to know you. You are priceless, Jesus, the tree of life.

Have a blessed day, beautiful people. Enjoy the riches of the tree of life.

These Words Calm the Soul

Good morning, beautiful people, good morning. Last evening, I was talking to my granddaughter about using her words to tell me what she wanted. She knows if she points to it, it is easier. However, I want to help her develop her words.

The same thing is true about the Word of God. As we mediate on the Word and speak the Word, we begin to believe the Word. I remember a time as I was meditating on a scripture, I just couldn't get myself to believe it. I went to my pastor and inquired, "Do you think I can really believe this scripture?"

He nodded his head slowly as I think he was probably saying to himself, Oh boy, what is she up to now? He knew if I believed something, I was going for it.

Today let's pray and speak some words together.

Father, thank you that you have come to give us life and life more abundantly (John 10:10). As we meditate on your Word and speak your Word, it becomes life to our bones. Second Corinthians 4:13 says that since we have the same spirit of faith, according to what is written, I believed, and therefore, I spoke, we also believe and therefore speak.

Father, thank you that we can speak the Word of God boldly as we are filled with the power of the Holy Spirit. It is your Word, O God, that accomplishes great things in our lives and the lives of others as we believe. Amen.

Have a blessed day, God's beautiful people. Read John 6:63 today and believe.

Things Change When He Is in the House

Good morning, beautiful people, let's thank God for change this morning.

Father, thank you for being in our lives today. Man has so many plans, but when you are involved, it's the best plan. Fear, pain, worry, sickness, and disease can all be laid down. You stir things up, Jesus. It doesn't need to look like what we think or desire, it's all about you and all for your glory. We are just blessed that you allow us to be a part of the work you are doing here on the earth. May we never take for granted the privilege it is to be part of building your kingdom.

Today, use us to be a light to the darkness in this world. God, use us to be carriers of hope. Jesus, we tear the roof off any doubt, fear, and unbelief for people all across this globe. Show yourself mighty today in their lives and ours too. You are the all-powerful, all-sufficient one.

All across this globe today, Jesus is in the house…No matter what your situation is, talk to him (pray) and get him involved. Amen.

Have a blessed day, God's beautiful people. Aren't you thankful Jesus is in the house?

A few days later, when Jesus again entered Capernaum, the people heard that he had come home. They gathered in such large numbers that there was no room left, not even outside the door, and he preached the word to them. Some men came, bringing to him a paralyzed man, carried by four of them. Since they could not get him to Jesus because of the crowd, they made an opening in the roof above Jesus by digging through it and then lowered the mat the man was lying on. When Jesus saw their faith, he said to the paralyzed man, "Son, your sins are forgiven." Now some teachers of the law were sitting there, thinking to themselves, "Why does this fellow talk like that? He's blaspheming! Who can forgive sins but God alone?" Immediately Jesus knew in his spirit that this was what they were thinking in their hearts, and he said to them, "Why are you thinking these things? Which is easier: to say to this paralyzed man, 'your sins are forgiven,' or to say, 'Get up, take your mat and walk'? But I want you to know that the Son of Man has authority on earth to forgive sins." So he said to the man, "I tell you, get up, take your mat and go home." He got up, took his mat and walked out in full view of them all. This amazed everyone and they praised God, saying, "We have never seen anything like this!" (Mark 2)

This Is Your Moment of Victory!

Good morning, beautiful people. This morning, I was thinking about how time goes by so quickly. Every day seems like a vapor. Every moment of our day is to enjoy and live as if it is our last. Our God has ordained our days before the foundations of the world. We choose to believe it, enjoy it, and be aware of his presence.

"How do you know what your life will be like tomorrow? your life is like the morning fog–it's here a little while, then it's gone" (James 4:14, NLT).

Let's pray.

Father, thank you for every moment of our lives. You, O Lord, know every detail, every step, and the plan you have for us. You empower us every day through your Holy Scriptures to believe. You tell us to call upon you, and you will answer us, and you will show us great and mighty things (Jeremiah 33:3).

Life is a beautiful gift. Every day we live is a gift from you. Each and every day is filled with wonder and new discovery. You ordained our days before the day we were born, and you know the plans you have for our lives. They are good plans according to Jeremiah 29:11, "For I know the plans I have for you, declares the Lord, plans to prosper you and not to harm you, plans to give you hope and a future."

Thank you for today, another new beginning, and a day to celebrate. Thank you for eyes to see as we see your plan unfold. Amen.

Have a blessed day, God's beautiful people. This is your moment of victory!

This Love Never Fails

Good morning, beautiful people, good morning. Today, let's pray and believe these scriptures on love.

For God so loved the world, that he gave his only Son, that whoever believes in him should not perish but have eternal life. (John 3:16)

No, in all these things we are more than conquerors through him who loved us. For I am sure that neither death nor life, nor angels nor rulers, nor things present nor things to come, nor powers, nor height nor depth, nor anything else in all creation, will be able to separate us from the love of God in Christ Jesus our Lord. (Romans 8:37–39)

But God, being rich in mercy, because of the great love with which he loved us, even when we were dead in our trespasses, made us alive together with Christ— by grace you have been saved. (Ephesians 2:4–5)

But God shows his love for us in that while we were still sinners, Christ died for us. (Romans 5:8)

But you, O Lord, are a God merciful and gracious, slow to anger and abounding in steadfast love and faithfulness. (Psalm 86:15)

Father, thank you for your love. Today all across this globe, may love abound. We pray that people who struggle to receive your love would have a deep revelation. You loved us while we were yet deep in our sin, even to die for us. Thank you for your Word and changing us more into your image each day. Oh, how you love us. So much you have us etched on the palm of your hands (Isaiah 49:16). Amen.

Have a blessed day, beautiful people. You are loved, people, you are loved.

Three, Two, One...It's Paid For

Good morning, beautiful people. Three dark days, but they couldn't hold him down. Thank you, God, for the resurrection power of Jesus Christ. Lives forever changed because our redeemer lives. Nothing could then, and nothing cannot now or will ever be in the future able to destroy the all-powerful anointed, Holy One, Jesus, light of the world. He paid the price. He willingly laid down his life that we could have it. Notice. I say willingly.

Father, thank you for Jesus. He made a public spectacle of our enemy. He defeated him at the cross. He paid the price for mankind's sins. Love's so amazing. Oh, the love of my Father.

The Love of My Father...

Oh Father, your love for me is so hard to comprehend, you died for me when I was yet a sinner.

Love, you had no boundaries, you took my sin, and you made me whole again.

Such love, the love of my Father.

When I chose the path of the evil one, you loved me and led me to your path again.

Such love, the love of my Father.

When I cried because of all the pain, you healed my pain and removed my shame. Oh, such love.

Where others wounded me, you bound up my wounds and filled me with joy.

Such love, the love of my Father.

When I needed guidance, you left me your Word and you're Holy Spirit.

Such love, the love of my Father.

Whatever the future holds for me is in your hands, for your love for me has made me whole.

My Father, you say in your Word that the footsteps of the righteous are ordered of the Lord. That's my future because of the love of my Father.

Have a blessed day, God's beautiful people. Receive the love of the father.

Time with the King

Good morning, beautiful people. This morning, I just wanted to continue to encourage you to persevere in prayer. This is no time to let up in prayer. We serve a covenant-keeping God. His Word is yes and amen, and he is watching over his Word to perform it (Jeremiah 1:12).

"So I say to you Ask and it will be given to you; seek and you will find; knock and the door will be opened to you. For everyone who asks receives; the one who seeks finds; and to the one who knocks, the door will be opened" (Luke 11:9–10). Another key is that we must have the right motive.

"You desire but do not have. You covet but you cannot get what you want, so you quarrel and fight. You do not have because you do not ask God. When you ask, you do not receive, because you ask with wrong motives, that you may spend what you get on your pleasures" (James 4:2–3). As God's people come together with a time of prayer and repentance, it will release the greatest outpouring of his spirit. It is time to intercede as never before as we stand in the gap on behalf of others, as well as entire nations. Invite others to join you in prayer. The power in the prayer of agreement from Matthew 18:19, "Again I say to you, that if two of you agree on earth about anything that they may ask, it shall be done for them by My Father who is in heaven."

This past Friday evening, I had the privilege to join my faith with others at the Caribou Meeting Place in Caribou, Maine, for the simulcast Cry Out, a three-hour nationwide prayer event for women. It was nice to see people from different denominations coming together praying for families, marriages, the unborn, etc. Maisie Grace (my granddaughter) and I were blessed to be a part.

Today, spend some time with the king. Today, get to know him more intimately. Let him speak to you and then obey. It will cost you but only time. Time with the king, there is no better way to start your day.

"Lift up your heads, O you gates! And be lifted up you everlasting doors! And the king of Glory shall come in. Who is the King of Glory? The Lord strong and mighty, the Lord mighty in battle. Lift up your heads, O you gates, lift up you everlasting doors! And the King of glory shall come in. Who is the King of Glory? The Lord of hosts, he is the king of Glory" (Psalm 24:7–10).

Have a blessed day, God's beautiful people.

Are You on God Assignment Today?

Good morning, beautiful people. Every day as we look into the eyes of people, we see their fear, their pain, and the years of buried hurt. Can you believe God himself would entrust such precious people to come into your life? Could he be desiring you to help them to find the hope they have in him? I believe so.

Today let's ask him to highlight at least one person that we could encourage, we could speak a timely word too. I love these God assignments, and you will too.

Father, thank you that you first loved us. Because of your great love, our lives are forever changed. We desire to be vessels for your love to flow through. At the end of every day, we want to know that we were more than Christian in just word but also in deed. Teach us, Holy Spirit, every day to walk in love. We want to walk in the love of Jesus Christ.

Today flow through us, Mighty God. May the world see you in action through our daily lives. Thank you for destiny. You truly are God with us. We believe. Amen.

Have a blessed day, beautiful people. Be secure in his love today and give some away.

"We love because he first loved us" (1 John 4:19).

Are You on Shaky Ground or Do You Believe?

Good morning, beautiful people. Are you on shaky ground or do you believe? I guess that's the question of the day. Recently I revisited some book reports I prepared for the International School of Mentorship in 2007. Judy Jacobs and the IIOM team, you are awesome. I was blessed to be a part and strengthen my belief there. It must be memory lane week as I spoke with a few ladies the other evening about a ministry opportunity I had journeyed a few years ago. I was part of a team in another state that helped feed the homeless.

As I walked up and down the sidewalks, inviting people along the beach area for a hot meal at the pier, one woman explained, "I'm cold. I just want a blanket."

I had helped pack the van that day, and there were no blankets on board. So I did the only thing I knew to do, I prayed with her for her a blanket. She then piped up and said, "Now what? Is that blanket going to fall from the sky?"

I told her probably not, but I just prayed and believed, and the Lord would provide a blanket. After doing the inviting up and down that beach area, I went across the street with another team member to some very nice hotels, inquiring about a blanket. I tried to persuade several hotels to let me buy a blanket, give me a blanket, etc., but the policies don't allow for such. I had just prayed, and I knew the creator of the universe could provide his daughter a blanket. I went back and joined the team as they ministered in song. I spoke a few words about my love for Christ and where he had brought me from.

As we were putting the empty trays, etc. in the van, the lady approached me once again and inquired, "Where's my blanket?" I must say I didn't have an answer, but I prayed and I believed with everything I had for her a blanket. I went to the team leader to discuss the issue with him, and he knew we had no blankets. He brought the whole team together as we closed in prayer; he inquired if anyone had any blankets. A few local folks joined the team late that I was unaware of, and one lady spoke up and said she had eight blankets in her trunk. She gave me those blankets, and as I walked up and down that beach area, I felt like I was giving a million dollars to those eight people. The lady I prayed with cried, hugged me, kissed me with thanksgiving. I accepted her thankfulness but told her it was not me who provided the blanket, it was the man that answers prayer. Somehow I remember that moment in time like it just happened yesterday.

This morning, I pack my suitcase to attend a woman's retreat along with my pillows and blankets. I take along the blanket I won at an Overcomers Conference with a ticket I didn't even buy. A friend had purchased a string of tickets and told me to pick one. I chose the middle one, and she said that one was hers to pick another, so I did. I had the winning ticket. The lady's hands, who made this blanket I will wrap myself in this weekend, are overcomers. They have been through very hard trials, some drug addiction, some abusive relationships, others pain beyond words. I feel blessed to have won that blanket. It has reminded me every day we are overcomers.

So today, what do you have need of? More than anything, you need a personal relationship with the man who created you. He said he would provide, and he does. If he can provide a homeless woman a warm blanket on a cool evening, he can help others overcome. What do you have need of this day? Can you believe? Let's pray.

Father, I thank you for every reader across this globe today. God, you are our provider. I lift each one up to you, and I join my faith with theirs. Whatever they have need of, Lord, you have the answer and the provision. I pray, Lord, you use me and everyone reading this post today to be a blessing to someone. We were created to be a team. Help us to be overcomers and help others overcome as well. We believe...

Have a blessed day, beautiful people.

"All things are possible only Believe" (Mark 9:23).

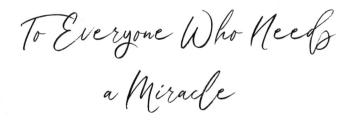

To Everyone Who Needs a Miracle

Good morning, beautiful people. Today let's join our faith together for everyone needing a miracle.

Father, you are the miracle worker. Today we continue to join our faith with others who are in need of a miracle. I particularly love the Christmas season because I seem to hear and see miracles all around.

God, you are the God of all possibilities. Your Word tells us with man, this is impossible, but with God, all things are possible (Matthew 19:26). Nothing is too difficult for you—no, nothing. Today, Lord, we ask you for (tell him what you have need of) my miracle.

In faith believing, we give you thanks for our miracle. For you said to call those things forth as though they are (Romans 4:17). We write your answer to our request by faith today.

Together all across this globe, we stand on God's Word for our miracle. We keep our eyes fixed on him. Amen.

Have a blessed day, God's beautiful people, and keep looking to the hills from whence your help cometh.

"I will lift up mine eyes unto the hills, from whence cometh my help. My help cometh from the Lord, which made heaven and earth" (Psalm 121:1–2).

Transformed by Love

Good morning, beautiful people. Today let's look at scriptures on love once again.

For God so loved the world that he gave his one and only Son, that whoever believes in him shall not perish but have eternal life. (John 3:16)

Greater love has no one than this: to lay down one's life for one's friends. (John 15:13)

You have heard that it was said, 'Love your neighbor and hate your enemy.' But I tell you, love your enemies and pray for those who persecute you, that you may be children of your Father in heaven. He causes his sun to rise on the evil and the good, and sends rain on the righteous and the unrighteous. (Matthew 5:43–45)

A new command I give you: Love one another. As I have loved you, so you must love one another. By this everyone will know that you are my disciples, if you love one another. (John 13:34–35)

Above all, love each other deeply, because love covers over a multitude of sins. Offer hospitality to one another without grumbling. Each of you should use whatever gift you have received to serve others, as faithful stewards of God's grace in its various forms. If anyone speaks, they should do so as one who speaks the very words of God. If anyone serves, they should do so with the strength God provides, so that in all things God may be praised through Jesus Christ. To him be the glory and the power forever and ever. (1 Peter 4:8–11)

So Jacob served seven years to get Rachel, but they seemed like only a few days to him because of his love for her. (Genesis 29:20)

Husbands, love your wives, just as Christ loved the church and gave himself up for her to make her holy, cleansing her by the washing with water through the word, and to present her to himself as a radiant church, without stain or wrinkle or any other blemish, but holy and blameless. In this same way, husbands ought to love their wives as their own bodies. He who loves his wife loves himself. (Ephesians 5:25–28)

Today my daughter and I were sharing about a young man we knew that his life had been transformed by love. This man was down to nothing and had very little hope. Today he has gained much ground. Why? Because someone loved him.

Father, the greatest gift is love. Today we thank you for perfecting your love in us and through us. As the body of Christ, there are so many divisions among us, and that shouldn't be. According to the book of James, chapter 4, you tell us this: What causes fights and quarrels among you? Don't they come from your desires that battle within you? You want something but don't get it. You kill and covet, but you cannot have what you want. You quarrel and fight. You do not have because you do not ask God. When you ask, you do not receive because you ask with wrong motives, that you may spend what you get on your pleasures. You, adulterous people, don't you know that friendship with the world is hatred toward God? Anyone who chooses to be a friend of the world becomes an enemy of God. Or do you think Scripture says without reason that the spirit he caused to live in us envies intensely? But he gives us more grace.

That is why scripture says: "God opposes the proud but gives grace to the humble." Submit yourselves then to God. Resist the devil, and he will flee from you. Come near to God, and he will come near to you. Wash your hands, you sinners, and purify your hearts, you double-minded. Grieve, mourn, and wail. Change your laughter to mourning and your joy to gloom. Humble yourselves before the Lord, and he will lift you up. Brothers, do not slander one another. Anyone who speaks against his brother or judges him speaks against the law and judges it. When you judge the law, you are not keeping it, but sitting in judgment on it. There is only one Lawgiver and Judge, the one who is able to save and destroy. But you? Who are you to judge your neighbor? Now listen, you would say, "Today or tomorrow, we will go to this or that city, spend a year there, carry on business, and make money." Why? You do not even know what will happen tomorrow. What is your life? You are a mist that appears for a little while and then vanishes. Instead, you ought to say, "If it is the Lord's will, we will live and do this or that." As it is, you boast and brag. All such boasting is evil. anyone, then who knows the good he ought to do and doesn't do it, sins.

Father, perfect this in us, we pray. Amen.

Have a blessed day, for this is the day the Lord has made, and we will rejoice and be glad in it. Love on someone today.

Whose Name Will You Call On?

Good morning, beautiful people. Today let's call on Jesus together.

Everyone who calls on the name of the Lord will be saved. (Romans 10:13)

To the church of God in Corinth, to those sanctified in Christ Jesus and called to be his holy people, together with all those everywhere who call on the name of our Lord Jesus Christ—their Lord and ours: Grace and peace to you from God our Father and the Lord Jesus Christ. I always thank my God for you because of his grace given you in Christ Jesus. For in him you have been enriched in every way—with all kinds of speech and with all knowledge—God thus confirming our testimony about Christ among you. (1 Corinthians 1:2–6)

Because he bends down to listen, I will pray as long as I have breath! (Psalm 116:2)

Father, thank you that you hear us when we call. You know our concerns before we even express them. You desire your people to call upon you. You have all the answers.

Today all across this globe, we call on Jesus. As we come to you each and every morning, your mercies are new. God, thank you that the answer is on the way. Forgive us, Lord, for when we called on others before you. Jesus, the greatest name we know. Amen.

Have a blessed day, God's beautiful people. Call on, Jesus.

Vision Beyond the Hurt

Good morning, beautiful people, good morning. There are so many hurting people among us. Devastation and brokenness have hit their lives. They begin to believe a lie that life is not worth living. Pain is only for a season, and then this too shall pass. Stay in the fight and begin to receive God's blessing and vision he has for your life. I know I say this often, but it is so true, he has the master plan. Let's pray.

Father, thank you that you have come to bind up the brokenhearted and set the captive free. No one is so far gone that they can't begin a new journey today. The hurt and pain will fade away as they begin to believe the promises of God over their lives. There is nothing that can separate a living soul from God (Romans 8:28–29), nothing if they believe. You can become their everything.

In loss, you bring peace and restoration. In hardship, you show yourself as Jehovah Jireh, our provider. In sickness, you reveal you are the healing Jesus. To the brokenhearted, you bring restoration and rebuild the ruins. It is true as the songwriter penned: You are our everything.

Father, today may many begin the journey with Jesus and believe deeper into the vision of God's promises for their lives all across this globe. Your vision for our lives is to live John 10:10. You have come to give us life and life more abundantly. You truly are our everything.

Have a blessed day, God's beautiful people. Let him be your everything!

You Are a Champion, Believe

Good morning, beautiful people. I love to tell me grandkids they are champions—they are. Every time they are in my presence, I remind them the greatness they have within. Champions have dreams; they work hard; they stay focused; and they make a difference in the world they live in. I refuse to let them speak negatively about themselves. I want them to learn to walk out the great plan God has for their sweet little lives.

Today let's pray for the greatness you have inside. If you are breathing, let's tap into the power that God himself has deposited within you. Pick up your dream and take a step. You are a champion…Believe.

Father, thank you that we can do all things through Christ who strengthens us (Philippians 4:13). Thank you for putting vision and dreams in every heart. May we never stop dreaming and making a difference in our world.

Thank you for strategies, teams, resources, and everything needed to fulfill the vision. You said in the book of James, we have not because we don't ask God. Today we ask, receive, and give you thanks. Amen.

Declare today, beautiful people, that you are a champion, and yes, you will win. Jesus Christ is on your team. He creates no losers, and you have everything you need to succeed in him. His Word is truth.

Have a blessed day, God's beautiful champion.

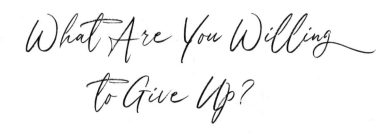

What Are You Willing to Give Up?

Good morning, beautiful people. Let's pray and ask God for faith to give up whatever he desires.

Father, thank you for the grace to give you full control of our lives. You don't want just a part of our lives, you want all of it. You will take our fully surrendered lives and bring about the plan and the destiny you have predestined for us. We give you thanks.

Father, we pray every church, every meeting place, and every person would surrender full control to you and the power of the Holy Spirit. Father, get us out of the way so you can have your way. Take full control.

O Heavenly Father, you know what is best for every life. You know the plans you have for each of us, the purpose we were designed to fulfill. As we surrender to your will and to your way, your plan unfolds step by step for our lives, one step at a time. Thank you for the master plan.

Today we just want to say, "God, we surrender all." (Can you honestly say that?) Every plan, every dream, and every desire, we surrender all. Do with our lives as you will. Your plan is our heart's desire. We will continue to keep our eyes looking up as you lead us. Unfold your will, God, for our lives, we pray. Amen.

Have a blessed day, beautiful people. Surrender it all to Jesus and believe. Tell him what you are willing to give up (sacrifice).

"Be still and know that I am God. I will be exalted among the nations, I will be exalted in the earth!" (Psalm 46:10).

Listen to the Voice of Truth

Good morning, beautiful people, good morning. In this world, there are so many voices. Everyone sees the answer through the lens of their own life experiences and where they are on their journey with God. Because we are all at different places in our walk with him, we must renew our minds with the washing of his Word. It is sometimes challenging to take all the knowledge we have obtained and set it aside and put on the new mind, the mind of Christ. I heard a pastor say before he begins to preach and minister, he sets his mind on the front pew and puts on the mind of Christ. Let's pray.

Father, thank you that you are a God of truth. You are the giver of life. Father, we ask for discernment and wisdom to determine the lies of the enemy of our soul. Father, you said to put on the mind of Christ.

Which things we also speak, not in words taught by human wisdom, but in those taught by the Spirit, combining spiritual thoughts with spiritual words. But a natural man does not accept the things of the Spirit of God, for they are foolishness to him; and he cannot understand them, because they are spiritually appraised. But he who is spiritual appraises all things, yet he himself is appraised by no one. For who has known the mind of the Lord, that he will instruct Him? But we have the mind of Christ. (1 Corinthians 2:13–16)

Father, thank you for the mind of Christ. Empower us today, and may all the knowledge we have gained to be setting on the front pew, and may the spirit of the Lord move through your anointed vessels for your glory. Amen.

Have a blessed day, God's beautiful people. Listen to the voice of truth.

A Little Stars Birthday

Good morning, beautiful people. This morning, I am awake early once again to pray my daily prayers and to petition the king of kings for everything that is on my heart for today. My mind wanders a bit as today is my second grandson's birthday.

Three years ago today, the world changed again as this little world changer made his debut. I thought about the post I wrote months ago now about making us fishers of men and used his sweet little picture. Just a short time ago, actually it was the evening after Memorial Day, I went to my daughter and son-in-law's home for a barbecue. As we were finishing our time together, and I was reading them a story and praying with them before bed, little Evan piped up and asked, "Grammy, who is Jesus?"

In as simple words I could find, I told him how Jesus lives in the heart of man. His big brother, now six, piped up and told him that Jesus lived in his heart, and that night, little Evan asked him in his. It brought tears to my eyes.

I thought about the Memorial Day post I wrote and attached Evan singing, "Have A Beautiful Day" from when he was barely two. Memories are precious, aren't they? I always wanted my children and grandchildren to have so much more than I had, but I have discovered on the journey it isn't material things. Yes, I like to buy them gifts, but the greatest gift I could ever give them is to teach them about Jesus.

Friday night, I took them shopping to discover what Evan would like for his birthday. We spent hours looking through the toy section as I watched them trying on cowboy hats, waving swords, and discovering Spiderman is a favorite. He put everything right back in its original place and was happy just looking and trying it out.

This is so different for me as I raised three very girly girls. Frilly dresses, anklets, dolls, and such filled our home. Memories, they truly do last a lifetime. I went back to the store alone yesterday and made my purchase (a Spiderman tackle box). It seemed the most appropriate as he likes to fish with his dad and big brother. Somehow I just know he is a fisher of men. So as little Evan sings it, "Have a beautiful daaay!"

"Children are a gift from God" (Psalm 127:3).

Nobody Wants to Tell You This

Good morning, beautiful people, good morning. I was asked this question yesterday: Is there hope and healing from abuse? My answer was yes. I believe God can and will rebuild your life and give you a new beginning. You can touch the hem of his garment and be made whole again. The process and journey for every broken heart is different. I don't even pretend to know or have all the answers. I believe when we surrender our heart, our lives, God himself will work everything out for our good. That's his promise to us in Romans 8:28. Our position must be in faith believing using the wisdom he provides.

Nobody wants to tell you they are being abused—nobody. They feel shame; they feel guilty; and they feel stuck. What little pride they muster up to make it through the day, gives them the courage to continue on the journey. If and when they can tell you, they water down the story, so it doesn't sound so bad. Abuse is a horrible evil.

I so wanted to reach through that phone and put my hand on that broken heart. I awaken early to intercede for this weeping soul. I am sure there are many more weeping just like her this morning. Will you join faith with me? Let's pray.

Father, we lift up every broken heart this morning. Christ the Healer touch hearts all across this globe today. You have a way like no other to apply the healing balm. Father, we stand against fear; we stand against rejection; and we stand against all the lies the enemy of their soul is speaking. You created them, call them beautiful, and have a plan for their lives.

Father, thank you for healing your people from the inside out. Nobody can touch our hearts like Jesus—nobody. May many feel your hand on their heart today and be made whole. You truly are the healer of the brokenhearted.

Father, we pray for courage to get help, to tell someone a way of escape, whatever is needed. You are the waymaker, miracle worker. Yes, yes, you are. O God, set your people free according to your Word. Amen.

Have a blessed day, God's beautiful people. Be kind to everyone, for you don't know the battle that lies within another person's heart, mind, and soul.

"Therefore, as God's chosen people, holy and dearly loved, clothe yourselves with compassion, kindness, humility, gentleness and patience" (Colossians 3:12).

Take the Road to the Good Life

Good morning, beautiful people, good morning. God's Word tells us in Isaiah 50:7, "Because the Sovereign Lord helps me, I will not be disgraced. Therefore, have I set my face like flint, and I know I will not be put to shame."

He promises to make even the hairiest days' work together for our good (Romans 8:28). He holds our lives in his hands. Let's choose to walk by faith in him, knowing that he holds the keys for today, and his promises will stand with us once again tomorrow.

His love is so amazing as we watch him make every crooked way straight on our behalf. "I will go before you and will level the mountains; I will break down gates of bronze and cut through bars of iron (Isaiah 45:2)." He will do what he has to do to break the chains and make the way for you if you can believe on his name and have faith in his promises. Let's pray.

Father, thank you for breaking all the bondages off us. The enemy of our soul can't have any hold on us, for we don't belong to him. Fear, depression, abuse, anger, hatred, doubt, bitterness, resentment, lies, shame, and guilt, you be gone in Jesus's name. Jesus paid the price for our freedom, and because he did, we can live John 10:10, "The abundant life."

Father, thank you for your faithfulness. Thank you for breaking chains across this globe today by the power of your Word. May people all across this world, in which you created, be set free because you live. Amen.

Have a blessed day, God's beautiful people. Break off your chains today!

Your Greatest Connection

Good morning, beautiful people. Let's pray to the greatest connection this world will ever have.

Father, you are the best connection any person on this earth could possibly have. For everyone who feels like there is no hope, you are their hope. For anyone who needs healing, you are their healer. For anyone who needs help, you send it from on high. To journey life with the creator of the universe is just downright amazing. We just can't wait to journey each and every day with you. You reveal yourself in the most amazing ways. Thank you for being our God.

We confess we don't always understand your ways, and your thoughts are so much higher than ours (Isaiah 55:8–9). We also don't get everything just right. You, O God, look at us and say, "They are mine. I love them with an everlasting love" (Jeremiah 31:3). "I paid the price" (1 Timothy 2:6). Doesn't that make our hearts sing for joy?

Today, God, thank you for fulfilling the purpose you have for our lives that you predestined before the foundations of the earth. Thank you for leading us, directing us, and making every crooked path straight. Thank you for being man's greatest connection. Holy Spirit, guide us, and may we leave a trail of blessings wherever you lead us this day. Amen.

Have a blessed day, God's beautiful people, and if you don't know him, you are only a few words away from the greatest connection your life will ever know (pray).

Tell him in your own words that you desire to journey life with him. He understands your language. You were created in his image (Genesis 1:27). He is your greatest connection.

"Therefore I tell you, whatever you ask for in prayer, believe that you have received it, and it will be yours" (Mark 11:24).

Shout Yes! The Winds Are Blowing

Good morning, beautiful people. Last night, the wind blew so hard, I wondered what would be standing this morning. Let's worship him together this morning, thanking him for this wave of God, this fresh wind and fire blowing throughout our land. Let's pray.

Father, in John 5:3–8, Jesus said, "Very truly I tell you, no one can enter the kingdom of God unless they are born of water and the Spirit. Flesh gives birth to flesh, but the Spirit gives birth to spirit. You should not be surprised at my saying, "You must be born again." The wind blows wherever it pleases. You hear its sound, but you cannot tell where it comes from or where it is going. So, it is with everyone born of the Spirit."

Thank you, Father, that your spirit is moving and drawing man to yourself. Thank you for changing people's lives by rebuilding the ancient ruins (Isaiah 61). O God, for every person who may be losing hope today send them someone (send us), give them help from on high. Father, we pray for the youth today. Spirit, sweep through this generation like never before. Set a fire, God, in their hearts for you who will turn this nation upside down. Strengthen our youth today, we pray.

Father, we thank you for the opportunity to work in your kingdom. Today we pray the prayer of Jabez once again from 1 Chronicles 4:10,

Just like Jabez cried out to you, we cry out to you for the youth of this nation. God of Israel, "Oh, that you would bless me and enlarge my territory! Let your hand be with me and keep me from harm so that I will be free from pain." And God granted his request.

Thank you for granting our request. We receive healing and deliverance for the youth of this nation. We declare and decree the drug issue that is waging war against this generation be destroyed. Every stronghold built up, we tear you down. The blood of Christ is against you. We draw the bloodline and say no more, you will go no further. These kids belong to Jesus, and we are taking them back. Blow, Spirit, blow…Amen. Have a blessed day, beautiful people. Bless a youth today. Let them know how important they are. They need your encouragement.

What Never Changes?

Good morning, beautiful people. Life changes fast, people change, circumstances change, and you wonder what remains, what stays the same. There is one thing that remains and never changes, Jesus Christ, the same yesterday, and today, and forever (Hebrews 13:8).

It seems like just yesterday, the children were small, and we were rushing to get everyone out the door for elementary school. A one-bathroom home made it a challenge with three girly girls and myself. The pink ribbons, curling irons, and a closet full of dresses turned into teen years of jeans, minds of their own, and new adventures. Then we journeyed wedding days, baby showers, and grandchildren. Oh, life is such a journey.

I decided some time ago now I was going to enjoy every day and live it to the fullest. God's Word tells us that this is the day the Lord has made, and we will rejoice and be glad in it (Psalm 118:24).

We can never get today back, so let's decide to live today and every day the very best we can. Let's make up our minds to be happy even in circumstances that are less than perfect. We will always have opposition, but we have someone who is always by our side. Amen? Amen!

Father, thank you that to everything, there is a season. There is a time for everything under the sun (Ecclesiastes 3:1). We thank you that the joy of the Lord is our strength (Nehemiah 8:10). No matter what comes our way today or in the future, we can rest assured you hold our future. Our lives are in your hands.

Thank you today, Father, for the grace to trust you more. You said to trust in the Lord with all thine heart and lean not to our own understanding, but in all our ways acknowledge you, and you will direct our paths (Proverbs 3:5–6).

We rest assured today that you see right where we are at, and you are saying, "No worries, my child. I hold the keys to your destiny." We say thank you, Father, we believe! Amen.

Have a blessed day, God's beautiful people. Enjoy your day! He holds your future.

Are You a Foot Washer?

Good morning, beautiful people. Let's pray about being a foot washer.

When he had finished washing their feet, he put on his clothes and returned to his place. "Do you understand what I have done for you?" he asked them. "You call me 'Teacher' and 'Lord,' and rightly so, for that is what I am. Now that I, your Lord and Teacher, have washed your feet, you also should wash one another's feet. I have set you an example that you should do as I have done for you. Very truly I tell you, no servant is greater than his master, nor is a messenger greater than the one who sent him. Now that you know these things, you will be blessed if you do them. (John 13:12–17)

Just as the Son of Man did not come to be served, but to serve, and to give his life as a ransom for many. (Matthew 20:28)

Sitting down, Jesus called the Twelve and said, "Anyone who wants to be first must be the very last, and the servant of all. (Mark 9:35)

For who is greater, the one who is at the table or the one who serves? Is it not the one who is at the table? But I am among you as one who serves. (Luke 22:27)

Each of you should use whatever gift you have received to serve others, as faithful stewards of God's grace in its various forms. If anyone speaks, they should do so as one who speaks the very words of God. If anyone serves, they should do so with the strength God provides, so that in all things God may be praised through Jesus Christ. To him be the glory and the power forever and ever. (1 Peter 4:10–11)

Father, thank you for laying down your very life for us. Just as you were a servant, Lord, our heart's desire is to be a servant too. (Tell him if this is true in your heart today.) Many will set at the table and look down on the lowly, Lord, help that never to be us. O God, the gift you have placed in your people all across this globe today, may they use it to serve one another.

Everything we are or will ever become, may we be found faithful servants of the Most High God, for your glory alone, Jesus, for your glory alone. We take up our cross and follow you. Amen.

Have a blessed day, beautiful people, for this is the day the Lord has made, and we will rejoice and be glad in it. Look for ways to serve today. Choose to be like Jesus.

He Will Stand with You

Good morning, beautiful people, good morning. Yesterday was Line Up for Life here in Presque Isle, Maine, sponsored by the Pregnancy Care Center of Aroostook to commemorate and mourn the immeasurable loss of more than sixty million lives since the Supreme Court decision of Roe v. Wade. The lineup had to be rescheduled from the Sunday prior as we were buried under much snow. I am so glad so many came to stand up for what they believe in under the direction of Charles Sullivan, executive director of the center.

This morning, my heart feels joy that from the Crown of Maine to seven continents of the world, we can declare. We are still standing. The best part of it all is we are not standing alone. The creator of the universe stands with us. Always stand for what you believe in, beautiful people, always. He will stand with you. Amen? Amen! Let's pray.

Father, thank you that life was your idea. Father, even though culture changes, your Word stands true. Thank you that even before we were in our mother's womb, you created us. Man has tried to determine life and death, but we know that life should be determined by you and you alone.

Father, you stood with us yesterday. You said to declare a thing, and it would be established for you so light will shine on our ways (Job 22:28). Let it be so, O God, according to thy Word. Amen.

Have a blessed day, God's beautiful people. Stand up, and he will stand with you.

Living beyond Ordinary

Good morning, beautiful people. I love living in Aroostook County, Maine. I know we are not supposed to brag, and I try hard not to, but sometimes it spills out. I see signs that say North of Ordinary at our local college, and it makes me laugh right out loud.

Every day, I declare it's going to be a good day. Sometimes the day gets a little hairy, but God's Word tell us that this is the day he has made it, and we will rejoice and be glad in it. I know that is not ordinary but living beyond the ordinary. It sure is a great way to live though, it sure is.

I was on a prayer teleconference on Saturday for the upcoming Healing Waters conference to be held in Bridgewater, Maine. I just kept hearing live, love, and laugh. We are supposed to enjoy our life. The abundant life of John 10:10. Dance, dance, dance (now I need work in this area. LOL.)

Today, make up your mind that it's going to be a good day. Declare it, decree it, and believe it. Job 22:28 states, "Declare a thing, and it will be established." So declare your day early and walk it out. Look for the new dance in your step today.

Have a blessed day, beautiful people. Live, love, laugh, and enjoy your day.

"A cheerful heart is good medicine, but a broken spirit saps a person's strength" (Proverbs 17:22).

Where Are You in the Puzzle Called Life?

Good morning, beautiful people, good morning. This morning, I was up early praying about the many issues of life. I was praying for the people I love, my family, friends, and for the many requests I have been asked to pray for. Life is complicated and challenging at times to stay in faith believing as we journey every day. It is so comforting to know that Jesus Christ ordained our days before the foundations of the earth.

Yesterday, a friend and I drove north to see the beautiful lake and to check out an island that I have heard so much about here in Maine. The lake was beautiful, and I kept thinking about the healing waters of Jesus Christ. All day, I sensed an ache in my heart that is hard to put in words. I put my hand on my heart and prayed for myself. Oh, what a joy journeying life with Christ the Healer.

Today no matter where you are in the puzzle called life, know that God's master plan is best. Ask him to continue to order your footsteps and put each piece of your life together according to his plan. God's plan and ways are higher than our ways, and he knows what's best. He alone holds each piece that completes the puzzle of our lives. God has a great future for us as we stay in faith believing.

Father, we come to you today in the name of Jesus Christ. No matter what we go through in life, you already knew. Every day was predestined before the foundation of the world. Each piece to the puzzle will come together as we stay in faith believing.

There is nothing or nobody that can separate us from the love of God. You have us engraved in the palm of your hand (Isaiah 49:16). Thank you for putting all the pieces together as we journey our lives with you. We thank you for destiny.

Wash over us once again with your presence and heal any brokenness or disappointments that may have come our way once again, we pray. Thank you for holding our world in your hands. We trust you will put each piece of our lives together as we continue to put our whole trust in you. Amen. Have a blessed day, God's beautiful people. Trust God's master plan for your life.

A Gem Called Mother

Good morning, beautiful people. Soon we will celebrate mothers. I think we could also call it celebrate life day. Without her, you just wouldn't be here. Last year, around the same time, I listened to a CD I won at a Joan Hunter Ministries meeting I attended. "Unleashing the Writer Within" by Wendy Walters inspires me to continue to write.

On this CD, Wendy speaks about the mantles in the bloodline that we are born in. I had to do a little research to find out about my bloodline. I can proudly say I come from a rich bloodline. Not in earthly wealth but a spiritual wealth that is beyond any dollar amount. My mother imparted to me more than I know even to this day. People have always told me she was the sweetest, kindest woman, and it made me proud to be her daughter. I have prayed many times; Father, I want to be just like her. She sounds amazing, God, and I want the gems she carried. My eight years with her wasn't long enough, God, but thank you for my sisters and the many spiritual mothers you have placed in my life. Father, please help me to be more like her. She must have truly walked close with you. Thank you for the mantle.

I look at her picture tonight, wearing her suit of sparkles, and I chuckle as I like glitzy myself. I pray the mantles in my bloodline continue to be passed down. I had the opportunity today to pray over my daughters, sisters, cousins, friends, and some of my grandchildren. My heart is truly blessed.

God certainly knew what he was doing the day you were born, beautiful people. Motherhood was his idea. Celebrate life.

"For you created my inmost being; you knit me together in my mother's womb" (Psalm 139:13).

Peace, Peace, God's Peace

Good morning, beautiful people. Yesterday, I drove to the St. John Valley to meet up with some of my ACTS sisters. There was such sweet peace up there. I enjoyed the drive up and back and the beauty that the valley beholds.

I kept thinking of this song this morning "Peace in the Valley." Isn't it great in Christ through Christ we can have peace, and at the end of our lives, we can enter into eternal peace? I love the peace of God and his journey of peace for our lives. Let's pray.

Father, thank you for peace, the peace that transcends all understanding (Philippians 4:7). Thank you that no matter what our journey entails, someday we will enter into your eternal presence in sweet peace. There is peace in the valley. Praise your name.

Today no matter what a reader is facing, we pray peace, we speak peace, and we declare peace over every life. The peace that the world can't give, medication can't give, it can only come from our God. No man, no enemy can take our peace. The world didn't give it to us, and the world can't take it away. Oh, the peace, sweet peace from our God. Amen.

Have a blessed day, beautiful people. Peace, abide in the peace of God today.

Love Shine Through Us

Good morning, beautiful people. Today let's pray God's love will shine and flow through us.

Father, thank you for light of Jesus Christ. Wherever you order our footsteps, our answer is yes. We too see a world that needs compassion. Thank you, God, for restoring lives to dream again. Not one person on planet earth you have not extended your mercy toward, no, not one. May they receive the love you have provided by the sacrifice of your Son, Jesus.

All across this world today, may the light of Jesus shine brightly through us, we pray.

Thank you, Father, for your amazing love for mankind. It truly is agape. Thank you for rebuilding the ancient ruins in our lives. Thank you for being a covenant keeper. May Christ reign in the hearts of man this Christmas. Amen.

Have a blessed day, beautiful people. You are loved. Let love flow through you today.

The Spirit of the Sovereign Lord is on me, because the Lord has anointed me to proclaim good news to the poor. He has sent me to bind up the brokenhearted, to proclaim freedom for the captives and release from darkness for the prisoners, to proclaim the year of the Lord's favor and the day of vengeance of our God, to comfort all who mourn, and provide for those who grieve in Zion—to bestow on them a crown of beauty instead of ashes, the oil of joy instead of mourning, and a garment of praise instead of a spirit of despair. They will be called oaks of righteousness, a planting of the Lord for the display of his splendor. They will rebuild the ancient ruins and restore the places long devastated; they will renew the ruined cities that have been devastated for generations. Strangers will shepherd your flocks; foreigners will work your fields and vineyards. And you will be called priests of the Lord, you will be named ministers of our God. You will feed on the wealth of nations, and in their riches you will boast. Instead of your shame you will receive a double portion, and instead of disgrace you will rejoice in your inheritance. And so you will inherit a double portion in your land, and everlasting joy will be yours. "For I, the Lord, love justice; I hate robbery and wrongdoing. In my faithfulness I will reward my people and make an everlasting covenant with them. Their descendants will be known among the nations and their offspring among the peoples. All who see them will acknowledge that they are a people the Lord has blessed." I delight greatly in the Lord; my soul rejoices in my God. For he has clothed me with garments of salvation and arrayed me in a robe of his righteousness, as a bridegroom adorns his head like a priest, and as a bride adorns herself with her jewels. For as the soil makes the sprout come up and a garden causes seeds to grow, so the Sovereign Lord will make righteousness and praise spring up before all nations. (Isaiah 61)

Amazing, Downright Amazing Love

Good morning, beautiful people, good morning. This morning, I was reflecting once again about God's love and forgiveness. His love toward me brought me to a place of such peace knowing he has my life in his hands.

God's love for mankind is so hard to comprehend. He died for us when we were in the depth of our sin. This is so hard for people to grasp. It was so hard for me to grasp. Every day, I am amazed at his love and tender care for me. The Good Shepherd watching over his people draws me to want to know him better than the day before. Oh, such amazing love, the love of my Father.

If I could give you a gift today, I would give you the gift of knowing Jesus. There's nothing more important in life, no possession you will ever own, that will measure up to journeying life with him. However, it is a decision you need to decide for yourself.

It doesn't matter where you have been, what you have done, it only matters where your end will be. Decide today to accept his free gift. Full of love and forgiveness, the Good Shepherd will lead you beside still waters. He will bring you to the healing waters of Jesus Christ, and he will set you free. Yes, yes, he will.

Can't you hear him calling your name? Let's pray.

Father, together we pray this prayer. John 14:6 tells us, "Jesus is the way and the truth and the life. No one comes to the Father except through Him." We ask Jesus to come into our lives today. We ask for forgiveness of our sins. Romans 3:23 tells us, "All have sinned and fallen short of the glory of God." We receive the free gift of salvation.

Come into our hearts today and give us a new beginning, we pray. Fill us with your Holy Spirit and lead us and guide us each and every day. We make the decision to accept Jesus Christ into our lives and allow him to set us free (John 8:36).

Thank you, Father, for the abundant life according to John 10:10. Amen.

Have a blessed day, God's beautiful people. You have made the right decision to follow Jesus Christ! He loves you, he loves you, he loves you.

Will You Be Overtaken?

Good morning, beautiful people. This morning at church, a lady sang this song on being an overcomer. Something stirred within me. He has, indeed, given us power. Rise up, Christians, it's time to rise up. Don't be just a casual Christian or a lukewarm Christian. You are either all the way in the kingdom of God, or you are not. He said in Revelation 3:16, "So, because you are lukewarm—neither hot nor cold—I am about to spit you out of my mouth." Nobody should have to guess where you stand—nobody.

God has given us power according to his Word. In 1 Corinthians 4:19–20, "But I will come to you soon, if the Lord wills, and I shall find out, not the words of those who are arrogant but their power. For the kingdom of God does not consist in words but in power." In Matthew 10:7–8, "And as you go, preach, saying, 'The kingdom of heaven is at hand. Heal the sick, raise the dead, cleanse the lepers, cast out demons. Freely you received, freely give. Do not acquire gold, or silver, or copper for your money belts, or a bag for your journey, or even two coats, or sandals, or a staff; for the worker is worthy of his support.'"

In Acts 3:12, "When Peter saw this, he said to them, "Fellow Israelites, why does this surprise you? Why do you stare at us as if by our own power or godliness we had made this man walk?" Again in Ephesians 6:12, "For our struggle is not against flesh and blood, but against the rulers, against the authorities, against the powers of this dark world and against the spiritual forces of evil in the heavenly realms." Then in Luke 10:19, "I have given you authority to trample on snakes and scorpions and to overcome all the power of the enemy; nothing will harm you."

Father, your Word is powerful. Your spirit living in us is powerful. Today we will rise up. We will take a stand. (Will you?) Not my will, Lord, but thine be done. It's all about your kingdom, and it's for your glory alone. Show your glory, your power through us today. Christians, rise up, join your faith together with other believers across this land. Speak the Word, declare the Word, and we should experience some powerful testimonies. It should look like a hurricane of souls being saved and miracles happening, for he said in Mark 16:15–18,

He said to them, "Go into all the world and preach the gospel to all creation. Whoever believes and is baptized will be saved, but whoever does not believe will be condemned. And these signs will accompany those who believe: In my name they will drive out demons; they will speak in new tongues; they will pick up snakes with their hands; and when they drink deadly poison, it will not hurt them at all; they will place their hands-on sick people, and they will get well.

Jesus, living in us, is powerful. Amen.

Have a blessed day, beautiful people. You will not be overtaken.

Rejected No More

Good morning, beautiful people, good morning. As I prepare for a meeting today for a group of people and during prayer this morning, the word rejection seemed highlighted in my spirit. Let's pray together about this issue. We are a loved people, and we are accepted in Christ. When we believe these lies, it makes people feel all alone and rejected. Some forms of the lies that come our way to see if we will believe them are I don't fit in, I can't overcome the obstacles in my life, I am a failure, I will never be good enough, I can't do this, who do we think we are? This makes people feel hopeless and full of self-hatred with no future. Lies, lies, lies, all lies.

Father, thank you that you love us unconditionally. Our acceptance does not depend on how we look, dress, feel, or think. Your Word is the final authority, and you say we are accepted in the beloved (Ephesians 1:6). Thank you for exposing all lies we are believing that the enemy of our soul plants in our minds.

Father, today we declare right out loud, "I am accepted in the Beloved." Jesus loves and accepts me, and he has a great plan for my life. It doesn't matter how others view us, it matters what our Creator says about us. He said we are fearfully and wonderfully made (Psalm 139:14).

Today all across this globe, we will renew our minds with the washing of the Word. We will believe God's Word. Rejection is not our portion. Lies be gone.

If you don't know him, then today is the day to make the most important decision you will ever make in life. Invite him in. Amen.

Have a blessed day, God's beautiful people. Tell him how much you love him today and let him love on you. Believe his Word, beautiful people, believe.

Thank, God, For Friends

Good morning, beautiful people, good morning. I was thinking about how good God has been to me. He has given me a lot of good friends. It doesn't matter what season of life I am in; my friends have journeyed life with me. I have been blessed to be a friend and to receive friendship.

Jesus is a friend that sticks closer than a brother (Proverbs 18:24). He is the very best friend and Father that you will ever know. He will never leave you nor forsake you (Hebrews 13:5). You have his word on that.

As you begin your day today, no matter what challenges you face, know that Jesus Christ is desiring to be your best friend. He is only one prayer away. Let's pray.

Father, thank you for life. Thank you that your love and friendship never cease. Your love for us is just downright amazing. How do we ever thank you? By praising you both day and night.

There is nothing that can separate us from your love. "For I am persuaded, that neither death, nor life, nor angels, nor principalities, nor powers, nor things present, nor things to come, nor height, nor depth, nor any other creature, shall be able to separate us from the love of God, which is in Christ Jesus our Lord" (Romans 8:38). Amen.

Bask in his love today, beautiful people. Jesus Christ will always be your best friend. He loves to journey life with you.

A Heart of Gold

Good morning, beautiful people, good morning. I am pretty certain everybody will have the opportunity to practice forgiveness this Christmas season. I don't believe there is a person alive who escapes this experience. Life has a way of bringing trials. I recently listened to a prophetic word I received while attending a meeting in Canada. These total strangers said God would bring justice to me for unjust things that were done. I ponder what that looks like at times in my life. One thing for sure, I know God does all things well. He is the God of payback. As we continue to forgive and let things go, it keeps our spirits free. Today let's choose to forgive and let God himself pay us back. Let's pray.

Father, thank you for being a God of justice. Thank you for the grace to forgive so that we may be forgiven. No matter how difficult the circumstance, your grace is sufficient. First Corinthians 12:9 tells us that your grace is sufficient for us; your power is made perfect in our weakness. Thank you for the strength to lay it all down once again.

Father, thank you for peace. The peace that transcends all understanding. We receive it today. Amen.

Have a blessed day, God's beautiful people. Choose to walk in forgiveness and be forgiven. Embrace a heart of gold.

"For if you forgive other people when they sin against you, your heavenly Father will also forgive you. But if you do not forgive others their sins, your Father will not forgive your sins" (Matthew 6:14–15).

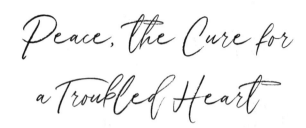

Peace, the Cure for a Troubled Heart

Good morning, beautiful people. Today let's thank God; he is the answer for a troubled heart.

Father, thank you that the peace we have as Christians, the world didn't give it to us, and the world can't take it away. John 14:27 tells us, peace, you leave us. It's your peace you give to us. You tell us not to be troubled or afraid.

Thank you for the peace that transcends all our understanding. The peace of God that guards our hearts and minds in Christ Jesus (Philippians 4:7).

Father, you tell us not to worry. We are instructed to cast all our cares on you because you care for us. (1 Peter 5:7). You tell us our sleep should be sweet. (Proverbs 3:24) Since you know the number of hairs on our head (Luke 12:7), and you know when we sit and when we rise (Psalm 139:2), we must believe you have our lives in your hands.

Father, we will cast down every imagination and every high and lofty thing that exalts itself against the knowledge of God, and we take captive every thought to make it obedient to Christ (2 Corinthians 10:5). We receive our peace as we cast all our care on you, for you care for us, Good Father. Amen.

Have a blessed day, God's beautiful people. No worrying, no stressing, and no anxious thoughts. Declare, "Jesus has my life." Sleep well tonight, he has your life covered.

"Return to your rest, my soul, for the Lord has been good to you" (Psalm 116:7).

Something Sweet for your Soul

Good morning, beautiful people. The blizzard weather has started this morning in Maine. The cancellation list is very long. Even church is cancelled on this blistery morning. Yesterday, I attended a training, and the folks who came in from Texas will be in the beautiful state of Maine for a few extra days. No flights in, no flights out. A good day to wrap in a blanket and spend some time filling your soul with God's Word and worship him in spirit and in truth. Everything seems to be on hold for a bit. That is everything but time with our King. Nobody can fill our souls like Jesus. How sweet it is. Let's pray.

Father, thank you for your love. You tell us to "taste and see that the Lord is good; blessed is the one who takes refuge in him" (Psalm 34:8). There is no storm you won't bring us through. Psalm 148 tells us to,

Praise the Lord. Praise the Lord from the heavens; praise him in the heights above. Praise him, all his angels; praise him, all his heavenly hosts. Praise him, sun and moon; praise him, all you shining stars. Praise him, you highest heavens and you waters above the skies. Let them praise the name of the Lord, for at his command they were created, and he established them for ever and ever—he issued a decree that will never pass away. Praise the Lord from the earth, you great sea creatures and all ocean depths, lightning and hail, snow and clouds, stormy winds that do his bidding, you mountains and all hills, fruit trees and all cedars, wild animals and all cattle, small creatures and flying birds, kings of the earth and all nations, you princes and all rulers on earth, young men and women, old men and children. Let them praise the name of the Lord, for his name alone is exalted; his splendor is above the earth and the heavens. And he has raised up for his people a horn, the praise of all his faithful servants, of Israel, the people close to his heart. Praise the Lord.

Father, thank you that you love us so deeply. There is nothing that compares to your agape love. You fill every empty place in our hearts and fill our souls with the richness of your Word. Father, we praise you for you are so worthy. Amen.

Have a blessed day, God's beautiful people. Let's fill our lives with the sweetness of his Word and praise him today. He will get us through every storm.

Always Stand for What You Believe In

Good morning, beautiful people, good morning. Today it is Hands Around the Capital here in Maine. The Forth-Sixth Memorial Anniversary of Roe v. Wade. Today we will come together and publicly recognize and mourn the Supreme Court decision of Roe v. Wade. The capitol bell will ring forty-six times, representing the number of years since Roe v. Wade was enacted. The Maine Right to Life Committee organizes this event each year. I will go with some friends who want to support as well.

Jeremiah, my aborted son, I will always be your voice.

Jeremiah, God knit you together in my womb, knowing the plan ahead for you. He knew I would abort you, and you would be a baby in heaven. I am so very sorry for that choice I made. I truly didn't understand. Now that I do, I ask for forgiveness from you, my aborted child. Jesus has forgiven me; I received his forgiveness; and now I ask of you. My decision took away all your rights here on earth, and the days you would have enjoyed. I truly am sorry. I truly regret. I live my life for Christ now. I truly feel his love. The love I thought I would feel from premarital sex didn't fill the void in me. I was a wounded girl, just looking for love, and I finally found it in him. Again, I say I'm sorry, Jeremiah, my aborted child. Again, I wish I had made a different choice. I know I will see you in heaven someday, but until then, I will be your voice.

May God use me in any way he can to speak regarding life and his plan. "For I know the plans I have for you, plans to prosper you and not to harm you, to give you hope and a future. I love you Jeremiah!" (Jeremiah 29:11).

Have a blessed day, God's beautiful people. Enjoy life.

Are You Anointed to Bring Freedom?

Good morning, beautiful people. Let's pray about God using us to set others free.

Father, thank you for Jesus. Thank you that you are the all-powerful, all-sufficient one. There is no God like our God. Thank you for the power to break every chain. You said greater things we would do in your name. Thank you for freedom for your people. You said in John 14:12, "Very truly I tell you, whoever believes in me will do the works I have been doing, and they will do even greater things than these, because I am going to the Father." Thank you for the anointing that breaks yokes off your people. (Thank him again.) Your Holy Scripture tell us in Isaiah 61,

The Spirit of the Sovereign Lord is on me, because the Lord has anointed me to proclaim good news to the poor. He has sent me to bind up the brokenhearted, to proclaim freedom for the captives and release from darkness for the prisoners, to proclaim the year of the Lord's favor and the day of vengeance of our God, to comfort all who mourn, and provide for those who grieve in Zion—to bestow on them a crown of beauty instead of ashes, the oil of joy instead of mourning, and a garment of praise instead of a spirit of despair. They will be called oaks of righteousness, a planting of the Lord for the display of his splendor. They will rebuild the ancient ruins and restore the places long devastated; they will renew the ruined cities that have been devastated for generations. Strangers will shepherd your flocks; foreigners will work your fields and vineyards. And you will be called priests of the Lord, you will be named ministers of our God. You will feed on the wealth of nations, and in their riches you will boast. Instead of your shame you will receive a double portion, and instead of disgrace you will rejoice in your inheritance. And so, you will inherit a double portion in your land, and everlasting joy will be yours. "For I, the Lord, love justice; I hate robbery and wrongdoing. In my faithfulness I will reward my people and make an everlasting covenant with them. Their descendants will be known among the nations and their offspring among the peoples. All who see them will acknowledge that they are a people the Lord has blessed."

Father, thank you for rebuilding lives. Thank you for setting the captives free. Thank you for being a God of justice. Thank you for a double portion. Thank you for being a covenant-keeping God. Thank you for the Holy Scriptures. Thank you for the anointing who breaks yokes. Thank you for being a chain breaking, God. Thank you for using us today to set others free. Amen.

Have a blessed day, beautiful people. Be free.

"So, if the Son sets you free, you will be free indeed" (John 8:36).

Enjoy your freedom!

Are You an Overcomer?

Today let's pray about overcoming our circumstances.

For whatever is born of God overcomes the world, and this is the victory that has overcome the world-our faith. Who is the one that overcomes the world, but he who believes that Jesus is the son of God. (John 5:4–5)

He who overcomes, and he who keeps My deeds until the end. To him I will give authority over the nations. (Revelation 2:26)

He who overcomes, I will grant to him to sit down with Me on My throne, as I also overcome and set down with My Father on his throne. (Revelation 3:21)

Father, thank you that we are overcomers today. Lord, your Word is life to our bones. Our hope, our faith is in you. To everything, there is a season, and for people all across this globe that have entered or going to enter a new season in their lives, they will make it. You will never leave us nor forsake us. That is your promise to your people.

Together all across this globe, we declare we are overcomers by the blood of the Lamb, and by the word of our testimonies (Revelation 12:11). Amen.

Have a blessed day, for this is the day the Lord has made, and we will rejoice and be glad in it.

Your Song Doesn't Need to End

Today lets thank God for Jesus the risen one.

I am he that liveth, and was dead; and, behold, I am alive for evermore, amen; and have the keys of hell and of death. (Revelation 1:18)

After the Sabbath, at dawn on the first day of the week, Mary Magdalene and the other Mary went to look at the tomb. There was a violent earthquake, for an angel of the Lord came down from heaven and, going to the tomb, rolled back the stone and sat on it. His appearance was like lightning, and his clothes were white as snow. The guards were so afraid of him that they shook and became like dead men. The angel said to the women, "Do not be afraid, for I know that you are looking for Jesus, who was crucified. He is not here; he has risen, just as he said. Come and see the place where he lay. Then go quickly and tell his disciples: 'He has risen from the dead and is going ahead of you into Galilee. There you will see him.' Now I have told you." So the women hurried away from the tomb, afraid yet filled with joy, and ran to tell his disciples. Suddenly Jesus met them. "Greetings," he said. They came to him, clasped his feet and worshiped him. Then Jesus said to them, "Do not be afraid. Go and tell my brothers to go to Galilee; there they will see me." While the women were on their way, some of the guards went into the city and reported to the chief priests everything that had happened. When the chief priests had met with the elders and devised a plan, they gave the soldiers a large sum of money, telling them, "You are to say, 'His disciples came during the night and stole him away while we were asleep.' If this report gets to the governor, we will satisfy him and keep you out of trouble." So the soldiers took the money and did as they were instructed. And this story has been widely circulated among the Jews to this very day. Then the eleven disciples went to Galilee, to the mountain where Jesus had told them to go. When they saw him, they worshiped him; but some doubted. Then Jesus came to them and said, "All authority in heaven and on earth has been given to me. Therefore, go and make disciples of all nations, baptizing them in the name of the Father and of the Son and of the Holy Spirit, and teaching them to obey everything I have commanded you. And surely, I am with you always, to the very end of the age. (Matthew 28)

Father, thank you that you are alive today. We are overcomers because of the power of the cross and the power of your shed blood. Today anyone needing mercy, hope, and a future, Jesus, you are the answer. Yes, indeed, to the whole world, seven continents, we declare Jesus is alive and wants to put a new song in your heart today. Press in, believe the Word of the Lord. Let him bring you alive today.

All authority in heaven and earth belongs to Jesus. We believe. We can face every day fearless because he holds our lives in his hands.

Have a blessed day, God's beautiful people. For this is the day the Lord has made, and we will rejoice and be glad in it. Yes, he's alive!

Mary, a Woman Trusted with Much...

Good morning, beautiful people, good morning. As I watched the movie, The Nativity Story, I kept thinking how much God trusted Mary. I ponder this morning what God could trust to us. Let's hope and pray he will find us faithful with all he desires for us and through us. Let's pray.

Father, thank you for the faithful life of Mary, mother of Jesus. She heard your angel's voice. She trusted, obeyed, and carried out the plan God had for our salvation. Thank you for the life of Jesus. Because his life, death, and resurrection, it has changed our lives forever. Father, thank you that you are a God of love for mankind. Because of Jesus, we have hope, life, and eternal life to come. The cross made salvation a reality for all and not just a dream we could not obtain on our own.

Father, we pray today you will find us obedient to listen for your voice, obey, and carry out the plan that you have for our journey here on earth. May we always say yes to whatever you ask us to do, wherever you ask us to go, and may our hearts be filled with gratitude that God himself would desire to use us.

Father, may Christmas this year be awakened in a new, fresh way in the hearts of mankind. May many return to their first love that may have grown cold throughout time. May the world know and receive the love and warmth of Mary's son, Jesus. Amen.

Have a joyous day, beautiful people. Jesus lives!

The angel said to her, "Don't be afraid, Mary; God has shown you his grace. Listen! You will become pregnant and give birth to a son, and you will name him Jesus. He will be great and will be called the Son of the Most High. The Lord God will give him the throne of King David, his ancestor. He will rule over the people of Jacob forever, and his kingdom will never end." (Luke 1:30–33)

Are You a Powerhouse?

Good morning, beautiful people, good morning. Let's ask for power.

Very Truly I tell you, whoever believes in me will do the works I have been doing, and they will do even greater things than these, because I am going to the Father. (1 John 4:4)

But you will receive power when the Holy Spirit comes on you; and you will be my witnesses in Jerusalem, and in all Judea and Samaria, and to the ends of the earth. (Acts 1:8)

Father, thank you for giving us power. You said in Luke 10:19, you have given us power and authority. Teach us Holy Spirit how to walk in that power so we can be powerhouses for your kingdom.

Thank you, Holy Spirit our Helper, whom the Father sent in his name, teaches us all things and brings to our remembrance all that he said according to John 14:26.

Fill us with your power, God. Amen.

Have a blessed day, beautiful people. Be filled with his power and be a good witness.

No More Silent Nights

Good morning, beautiful people. Just as the season has changed, and the white powdery snowflakes come down quite frequently here in Maine, I must say I sense a shift. A time that will go down in the history of the United States of America. Today let's pray for our great nation once again.

Father, thank you for Christmas. Thank you for the greatest awakening this country has ever known, not because we deserve it but because of your great love and mercy for our nation.

Father, forgive us for being silent when they were removing your great name. Forgive the poor decisions that we personally have made, as well as our leaders. O God, we ask for forgiveness on behalf of the churches across this nation. Some of your own places that carries your name doesn't even recognize that your spirit left a long time ago. They are left with mere religion, filled with rules and regulations, instead of the precious relationship with your Son, Jesus Christ. The price you paid was enough for mankind's sins. You said it was finished.

Father, thank you for pouring out your spirit on our land once again. Just as we receive the white fallen snow, thank you for new beginnings and cleansing our nation. You are a merciful God, and we are in need and receive your grace.

Father, we ask for the wisdom of Solomon for us all today. May we hearken to the voice of our Lord. We join our faith all across this globe today for America. We declare and decree there will not be another silent night. We declare today, America has made room for our king. Amen.

Have a blessed day, God's beautiful people. May Christ in Christmas be alive in you today.

And she gave birth to her firstborn, a son. She wrapped him in cloths and placed him in a manger, because there was no guest room available for them. And there were shepherds living out in the fields nearby, keeping watch over their flocks at night. An angel of the LORD appeared to them, and the glory of the LORD shone around them, and they were terrified. But the angel said to them, "Do not be afraid. I bring you good news that will cause great joy for all the people. Today in the town of David a Savior has been born to you; he is the Messiah, the Lord. This will be a sign to you: You will find a baby wrapped in cloths and lying in a manger."

Suddenly a great company of the heavenly host appeared with the angel, praising God and saying, "Glory to God in the highest heaven, and on earth peace to those on whom his favor rests." (Luke 2:7–14)

Are You a Loyal Person?

Good morning, beautiful people. Today, let's pray about being loyal.

Be devoted to one another in brotherly love. Honor one another above yourselves. (Romans 12:10)

And may your hearts be fully committed to the LORD our God, to live by his decrees and obey his commands, as at this time. (1 Kings 8:61)

However, I consider my life worth nothing to me; my only aim is to finish the race and complete the task the Lord Jesus has given me—the task of testifying to the good news of God's grace. (Acts 20:24)

Remind the people to be subject to rulers and authorities, to be obedient, to be ready to do whatever is good. (Titus 3:1)

Father, thank you for being loyal to your people. Today our heart's desire is to be found loyal in return. Is this true of you? Then tell him so.

Thank you for your Word of instruction. Today, as we meditate on these scriptures, may we be found faithful to share the good news of your grace, even if we can't use words. Today all across this globe, we declare we are loyal people, honoring others above ourselves. We declare we will not be part of gossip or belittling others. We will choose the high road of being a leader in whatever atmosphere we find ourselves in. Atmospheres will not change us; we will change the atmosphere.

Thank you for ordering our footsteps. Amen.

Have a blessed day, God's beautiful people. Let's be loyal.

Isn't It Time to Come to the Table?

Good morning, beautiful people, good morning. Yesterday, I ran into a person who has battled drug addiction. I don't know if this person has ever journeyed with Jesus. We exchanged glances, and I said a prayer under my breath that God himself would draw them and set this individual free. I know that in Christ, there is freedom. Somehow as a youth, this person was taken captive, and drugs became their best friend. Today let's join our faith for those battling.

Father, thank you that you don't reject anyone. Any person struggling with any issue can come to your table, dine with you, and you bring the change. This journey is different for every person. Your love goes deep into the recesses of hearts and souls and heals the broken places. You open new doors, close old ones, and write new stories on people lives every day.

Father, thank you for the table of love. May many across this globe today come and sup with you. "Here I am! I stand at the door and knock. If anyone hears my voice and opens the door, I will come in and eat with that person, and they with me" (Revelation 3:20).

Father, thank you that there is always room at your table. There is no one who can't join you; all are welcome. Father, we ask you draw many to yourself who are battling life issues. May they begin the journey of freedom in Christ, through Christ, all because you paid the price. Amen.

Have a blessed day, God's beautiful people. Come to the table every day. Everyone is welcome.

A Father's Footsteps

Good morning, beautiful people. Today let's pray together once again the Lord's Prayer:

Our Father which art in heaven, hallowed be thy name. Thy kingdom come, thy will be done in earth, as it is in heaven. Give us this day our daily bread. And forgive us our sins. (Matthew 6:9–13)

Jesus, we join our faith together today all across this globe and thank you for being a Father to the fatherless.

Today we declare restoration where there has been pain and offense. May many fathers return to their first love, Jesus Christ, today and allow you to put their lives in order.

We thank you for strengthening of Father's. They have very important shoes to fill. May they be men of character, integrity, and may they lead their families, communities, and world in the ways of the Lord. Amen.

Have a blessed day, for this is the day the Lord has made, and we will rejoice and be glad in it. Bless a father today.

No One Can Stand Between Us

Good morning, beautiful people, good morning. This morning, I think about how God's redemption of mankind is for all of us, not just certain people. There are people who would try to convince us that God's love is beyond our reach, that some sins cannot be forgiven. Sometimes we feel we don't seem to fit in a certain group or lifestyle; it doesn't make us less to God. He loved us enough to die for us when we were dead in our sins. He loved us too much to leave us in the mess we were in. He rescued us; he had the redemption plan through the blood of Jesus Christ.

Unfortunately religion has tried to conform us to just that—religion. Jesus is all about relationship. He truly is the lover of man's soul. Today let's ask him for clarity, discernment, and understanding by the power of his Holy Spirit. Let's journey every day with him and allow him to change us more into his likeness. You will soon discover that no one can make a difference in your life like Jesus.

Today we are where we are because of his great love. If you need rescuing, he is your rescuer. If you need anything, talk with him today. The greatest gift you have ever been given is the gift of salvation. His blood was enough. Amen? Amen!

Have a blessed day, God's beautiful people. You are loved. Have a joyous day.

"In him we have redemption through his blood, the forgiveness of sins, in accordance with the riches of God's grace" (Ephesians 1:7).

Nobody Like Him, Nobody!

Good morning, beautiful people, good morning. It doesn't matter what things look like all around you this morning, keep your eyes fixed on Jesus. He is the author and finisher of our faith.

He said if we had faith as a mustard seed (that's just a little), we could speak to the mountains in our lives, and they must come down. Anything that exalts itself against the knowledge of God will be brought low. Our position must be in prayer, thankful, and believe he is enough to satisfy the longings of our soul.

Whatever you have need of today, worship him until he brings you the answer. Once you ask him in prayer, thank him every day for his answer. He is enough, you are enough, and the answer will come, not because I say so but because his Word says so. Believe? Believe. Let's pray.

Father, you tell us to pray, to believe, and to receive (Mark 11:24). You tell us, O God, to trust in you with all our heart and not lean on our own understanding (Proverbs 3:5). You have given us authority to trample on snakes and scorpions and all the powers of the enemy (Luke 10:19). Since all power belongs to you in heaven and on earth according to Matthew 28:18, and you live in us, we are victorious. Thank you for victory every day.

Father, you tell us your sheep know and hear your voice, and they follow you (John 10:27). Lead us this day, O God, as we submit our lives to you our victorious King. Amen.

Have a blessed day, beautiful people. You are powerful in Jesus, through Jesus because his spirit lives in you! Somebody shout he reigns forevermore!

Not Debatable, Life

Good morning, beautiful people. Today let's pray for the unborn.

Yet you brought me out of the womb; you made me trust in you even at my mother's breast. From birth I was cast upon you; from my mother's womb you have been my God. (Psalm 22:9–10)

For you created my inmost being; you knit me together in my mother's womb. I praise you because I am fearfully and wonderfully made; your works are wonderful, I know that full well. My frame was not hidden from you when I was made in the secret place. When I was woven together in the depths of the earth, your eyes saw my unformed body. All the days ordained for me were written in your book before one of them came to be. (Psalm 139:13–16)

This is what the LORD says, "He who made you, who formed you in the womb, and who will help you." (Isaiah 44:2)

The word of the LORD came to me, saying, "Before I formed you in the womb, I knew you, before you were born, I set you apart; I appointed you as a prophet to the nations." (Jeremiah 1:4–5)

Father, we thank you for life. Today we join our faith across this globe and pray for the unborn. God, you are a God who loves children. Today we pray you strengthen the women who are carrying a child.

Father, we join our faith and declare safe houses for women and children will open all across this globe. We pray a hedge of protection around the unborn. Give every woman wisdom, Lord, and send them help from on high. May they know the truth and don't buy into the world's lies.

Father, for women who have suffered from abortion and the aftermath and all the devastation that came to them from that choice, we bring them to the healing waters of Jesus Christ today. Lord, thank you for making your women whole again. There is, therefore, no condemnation for those who are in Christ Jesus (Romans 8:1). Only you, O God, can accomplish this in a woman's life, only you.

Father, you are our Father, and you know every detail of our lives, even to the number of hairs on our heads (Matthew 10:30). You know what your people need to be whole again. Thank you for setting this up for your people who have bought into the lie—it wasn't a life. Your Word is not debatable.

Thank you for hearing and answering our prayer today. Amen.

Have a blessed day, God's beautiful people. Life is not debatable.

Not Impossible

Good morning, beautiful people. Today let's thank God for the journey we are on with him. He makes all things possible.

Ah Lord God! Behold, thou hast made the heaven and the earth by thy great power and stretched out arm, and there is nothing too hard for thee. (Jeremiah 32:27)

But Jesus beheld them, and said unto them, with men this is impossible; but with God all things are possible. (Matthew 19:26)

I can do all things through Christ which strengtheneth me. (Philippians 4:13)

And Jesus looking upon them saith, with men it is impossible, but not with God: for with God all things are possible. (Mark 10:27)

Jesus *said unto him, if thou canst believe, all things are possible to him that believeth.* (Mark 9:23)

Father, thank you that with man, some things are just plain impossible, but with you, all things are possible. Today wherever we journey and whatever our lot in life is, help us to never to stop dreaming. Sometimes you take those dreams and sprinkle your blessing on them, and they are fulfilled. You love to give your children good gifts. You gave us the best gift we could ever receive when you gave us your Son, Jesus. The price on the cross cost you everything and us nothing. May we never take that gift for granted.

Today for all the dreamers, keep dreaming. For those on the journey toward fulfillment, we join our faith with yours and petition the man who placed the dream inside of you in the first place to bring it to fruition. Your dream is possible, and if it's his will, definitely a yes.

All across this globe today, we declare our Jesus is limitless, and all things are possible. We declare his Word, for it is yes and amen.

Have a blessed day, God's beautiful people. Today may be the day your Savior says yes to your dream. Believe.

More of Him, Less of Me

Good morning, beautiful people. Today let's pray together about asking God for less of us and more of him. Let's give him permission to set a fire in our soul.

It is good to praise the Lord and make music to your name, O Most High, proclaiming your love in the morning and your faithfulness at night, to the music of the ten-stringed lyre and the melody of the harp. For you make me glad by your deeds, Lord; I sing for joy at what your hands have done. (Psalm 92:1–4 and 12–15)

He must become greater; I must become less. (John 3:30)

Now the Lord is the Spirit, and where the Spirit of the Lord is, there is freedom. And we all, who with unveiled faces contemplate the Lord's glory, are being transformed into his image with ever-increasing glory, which comes from the Lord, who is the Spirit. (2 Corinthians 3:17–18)

Father, thank you for more of you in our lives. It is your will that we have fruitful lives for your glory. Today may someone be drawn to the light that lives in each of us because we are Christians. It is all about you, O God, and all the glory goes to you. Thank you for allowing us to work in your kingdom.

Today all across this globe, we declare we need more of you and less of us. Change us to be more like you. We want more of you, Lord, in our lives. Set our souls on fire and let the fire spread. More of you is our prayer today and less of us. Amen.

Do you want more of him? Tell him so.

Have a blessed day, beautiful people, for this is the day the Lord has made, and we will rejoice and be glad in it. *Receive more of him.*

Now That's the Truth...Believe!

Good morning, beautiful people. Romans 8:38–39 tells us, "For I am convinced that neither death nor life, neither angels nor demons, neither the present nor the future, nor any powers, neither height nor depth, nor anything else in all creation, will be able to separate us from the love of God that is in Christ Jesus our Lord."

I wanted to share my first writing once again.

The Love of My Father

O Father, your love for me is so hard to comprehend; you died for me when I was yet a sinner.

Love you had no boundaries; you took my sin; and you made me whole again.

Such love, the love of my Father.

When I chose the path of the evil one, you loved me and led me to your path again.

Such love, the love of my Father.

When I cried because of all the pain, you healed my pain and removed my shame. Oh, such love.

Where others wounded me, you bound up my wounds and filled me with joy.

Such love, the love of my Father.

When I needed guidance, you left me your Word and your Holy Spirit.

Such love, the love of my Father.

Whatever the future holds for me is in your hands, for your love for me has made me whole.

My Father, you say in your Word that the footsteps of the righteous are ordered of the Lord. That's my future because of the love of my Father.

Have a blessed day, God's beautiful people. "Jesus is the way, the truth and the life. No one comes to the Father except through Him" (John 14:6). Believe!

O God, I Am Letting You Out of the Box

Good morning, beautiful people. Today I will continue to interview team members from Global Awakening. I get so frustrated at myself at times for how I limit God. He doesn't always do things the way we want him too, and it doesn't always look like what I think it should. I have grown not to care really how it gets done as long as he is involved, and his people get their miracle. Just when I think I may have a little more figured out about him, I see him working in a whole new dimension.

At this meeting, so many people have received healing. I love to see the miraculous, and I love to be part of it too. I have made up my mind once again; I am letting him out of the box. My limited thinking is just that limited.

Father, thank you for being the God of impossibilities. Lead us out of the box this day. You have the keys, the divine appointments, and the divine connections, you are the all-sufficient one. Lead us to our destinies, we pray.

Forgive us, God, when we only gave you a small box or a small window of opportunity in which to move. Limitless Jesus, take the limits off our thinking today. We believe Luke 1:37 that tells us with you, O God, nothing shall be impossible.

We pull down every hindrance, everything and anything that would hold us back from moving according to your Word and spirit. You are our God, and we are your people. In you, there are no limits, no time, no boundaries, just freedom.

We walk with the highest authority on the earth, the authority of Jesus Christ. Even the wind must obey. Help us, Lord, to put aside our thinking and put on the mind of Christ.

Together all across this globe today, we declare revival fire. Our destinies are coming to pass. This is our season. This is our time. There are no limitations as we let Jesus out of the box.

Father, the world shows us every day what they can do. Today, O God, show the world what you can do through us your people. Amen.

Have a blessed day, beautiful people. Never forget Jesus's Words in Luke 18:27, "What is impossible with man is possible with God." Let him out of the box of your limited thinking today.

Oh No! What Have I Done?

Good morning, beautiful people This morning, my eyes were drawn to the portrait so beautifully framed as a gift to me, that's hanging on my dining room wall. It captured my attention this day like never before.

The teenage artist, Gabriella from central California, was bringing forth a message through the gift she has been given by God. The sketch in which she titled, "Oh No! What Have I Done," made my mind ponder the terrible mess this young artist was thinking about when she was painting this portrait.

Standing in muddy waters, this once beautiful girl now with a tattered pink dress had a look of despair. She was now glaring at her right hand as she realizes her life has been tainted by sin.

She had gotten herself in a bad situation, a dark place, a frightening dilemma that was now beyond her own control. Only God himself could help her and put her life's journey on a better course.

On the back of the portrait were the Bible verses: "Do not be deceived, evil company corrupts good habits" (1 Corinthians 15:33). Also "And do not be conformed to this world but be transformed by the renewing of your mind, that you may prove that is good and acceptable and perfect will of God" (Romans 12:2).

These scriptures say it well. If we only would have adhered to them. However, we all have made poor choices, bad decisions, and sometimes just plain old stupid mistakes. I am so thankful for a loving Heavenly Father who died on a cross for us when we were yet sinners.

I thank God for his grace he so mercifully gives to each of us. I remember being at a crossroad just like the girl in the portrait. Many words were spoken about my past sins and hurtful words about my current appearance. I no longer wore the size someone else thought it should be, and yes, as a teenager, I had made some bad choices as well.

It did leave its mark on my life, but years ago, I had met Jesus, my redeemer. I looked in the mirror the very next morning as I was preparing for work. Applying the makeup that would cover the tear-stained face from the painful words that were spoken; I talked to God, the creator of the universe about how he saw me. I remember that morning just like it was this morning. Beautiful was his reply. I then quickly found a pen and paper to write, and this is what flowed.

Ashes no more. Jesus, lover of my soul, creator of my image, lifter of my head, my name is beautiful. Pure, holy, undefiled, sanctified, set apart, journeying with Jesus. A path, narrow and straight. Ashes no more. Trusting her master, her maker, the lover of her soul. Skipping on the journey with childlike faith, believing her Father knows what's best. The morning dew, the night's crisp air reminds her of the kisses from above. Jesus, the ultimate man, the lover of her soul. Beautiful, a receiver of his glory, ashes no more.

I am so thankful for a loving Heavenly Father who speaks to his children and sets the course of destiny for each of our lives. Today no matter what you have done, where you have been, or where you now find yourself, know that you are loved. Just like the girl with the tattered pink dress that sin had left its mark, today Jesus is saying, "Come journey with me and let me give you a new beginning. I am your redeemer." Let's pray.

Father, thank you for the Word of God (Bible). Thank you that you are our redeemer. Thank you for paying the ultimate price for our sins. Thank you for grace. Father, today we pray for every girl, every woman who is caught in a bad situation that needs intervention. For every person today, O God, that sin has lefts its mark.

We pray by the power of your Holy Spirit, you draw them to yourself, and may they know you as their redeemer. We pray for shackles to be broken all across this globe. May the love of Christ flow freely to people, we pray, as you write beautiful created in my image (God) on their mirror this day.

Jesus, the ultimate man, the lover of our soul, thank you for new beginnings this day, we pray. Amen.

Have a blessed day, beautiful people. He calls you beautiful.

One Decision Can Change Your Life

Good morning, beautiful people, good morning. Every day we make decisions that impact our lives. A decision to enjoy our day or not. A decision to let others dictate how our day will go. A decision of where we will live, work, who we will marry, etc. Life is full of decisions.

Today let's pray about the decisions we have made. Have you made the decision to be a follower of Jesus Christ? Have you made the decision in word only and not in deed? Are you a little in or have you made the decision to be sold out? Decisions, decisions, decisions.

Father, thank you that you gave us free will to choose and make our own decisions. You force your will on no one. The choice, the decision, is ours. We can choose to sing, or we can choose to worship. We can choose to sit in a pew one day a week, or we can choose to be a follower of Jesus Christ every day.

Father, empower us to make the right decisions today. The decision to take the high road when we can take the low one. The decision for our future, the decision for our families, and the decisions according to your Word.

Father, may many make the decision to follow you and experience a life in Christ with Christ and eternal life forever more. Amen.

Have a blessed day, beautiful people. What's your decision?

"If you declare with your mouth, "Jesus is Lord," and believe in your heart that God raised him from the dead, you will be saved" (Romans 10:9).

One of a Kind

Good morning, beautiful people, good morning. When God created you in his image, he threw the mold away. You are one of a kind.

Today let's start our prayer time together with a praise song and giving the Lord permission to mold and shape us into his image.

Yet you, LORD, are our Father. We are the clay, you are the potter; we are all the work of your hand. (Isaiah 64:8)

But we all, with unveiled face, beholding as in a mirror the glory of the Lord, are being transformed into the same image from glory to glory, just as by the Spirit of the Lord. (2 Corinthians 3:18)

The words of the Lord are pure words: as silver tried in a furnace of earth, purified seven times. (Psalm 12:6)

Father, we thank you for creating us into your image. Thank you for molding and shaping us, setting us apart, calling and equipping us to do your work here on earth.

Father, we thank you for your Word that transforms us daily. Thank you for enlarging our territories as you work out your plan for our lives.

Father, we thank you for pouring out your spirit on all mankind. We join our faith together and declare the works of your hands all across this globe. May many come to know you today, Lord. Draw them to yourself, we pray. Amen.

Have a blessed day, God's beautiful people. You are one of a kind.

Only Be Overwhelmed by This

Good morning, beautiful people. Everywhere I go lately, people seem to be overwhelmed by politics, family discord, marital issues, financial strains, and the list is endless. Today let's be overwhelmed by God's goodness, his mercy and love for us.

Father, thank you for mercy. Thank you for your love for mankind. You are an amazing God, and we are overwhelmed by your goodness to us. May we all stay focused on how great our God is. May we only be overwhelmed by your presence.

Father, may we "hold fast the confession of our hope without wavering, for he who promised is faithful" (Hebrews 10:23).

Thank you for your faithfulness. We are overwhelmed with your goodness.

Have a blessed day, beautiful people. Be overwhelmed with him today, him only.

Open Your Door, Fire

Good morning, beautiful people, good morning. Let's pray for open doors.

Father, thank you for opening our hearts so people will feel loved and cared for. God, thank you for making our hearts an open door. Open our hearts wide, open them wider today, O God. May the world see you in our lives because of the love and care we have for your people. It doesn't matter what race, what economic status, you loved people. Father, help us to love what you love, people.

At the end of the day, it doesn't matter who is right or who is wrong, it matters that people feel valued and cared for. Empower us to lay down our rights so that others may experience the love of Jesus Christ. It cost him his very life; may it cost us all laying down our pride, our agendas, our pretense, our need to be right, and every other thing that exalts itself against the knowledge of God.

Father, you were all about people. May our day look different today because we spread some of what you gave us—love. May our heart be filled with the same love. Do a work in all of our hearts today, God. We give you permission. (Tell him if you are willing.) Thank you for the grace to let everything up until this very moment go. The hurts, the wounds, and the pains that others have inflicted, we release it to you, Father. Fill the hurt with your love. We want more of you flowing through our daily lives.

May the love of Jesus Christ spread like wildfire through the body of Christ today. May we give some of the love he fills our hearts with away today all across this globe. Amen. Somebody yell open doors! Somebody yell fire!

Hope does not put us to shame, because God's love has been poured out into our hearts through the Holy Spirit, who has been given to us. You see, at just the right time, when we were still powerless, Christ died for the ungodly. Very rarely will anyone die for a righteous person, though for a good person someone might possibly dare to die. But God demonstrates his own love for us in this: While we were still sinners, Christ died for us (Romans 5:5–8).

Have a blessed day, God's beautiful people. Open the door to your heart and let the fire blaze.

Our Joy Is in the River

Good morning, beautiful people, good morning. I was thinking about the light in the eyes of every soul. You can see when the light is dim, hurting, and when the light is full of joy. You can tell a lot about people by looking them in the eyes.

"The eye is the lamp of the body; so then if your eye is clear, your whole body will be full of light" (Matthew 6:22).

Father, thank you for the joy in the river. This joy is so hard to contain. I love how the rocks can't stop the river from flowing. You take care of it all. We can dance in the river; we can sing in the river. The joy of the Lord is our strength as we wait upon you (Nehemiah 8:10).

Father, I get so excited as I wait upon your answers. I'm just like the child going to the candy store for the first time. You always give us so much more than what we could ever think or ask.

Thank you for the river. Thank you that it is flowing. Thank you we can dance in the river. Thank you that we can put our trust in you. You are God over everything!

From the Crown of Maine to seven continents of the world, the river is flowing. Now that's something to dance about! Amen.

Have a blessed day, God's beautiful people.

"Light in a messenger's eyes brings joy to the heart, and good news gives health to the bones" (Proverbs 15:30).

Out with the Old and In with the New

Good morning, beautiful people, good morning. I was thinking this morning about how fasting, prayer, and the Word of God radically changes lives. I like to pray for all the ministries I know that are making a difference in people's lives. I pray for lost souls. I pray for my family. I pray for my prayer partners. I pray for the world, and I also pray for myself. I pray to know the heart of my God every day. I want to continue to be a carrier of his power and anointing to touch the hurting and wounded among us. I want to go wherever he wants me to go, to say whatever he wants me to say, and to do whatever he wants me to do. If that is your heart's desire too, join me in prayer this morning.

Father, thank you for making us vessels full of your new wine. We want to be carriers of freedom, of life, carriers of your new wine. Take us up higher, Jesus. In our weakness, you are made strong. You change us from glory to glory.

Father, we lay down our lives today as an offering to you. Show us, God, our daily assignments. Highlight the people who are losing hope so that we may be your vessels of life. You have come to give the world life and life more abundantly (John 10:10). Use us today to give that life to a lost person we will encounter today. You are the way, the truth, and the life (John 14:6).

Father, thank you that signs, wonders, and miracles are performed through the name of Jesus. You said signs, wonders, and miracles should follow us. Thank you for this power. Then as Peter said in Acts 3:6, "Silver or gold I do not have, but what I do have I give you. In the name of Jesus Christ of Nazareth, walk." Thank you for the anointing.

All across this globe today, take Jesus at his Word. Believe!

Have a blessed day, beautiful people. Your faith has made you well. "According to your faith let it be done to you" (Matthew 9:29).

Overcome your Circumstances by Worship

Good morning, beautiful people. This is the day the Lord has made. I will rejoice and be glad in it (Psalm 118:24). Yes, I will. I have made my choice again today. Yesterday I came home from church after an amazing service both rich in Word (Bible) and worship and praised some more. I began to put music on and sing and worship my King. I want to know him. I want to know him the best I possibly can know him. I want to know the heart of my God. Even through difficult times, he is worthy of our praise. We all have or will have circumstances that we will need to overcome.

I was invited to attend an overcomer's conference a few years ago with Evangelist Tanya Jalbert. I prayed for women who had overcome the most horrific situations. Through an interpreter, I prayed for strength, peace, and joy for these dear women. I declared the Word of the Lord over each of their lives. I took along my writings and gave them free to anyone who desired them. Jesus was a free gift to me; he cost me nothing in dollars and cents; and I wanted to freely give them the same hope. That's where I first heard Robert Philibert as he humbly played his guitar for worship. I was blessed at his pure heart as he led the worship in both English and French. Robert recently, along with Tanya Jalbert and a few other worshippers, began launching a CD called Intimate. You can listen to their samples on www.reachoutworship.com and meet them both on YouTube. As I listened to one of their songs yesterday, "Apart from You," I began to reflect what my life was like before surrendering to Jesus. Yes, I believed in God; yes, I believed there was more than just going to church; and yes, I wanted to embark on the fullness of the journey.

The trials came, and I soon learned that I could do nothing apart from Christ, just like the song said. According to the Word (Bible) in Psalm 34 it states, "Praise him in all things," and in James 1:2, "To consider it all joy the various trials, knowing that the testing of your faith produces endurance." In simple everyday language, he is saying, "Trust me, praise me," and his joy would be our strength. Wow, so easy to read, but it's our obedience to his Word that brings change.

Today whatever circumstance you find yourself in, can you step out and praise him? You were created to praise him. Worship is a personal choice; no one can force you; and no one can do it for you. You choose when, you choose how, but in the end, you will receive the blessing. You will feel revived, refreshed, and the barriers built up in your heart will be torn down.

Today let God pour more of himself into your heart. Let his love flow freely from the throne room into your heart. Then you will be a conduit of his love to others in the world where so many are hurting.

A few years ago, I read the book, It's Time to Move Now by Tanya Jalbert (check it out on Amazon). I must agree the time to step out and walk in obedience and worship the King is now.

Yes, we have all been done wrong, and if you haven't yet let me tell you, it will happen. So the time to let go is now, the time to move on is now, the time to praise his name is now. Now is the time to worship the Father in spirit and in truth, for the Father is seeking such to worship him (John 4:23).

Don't you feel like praising him? Come on, step out, the time is now. Let's pray.

Father, thank you for your Word. In Psalm 9:1–2, it states, "I will give thanks to you, Lord, with all my heart; I will tell of all your wonderful deeds. I will be glad and rejoice in you; I will sing the praises of your name, O Most High."

Today, I choose to rise above any and all circumstances and sing my praises to you. I will trust you at all times. You are a good Father, and I will praise your name. I thank you for your joy that is my strength (Nehemiah 8:10). I choose to praise you, to worship you, and to bless your Holy name, Jesus. Amen.

Have a blessed day, God's beautiful people. Praise him!

Pardoned?

Good morning, beautiful people. Don't you wish we were a perfect people and did everything 100 percent right all the time? Believe me, I have had my share of trying. No matter how good we are, or think we are, we are only saved by his grace and his grace alone. It's when we give up and let him live his life through us, we have the victory. Oh, how I love Jesus! Let's pray.

Father, thank you for Jesus. Thank you that because he lives, because he paid the ultimate price, we can face every day with confidence. We have been pardoned, and we don't need to live in fear. Our future, our tomorrows are in his hands. Thank you for ordering our footsteps.

Father, thank you for mercy and grace. Thank you that we are only saved because of Jesus. Our righteousness is as filthy rags (Isaiah 64:6). Let the love of God that is shed abroad in our hearts pour out on others today. May we give from the abundance, the overflow through the power of the Holy Spirit to a hurting world.

May hope arise all across this globe today, not because of who we are but because Jesus lives. Because he lives, there is nothing we can't face with him by our side. At the end of our lives to see him face-to-face, that's what we live for. Only he knows the day and hour, but until then, we walk boldly and confidently through the power of the Holy Spirit. Lead us beside still waters today, we pray. Amen.

Have a blessed day, God's most beautiful people. Talk to him about anything, share your heart with him, for he cares for you. You have been pardoned. Be free.

Perfection or Grace

Good morning, beautiful people, good morning. This morning, I was thinking of some of the decisions and choices I made as a teenager. Although I was created in the image of God, I wasn't and will never be perfect. I am thankful for God's grace.

If you are breathing, and you are being truthful, you would have to admit the same. It is easier to look at the speck in someone else's eye than the plank in yours (Matthew 7:5). I have had to revisit this place many times in my walk with God. We are not perfect, and we will never be until we reach the other side. Let's pray.

Father, thank you for the providential plan for everyone living. For God knows there are so many who are not even among us that should be. So many lives have been taken with world views instead of God's plan.

Father, thank you for mercy and grace. We are not ashamed of the Gospel of Jesus Christ. Today we declare all across this nation and to the nation/s of the world, all seven continents, that you are alive and well, and your spirit is moving on the earth today.

Your Word does not return void, and you are watching over it to perform it. From the White House to every court house and to every home all across this land… BELIEVE… "Jesus is the way the truth and the life" (John 14:6).

Have a blessed day, God's beautiful people. Thank him for Grace.

"The Word became flesh and made his dwelling among us. We have seen his glory, the glory of the one and only Son, who came from the Father, full of grace and truth" (John 1:14).

Praise Him and Trust Him Even in the Storm

Good morning, beautiful people. This morning, I was thinking on how easy it is to praise him when things are going well. However, when life presents challenges, and things aren't going as planned, it is easy to get our eyes on the circumstances of the moment and not keep our eyes fixed on the promises of God. We fail at times to remember his track record. He is a faithful God, and he is watching over us. He is a God of love, compassion, and mercy.

He doesn't cause the difficulties in our lives, but praising him in the storm will bring us through. We can trust the man who laid down his life for us. When difficulties strike us, we need to be like Job 1:20–22.

At this, Job got up and tore his robe and shaved his head. Then he fell to the ground in worship and said: Naked I came from my mother's womb, and naked I will depart. The Lord gave and the Lord has taken away; may the name of the Lord be praised. In all this, Job did not sin by charging God with wrongdoing.

Father, we praise you, and we trust in you, and we take you at your Word every day. We know from the prayers you have already answered, you are trustworthy. Your promises will come to pass as we put all our trust in you. Your Word does not return void, it is forever settled.

As we journey every day, we will keep our eyes lifted to the hills from whence our help cometh. "Our help cometh from the Lord, which made heaven and earth" (Psalm 121:1–2). Amen.

Have a blessed day, God's beautiful people. Praise Him!

Releasing Control of Your Destiny

Good morning, beautiful people, good morning. Isn't it great we journey life with a man who is in control of our lives? Whatever concerns our hearts and minds, he has it all under his control.

Even when others try to control our destinies, we must stay close to God and follow the direction he has for us. God knows the ending of our lives before we were in our mother's womb (Psalm 139). Opinions, good intentions of others are appreciated, but we must keep our eyes fixed on Jesus, the author and finisher of our faith. No one can take our destiny away from us, unless we release to them the power.

Today let's surrender once again full control of our lives to the next step in fulfilling our destiny. Jesus knows what's best. Let's pray.

Father, thank you that you, O God, order our footsteps. Direct us, Lord, each and every day. As you have filled our lives full of destiny moments before the foundations of the earth, give us eyes to see them each and every day.

Father, your plan is always the best. We take our hands off and release our lives to the man who breathed life in us. Take over every plan and every detail of our lives. We release full control and will walk according to your will and your way. Amen.

Have a blessed day, beautiful people. Release control of your future to him.

"In their heart's humans plan their course, but the Lord establishes their steps" (Proverbs 16:9).

Say No to Gossip

Good morning, beautiful people, good morning. This morning, I was thinking how hard it is at times to get out of conversations that are not edifying or building up of another person. It is hard today to find people who you can trust, wholeheartedly trust.

Since every person is important to God, we must keep our tongues in check. Only praying and believing the very best for one another. He desires freedom for all his children.

"A gossip betrays a confidence, but a trustworthy person keeps a secret" (Proverbs 11:13).

Father, thank you that we are children of the Most High God. Thank you for trustworthy people in our lives. May we be found trustworthy as well. Empower us to guard our mouths and speak only words that build up, edify and exhort one another to be the very best we can be.

Father, as you trust us with people from diverse backgrounds, diverse struggles, may we be vessels fit for the master's use. Never forgetting our own struggles and how we overcame. May we be the safe person today that someone who is hurting could share their burden.

Father, purify our hearts, purify our mouths, and as we journey today with our family, friends, coworkers, and people in our communities, help us to remain optimistic, always looking for the best in one another. Amen.

Have a blessed day, God's beautiful people. Say no to gossip and yes to building one another up.

See your Life through God's Eyes

Good morning, beautiful people, good morning. Life is such a journey. I dropped my glasses and cracked my lens recently. It made life look a bit hazy. As I traveled north yesterday, I stopped and purchased a new pair. Wow! Isn't it amazing how quickly things look differently? It's the same with our journey with God.

There are times that we can't see our way, but we take him at his Word. As we put our trust in him, he makes every crooked way straight. We walk blindly with our God through faith. Let's pray.

Father, thank you for new beginnings. As we journey every day with you, we can rest assured you hold our lives in your hands. Perfect love casts out all fear. We do not have to fear the future, for fear has lost its grip on us. You work all things together for our good as we put our trust in you. We can wake up confidently every day, knowing you carry the master plan.

Father, lead us today by still waters and refresh our soul. Highlight the path you have for us as we put our trust in you. Amen.

Have a blessed day, God's beautiful people. See your life through God's eyes. His Word is very clear.

"For I know the plans I have for you," declares the Lord, "plans to prosper you and not to harm you, plans to give you hope and a future" (Jeremiah 29:11).

Sharpen Us Up, God

Good morning, beautiful people, good morning. Let's ask God himself to make us sharp.

Father, thank you for the Word of God. John 1:1 says, "In the beginning was the Word, and the Word was with God, and the Word was God." You said to meditate on it day and night and to be careful to do everything that is written in it. Then we will be prosperous and successful (Joshua 1:8). Thank you, Holy Spirit, for bringing the Word to remembrance today as we need it (John 14:26). O God, speak the truth to us as the Word sharpens us. For the Word of God is alive and active sharper than any double-edged sword, it penetrates even to dividing soul and spirit, joints and marrow; it judges the thoughts and attitudes of the heart (Hebrews 4:12). Sharpen us, God, sharpen us up. May our hearts be pure before you. Cleanse us and make us fit for the master's use. Amen.

Have a blessed day, beautiful people. Read your Bible and ask the Holy Spirit to make you sharp and ask him to sharpen me up too.

Praise Him

Good morning, beautiful people. I just had to share this once again. Praise is on my mind today. Let today be a day of praise to our King. This is from my prayer experience at a local church I attended.

We traveled the stations all based on *the Lord's Prayer* from Matthew 6:9–13. We traveled stations: adoration, thanksgiving, penitence, oblation, petition, and intercession, and the final station was the praise station.

Our Father, which art in heaven, Hallowed be thy Name. Thy Kingdom come. Thy will be done in earth, as it is in heaven. Give us this day our daily bread. And forgive us our trespasses, as we forgive them that trespass against us. And lead us not into temptation, but deliver us from evil. For thine is the kingdom, The power, and the glory, Forever and ever. Amen.

I picked up a paper that read, "Praise in this station." We praise God not to obtain anything but because God's being draws praise from us.

For thine is the kingdom, the power and the glory (Lord's Prayer).

Prayers of Praise

O praise the Lord, all ye nations: praise him in the firmament of his power. Praise him for his mighty acts: praise him according to his excellent greatness. Praise him with the sound of the trumpet: praise him with the psaltery and harp. Praise him with the timbrel and dance: praise him with stringed instruments and organs. Praise him upon the loud cymbals: praise him upon the high-sounding cymbals. Let everything that hath breath praise the Lord. Praise ye the Lord. (Psalm 150)

What is praiseworthy around you? What glimpse of God of his presence and his promise have you seen lately? Take a few moments and write out or speak out loud praises to the Lord.

Here's my prayer for us today.

Father, we praise you. We praise you in the morning. We praise you throughout our whole day. Your praises are continually on our lips. From the rising of the sun to the going down of the same, the name of the Lord shall be praised (Psalm 113:3).

We come today not asking for anything but just lifting up our voices of praise. You have blessed us beyond measure, and our cup runneth over. We just have to praise your holy name. You are a good God, and your presence is everything to us.

All across this globe today, praise the Lord. Amen.

Have a blessed day, beautiful people...praise him!

Shhh! It's a Secret

Good morning, beautiful people, good morning. I was talking with a friend in Walmart last evening about giving. If you want some joy in your life, give something to someone who really needs it and could never pay you back. Don't tell anyone, let it be between you and God alone. Even kick it up a notch and ask Jesus to show you the person, and he will. He will highlight someone, bring a name to your mind, bring them to you, or you will run into them. He will give you an assignment. It doesn't even need to cost money. It could be a visit, a kind word. It could be something you have, or it could be something you will buy.

I love God's assignments. Then hush is the word, don't tell anyone. Let the love of Christ flow across the earth today.

Father, you said in Matthew 6:1–5,

Be careful not to practice your righteousness in front of others to be seen by them. If you do, you will have your reward from your Father in heaven. When you give, do not announce it with trumpet's, as with the hypocrites do in the synagogues and on the streets, to be honored by others. Truly, I tell you they have received their reward in full. But when you give, do not let the left hand know what the right hand is doing, so that your giving may be in secret. Then your Father, who sees what is done in secret, will reward you.

Thank you for God's assignments today. Thank you for highlighting and showing us the need. We want to know your heart, Father, today for your people. We want to love them and be your hands extended to them. Thank you for teaching us how to love as you do.

Thank you for being our God, and we your people. Amen.

I can still see that sign from a home I visited a short time ago, learn to love by loving… Oh, beautiful people, read the book of life today (Bible), our instructions for daily living. Let's fill our world full of love. Let's keep it a secret; nobody needs to know. Jesus sees it all. Receive joy in your heart from him that is priceless. No man and no dollar amount can place that in the heart of man. It's the great reward from the creator himself.

Stay blessed and bless others today, beautiful people.

Shine, Shine, Fire

Good morning, beautiful people. Tuesday night, I attended Bible study, and we discussed our thoughts and scriptures about our thoughts. They all laughed as I said, "Every morning, I get up and start my day and declare fire."

Wednesday morning came, and a dear lady called and shared these scriptures and again last evening another individual called and shared the same scriptures. I am going to share them with you today.

"Arise, shine for your light has come, and the glory of the Lord rises upon you. See the darkness covers the earth and thick darkness is over the peoples, but the Lord rises upon you and his glory appears over you. Nations will come to your light, and kings to the brightness of your dawn" (Isaiah 60:1–3).

Father, this is the day that you have made, and we will rejoice and be glad in it. We are blessed to wake up every morning and be a carrier of your glory. Holy Spirit, shine through us today. May our light shine bright, and the world see you in us for your glory and your glory alone.

Father, you said it is not by might nor by power but by your spirit (Zechariah 4:6). Thank you for pouring out your spirit. Blaze, Spirit, blaze.

Thank you for God's assignments today. Order our footsteps and lead us right into destiny. Amen.

Have a blessed day, beautiful people. Look in the mirror and yell fire. Be on fire for Jesus today. Share your faith; someone in your path needs hope.

Nothing Is Too Difficult

Good morning, beautiful people. Today let's declare Jeremiah 32:27 that states, "You are the Lord of all mankind. Nothing is too hard for you!"

Father, we lift up every need, problem, injustice, and circumstance to you and join our faith together for every reader across this globe. Nothing is too hard for you according to your Word—no, nothing.

Father, today we ask you to intervene, to provide, and to show yourself strong (tell him your need and your situation) on behalf of all mankind.

Father, thank you that you are the Lord who knows and sees it all. Together we believe. Forgive any unbelief that has crept in our lives. Yes, yes, we believe. Yes, indeed.

Have a blessed day, God's beautiful people. This is the day the Lord has made, rejoice and be glad in it. Have a blessed day!

Beautiful Pumpkin

Good morning, beautiful people. Fall time is so beautiful here in Maine, and here I go bragging again. The leaves are changing different colors every day, and pumpkins are everywhere. This precious pumpkin, Maisie Grace, is truly a blessing from the Lord.

The best gift a grandmother can give their grandchildren is to pray for them, and that I do. I have prayed faithfully for Maisie since the day her mother and father announced they would be bringing a child into the world.

Maisie and I have prayed a lot together for all the children around the world. She usually gives a big smile when I ask her if she wants to pray with her grandma.

"Behold, children are a heritage from the Lord, the fruit of the womb a reward" (Psalm 127:3).

Today, the world is pulling for our children and grandchildren at a young age. The best gift a parent can give their child is to train them up in the ways of the Lord. Material items will fade away, but God's Word does not return void. So today, let's take a moment and thank the Lord for the blessing of children and grandchildren all across this globe. Let's join our faith for protection, for health, for a joyful life, rich in love and blessing and his Word.

Father, thank you for the gift of children and grandchildren. Today, we join our faith, O God, that you would dispatch your angels to watch over them. That they would not just learn about you God but truly know you intimately.

We pray they would learn your Word at an early age, and according to your Word, they will not depart from it.

"Train up a child in the way he should go; even when he is old he will not depart from it" (Proverbs 22:6).

Thank you for a harvest of children and grandchildren across this globe. It truly is harvest time. Amen. Stay blessed, beautiful people.

Think Positive, Speak Positive

Good morning, beautiful people, good morning. I was driving to work a few towns away on Friday of last week. I began to reminisce about the play I took my grandson, Mason, to see at Presque Isle High School as I made my way for the one-hour commute. We were wowed at an outstanding performance of Willy Wonka. I still can hear the young man as he played the part of Charlie Bucket and sang the song, "Think Positive."

Mason, being four, has a lot to learn in life, and it's my prayer he will learn early ways that will make life fulfilling for him. Life has many bumps in the road, trials, tragedies, and disappointments, but the journey must go on. It brings to mind the scripture in Philippians 4 verse 8, "Finally, brethren, whatever things are true, whatever things are noble, whatever things are just, whatever things are pure, whatever things are lovely, whatever things are of good report, if there is any virtue and if there is anything praiseworthy—meditate on these things."

It's amazing how a bad memory, a poor choice, or the world around us and all the negative reports we hear each day impacts us. Although it happened, it hurt, and the world seems to be growing darker; it doesn't change the Word of the Lord. People are losing hope today, and as Christians, we are to bring that hope. Romans 15 verse 13, a favorite scripture, "Now may the God of hope fill you with all joy and peace in believing, that you may abound in hope by the power of the Holy Spirit."

Declare today that no matter the negative influences that bombard your life, you will fill your bucket with good thoughts, good reports, and look for the positive. Today declare you will speak good things, and your words will bring hope that will encourage another. Declare today is going to be a good day. Don't forget to pass it on as well. Look for someone to bless, edify, build up, and encourage. Make today a good day for someone else and watch how your day unfolds. It's a good day already. Let's pray.

Father, I pray for every reader today. I declare that no matter what the circumstances are, your Word triumphs it. No matter the loss, no matter the disappointments, you are their hope. Today fill each reader with a fresh wind of hope. May you send someone to encourage them, to lift their spirits and bless them. May you send them to do the same for someone else. Today, God, we declare over it's a good day!

Have a blessed day, God's beautiful people.

Thirsty Soul?

Good morning, beautiful people. Thirsty? Let's pray.

"As the deer pants for streams of water, so my soul pants for you, my God. My soul thirsts for God, for the living God" (Psalm 42:1–2).

Father, we want more of you, more of you. Show us your glory, O God. To the nations of the world today, we declare Jesus is the way, the truth, and the life. No one comes to the Father except through him. Draw your people, we pray.

You fill the thirsty soul, and we want more, God, more of you. Rain down on us.

All across this globe today, we receive the outpouring. You are raining down, changing lives, bringing hope, and healing to your people.

Father, ignite every meeting place, your church, and fill every thirsty soul. Amen.

Have a blessed day, God's beautiful people. You are loved! Drink deep today in his presence. Today is your day to receive more of his living waters. It's raining.

Show the World You Care

Good morning, beautiful people. Our world is filled with so many issues. I have been pondering this morning in my heart a radio interview on Destiny Moments I had done with a pastor.

This morning, I thought about all the brokenness I live in and around. I think about the brokenness I experienced in my own life. I ponder in my heart lots of things this late morning. There are somethings you just know at heart's level. People can try to convince you this will work, that will work, but there are some things you just know because you know, because you know. Pray with me this morning once again for our nation to the nations.

Father, we humbly come before you today, thanking you for healing our land. Father, we lift up our leaders to you. It doesn't matter what party they are from, Democrat, Republican, Independent, may they seek you first for our nation. Many nations are depending on us to lead the way. We thank you for this move of God.

Father, forgive us, for how man (us) have messed up our world. Everybody thinking they had the answer, and they were right. What the world needs is more love, more caring for one another. People don't care how much knowledge we have, they want to know how much we care. Take us deeper today in our hearts, Lord. Deep calleth unto deep.

Father, every life is important to you. Even the ones that the world cast aside, you go after that one. Father, teach our nation to care and to love one another. Where there has been hurt, let forgiveness flow. Where there has been injustice, we pray for justice.

O God, thank you for the river. Thank you that love, caring, kindness, joy, hope, and forgiveness are all in the river. To that, we say amen.

Father, let the river flow from the Crown of Maine (New England is the womb of the nation) to the seven continents of the world. Flow, river, flow. We pray the prayer of St. Francis of Assisi once again.

Lord, make me an instrument of your peace. Where there is hatred, let me sow love; where there is injury, pardon; where there is doubt, faith; where there is despair, hope; where there is darkness, light, where there is sadness, joy. Oh divine master, grant that I may not so much seek to be consoled as to console. To be understood as to understand. To be loved as to love. For it is in giving that we receive; it is in pardoning that we are pardoned; and it is in dying that we are born to eternal life. Amen.

Have a blessed day, beautiful people. Let the river flow from your heart today. Show someone you care.

"Whoever believes in me, as Scripture has said, rivers of living water will flow from within them" (John 7:38).

Signs You Must Read

Good morning, beautiful people, good morning. I was driving by a church the other day in Fort Kent, Maine, and I just had to pull over and take a picture of these signs. I have never been inside that church; it is a little over an hour away from my home. I must put this on my calendar in the near future. I love that church already, and I haven't even been inside the doors. They have open written all over them as they boldly share what they stand for.

Women Deserve Better Than Abortion hangs a banner over the door at St. Louis Roman Catholic Church in Fort Kent, Maine. Abortion hurts women, kills children, and breaks hearts, the sign continues to read. Yes, abortion does.

Women make the choice to have an abortion for so many reasons, timing, fear, religion, fear of judgment, fear of the unknown, and the lies the enemy will feed us is endless. Believe me, I know firsthand. Women do deserve better. The aftermath of an abortion is something you never want any woman alive to experience.

Some women openly share they have had an abortion and are doing well and are happy at the choice they have made. Wait a few more years, it will affect you—it just does. I feel for you today; I know what is ahead. I, too, have walked it; no one is exempt. Let me recommend a book for you when you do reach this point. Forgiven and Set Free written by Linda Cochrane. Find a trusted friend, as I did, or visit the local pregnancy care center and journey the steps to freedom. You will be so glad you did.

The next sign I noticed was hanging in their parking lot. The sign read, God saw all he had made, and it was very good. The pictures of these babies put a smile on your face like no other. I am sure every one of these babies are named Precious, for they sure are.

What more can be said really? These signs say it all. Pray for the unborn today. No matter where you go to worship, hang these two signs on your heart. Oh, I forgot to tell you, I was born in Fort Kent, Maine.

Have a blessed day, beautiful people. Thank God today your mother choose life.

Silver or Gold

Good morning, beautiful people, good morning. Today let's pray these scriptures.

Delight thyself in the Lord: and he shall give thee the desires of thine heart. (Psalm 37:4)

The desire of the righteous shall be granted. (Proverbs 10:24)

What things soever ye desire, when ye pray, believe that ye receive them, and ye shall have them. (Mark 11:24)

Father, thank you for granting our heart's desire to do your will. Today *we declare your Word, silver and gold have I none, but what I have, I give to thee; in the name of Jesus Christ of Nazareth rise up and walk (Acts 3:6).*

Father, we declare these Holy Scriptures over our lives today. We believe them, and today we receive accordingly. Amen.

Have a blessed day, beautiful people. Rejoice, for you have the Word of the Lord. It is richer than silver or gold.

Some Days You Just Need to Laugh

Good morning, beautiful people. I rise early to pray this morning and write my daily post. I just begin to laugh out loud as I try to put some thoughts together between the hot flashes. A week or so ago, I told a coworker, I was going to write a post and call it "God, Are You Bigger than Menopause?" Then I thought, Gee, I might as well as spill it and ask it all. God, are you bigger than divorce, and by the way, God, when is the house going to sell?

I always tell people they can be real in their prayer life with God as he knows it all anyway. There is nothing hidden from him, no, nothing. I already know the answer to these questions. However, I'm human, and I like when he answers a little more speedily. He answers in his time, and I've learned it isn't always as quick as going through the drive-through. Yes, God is bigger than menopause. Yes, I will make it through tears and laughter in the same five minutes. Being twenty-nine isn't all it's cracked up to be (laugh out loud). Yes, God is bigger than divorce. He hates divorce as he knows how hard it is on families. Life goes on, and he continues to put the broken pieces of each of our lives back together again. Yes, God has a buyer for the home. He knows the right time, the right family, and the right price; he knows it all. It will all happen on the right day.

It really all comes down to this one word, TRUST. So I guess that should be the title of the post "Do We Trust Him?" Hmmm...sometimes I find myself asking him to forgive my unbelief.

Today no matter what you are going through, make a choice to enjoy the day you have been given. Life isn't always easy, and the wait for the answer is sometimes longer than we like. Today take this scripture and deposit it in your bank. That bank is your memory bank, beautiful people.

"Trust in the Lord with all thine heart; and lean not unto thine own understanding. In all thy ways acknowledge him, and he shall direct thy paths" (Proverbs 3:5–6).

Have a blessed day. Laugh out loud, do a kind deed, and believe the Word of the Lord.

Some Will Decide Tonight

This morning, as I prayed for the Pregnancy Care Center of Aroostook banquet dinner being held tonight, I wanted to ask you to join your faith for PCC Care Centers around this globe.

A Time to Heal so beautifully written on the invitation with a clock and beautiful flowers warms my heart this chilly morning. God himself wants to heal his people. He wants women who have had abortions to be set free.

Linda Cochrane, RN, will speak here tonight in our city. I hold back the tears as I wait expectantly to meet the woman who wrote the Bible study that God himself used to set me free. I so want to invite you all, but I know that is not possible.

Father, we pray from Presque Isle, Maine, to every place around this globe for women who have suffered an abortion. Sometimes we all make decisions too fast, scared, or overwhelmed with feelings of helplessness. Thank you for the healing power of Jesus Christ.

We thank you, Father, for safe houses all across this globe. For that woman who still holds the ache in her heart, will you set up her healing, O God. You said in your Word, you sent your Word and healed thee (Psalm 107:20). Thank you for healing your people.

In your presence, Lord, there is fullness of joy. I thank you "that there is therefore now no condemnation for those who are in Christ Jesus" (Romans 8:1). I thank you "for whom the son sets free is free indeed" (John 8:36).

Have a blessed day, beautiful people. Pray and believe.

Somebody Shout Fire!

Good morning, beautiful people. Hasn't the week gone by fast? I am so excited to see what this day will hold. When I wake up every morning, I look in the mirror, and I point my finger, and I yell fire. (Then I pray the neighbors don't call the fire department. LOL.) I pray every day that we all will be full of the Holy Ghost and fire. Life is a vapor, here today and gone tomorrow. No time to be woe is me, time to rise up and be the ambassadors we are called to be. Today let's thank the Lord for more of him in our lives. Let's thank him for more of the fire.

Whatever you are going through in your life today, get in his presence and stay there until he fills you with his fire. Let today be the day the power of God transforms your life so you can be the world changer you were created to be. (Yes, you!) If you can't do it alone, call another fire starter in the body of Christ. Don't find someone who will be pitiful with you. Find someone who will pray with you until you get the fire. Let's thank him for his Holy Ghost power and fire today.

Father, thank you that you said we can call on you, and you will answer (Jeremiah 33:3). Today we join our faith for every person around this globe who needs fresh fire, who needs direction, who needs vision, and who has a need of any kind. We bring them to you today. Father, thank you for pouring out your spirit. Thank you for Holy Ghost fire today. Fill us all afresh, God. We all need more of you in our lives. We receive it. Amen.

Have a blessed day, beautiful people. Stay in his presence until you receive what you need. Then look in the mirror, point your finger, and say watch out world, here comes fire!

John answered and said to them all, "As for me, I baptize you with water; but One is coming who is mightier than I, and I am not fit to untie the thong of his sandals; he will baptize you with the Holy Spirit and fire. "His winnowing fork is in his hand to thoroughly clear his threshing floor, and to gather the wheat into his barn; but he will burn up the chaff with unquenchable fire." (Luke 3:16–17)

And there appeared to them tongues as of fire distributing themselves, and they rested on each one of them. And they were all filled with the Holy Spirit and began to speak with other tongues, as the Spirit was giving them utterance. (Acts 2:3–4)

Refresh Us, God, and Fill Us with Your Power

Good morning, beautiful people, good morning. Do you need refreshing? Do you need your Creator to touch you and make you whole once again? Do you need him to empower you to make it through whatever is going on in your life? Simply come and ask and he will. He will fill you with his power. He is the good, good Father. He is not mean and ugly, waiting for you to mess up so you can be shipwrecked. If you declare with your mouth, "Jesus is Lord," and believe in your heart that God raised him from the dead, you will be saved (Romans 10:9). Also he is the propitiation for our sins and not for ours only but also for the sins of the whole world (1 John 2:2). He tells us to be filled with the Holy Spirit and receive power (Acts 1:8). He is a good Father. Let's pray.

Father, thank you for the free gift of salvation. Thank you for refreshing us, making us whole, and filling us with your Holy Spirit. Thank you that you paid for it all with the precious blood of Jesus Christ. Oh, the power of the cross. May we never take for granted what you have done for us.

Fill us fresh today with your Holy Spirt, and may we be sensitive to it as we go about our day. Show us things, God, that we could only know by the Holy Spirit dwelling within us. What you reveal, no man can dispute. To you, O God, be all the glory. For great things you are doing, will continue to do as we keep our eyes fixed on you. Amen.

Have a blessed day, beautiful people. Let's stay full of his Holy Spirit and power!

Somebody Shout Hallelujah

Good morning, beautiful people, good morning. I smile this morning as I listen to the recording of my grandson, saying, "Hallelulah." His sweet soft voice trying to get all the syllables together, exclaimed, "Hallelulah!" Oh, the joy of children. Let's pray.

Father, thank you for the innocence of children. Birth was your idea from the very beginning of time. This Christmas, may love abound in the hearts of people. We pray that no child would be forgotten, that no person would go hungry, that hearts would heal from the pain of brokenness, that kindness would be sprinkled everywhere, that the gifts given in love would be just right, that forgiveness would be present, that our hearts would be tenderized by the magic of the season all year long, that addictions would be broken, that life would be good for everyone. That's my prayer once again for our world. Peace on earth and good will to everyone. May it begin with each of us today.

May the spirit of Christ who dwells within us reign on the earth today. Hallelujah!

Father, thank you for pouring out your spirit on our land once again. Awaken the hearts of mankind. May the light of Christ shine brightly across the seven continents of the world like never before. O Emmanuel, how blessed we are to carry your presence to a hurting world. Holy Spirit, lead us this day. May the light that is within us beam brightly to all we meet. Amen.

Have a blessed day, beautiful people. Jesus is with us. Shout hallelujah!

Sometimes the Surprise Is on Us

Good morning, beautiful people, good morning. What a beautiful day here in Maine. The sun is out, and I went for my morning walk, praying for all the families that have suffered loss from the hurricanes. I went by a construction truck that had people working on our roads near my home. Madawaska was written on their truck door, and it caught my attention. I chuckled as it reminded me of a story I wanted to write about. So today's the day.

Last month, I wanted to surprise my youngest daughter for her birthday. I made the trip north on her special day to the beautiful town of Madawaska. She was not home but on vacation around the coast of Maine. I was disappointed. However, I stopped and prayed and shared my disappointment with God himself. I asked if there was anything I should do before I leave. Then I noticed a police vehicle, and it read, In God We Trust, on the back by the license plate. I got excited. I immediately said out loud, No wonder their school's marching band was chosen to go to Washington, DC, for the inauguration. I asked God to make a way for me to talk to the officer. She pulled up and parked a few blocks from me, and yes, I went right up to talk with her. She said some people don't like it, but the chief made the decision it would stay on the vehicle. What a chief! What a leader! I love his bold stand.

Sometimes I am just bold. I just had to stop at that police department and shake his hand. As I glanced up and read the vision statement on his wall, I was blessed. Sure made my heart happy. I wish I could remember it all, but I can't.

Then I thought I would go to the local grocery store and post about the Healing Water's Women's Conference. (It was amazing by the way.) I noticed a florist/gift shop named Daisies. I smiled as daisies was the decorations we were using for the conference. I continued to drive down Main Street toward home, but something kept drawing me back. I finally turned around and went in to see what Daisies was all about. I saw the most beautiful items and met the owner of the store. I was just amazed at all the beautiful things she had for baby dedications, christenings, weddings, etc. The decorative Bibles and babies in cradle musical globes and the believe necklaces made my heart covet a bit. (I'll be back.)

I inquired of the owner how she got the name daisies for her store. She said her grandson yelled out daisies as she and her husband were talking about possible names. Aren't kids amazing? I asked if I could pray a blessing over her store. I loved her creative ideas, and I loved her gifts for christenings and baby dedications. I loved the whole store.

I dropped my daughter's gifts off at her in-laws and headed home. Although I missed them, I am blessed, knowing God has them in the palm of his hands. I am thankful, even the police department is looking to God. I am thankful for meeting the owner of Daisies. I am thankful for their grandson who named the store. Life is good. In God, we can trust. Yes, yes, we can.

Father, help us to see and hear you working all around us. Your ways are higher than our ways; your thoughts are higher than ours (Isaiah 55:9). Empower us to have the grace to trust you more. We ask you to forgive us when unbelief has crept in. We believe, we believe, we believe. Oh, how I wish I could buy everyone in the whole world one of those believe necklaces from Daisies. Oh, how I wish I could buy every pregnant mother a globe with the baby in a cradle, singing. Since I can't, I thank you for the daisies in the field. Every time they see a daisy, God, I pray they know how much they are loved. I pray they know how precious life is. I pray they will believe your Holy Scriptures.

You always make my heart sing. I love journeying everyday with you, Jesus. Amen.

Have a blessed day, beautiful people. Enjoy your day. Jesus is the way, the truth, and the life (John 14:6).

Sometimes I Just Forget

Good morning, beautiful people. Yesterday I was driving to interview a young evangelist who had come to be part of some convention meetings in my area. As I left to make my way the twenty-minute drive, the rain just poured down so fast and furious I couldn't see. I pulled over and decided that I better reschedule and head back for home.

This morning, I was praying for this young evangelist, Carl, and his wife and beautiful family. I thanked the Lord that he orders their footsteps. I thanked the Lord that he opens the doors for this evangelist and provides everything he and his family needs. I sort of got a little mad at myself and asked myself, "Why didn't you pray and ask the Lord to hold the rain until you got there?" I just didn't think of it until this morning as I shook my head at myself.

I have a friend, Laurie, who asked the Lord to stop the rain for a man who was working on her brother's chimney. The man asked her, "Why don't you ask your God to stop the rain, and if your God does, I will go to church with you tomorrow."

So she did. She went home and prayed and asked God to stop the rain. Yes, God stopped the rain all around this house. The man came by and told her that it never rained at her brother's house until after he was all done. It rained at all the other houses around her brother's place. Needless to say, the man went to church with her the next day. That, my friend, is the God we serve. The all-powerful, Almighty God, master of the wind, and maker of the rain.

My friend, Heidi, would sing this song, "Master of the Wind" at Aglow International meetings when she was president here in this city. She made me a recording, but I wore it out. I guess it's time to request another copy to help me remember.

Don't I have amazing friends?

No matter what you have need of today, don't forget to pray. He is a God who answers prayer.

Read Mark 14 today. Focus in on verses 14–18. Have a blessed day, beautiful people. Jesus truly loves you.

Sparks Turn into Fire

Good morning, beautiful people. This morning, as I was sitting thinking about what to pray and what I would write about today, I really wanted to ask you to pray the words to this song to God himself for you, your family, and for the world.

Four years later from when I penned this, all I can say is this, what a difference a day can make.

The Flashlight and the Light of the World

I was preparing to take Mason and Evan, my two grandsons, to church. We started at 5:00 a.m. to get ready for the service that started at 10:00 a.m. Mason, almost four now along with a very strong mind of his own I might add, didn't want the dress outfit his mom had packed and thought his jeans and white T-shirt was sufficient. After much coaxing, I was able to get a sweater over the T-shirt. It was 10:15 a.m., and we were still working on the socks. He advised me due to the lines on the socks he was not going to wear them. So I advised him he could not take his boots off at church. So with his bare feet in fireman boots, along with Evan dressed like a king, we headed to church to worship and hear the Word of the Lord.

I managed to sing a few songs and then came the prayer. I closed my eyes as Evan vast asleep in his carrier snuggled next to me and Mason sitting on the other side quietly, I added my prayer along with the others to the creator of the universe. I was a bit tired and enjoyed the stillness and the connection for just a few moments.

I love to pray, and I believe in it so much I wanted to add mine. I opened my eyes to find Mason had unzipped his backpack and taken out his flashlight. He was shining it all around at the people with closed eyes. I might add he was standing proudly in his bare feet! I laugh when I think about it. It was a sight to see as he shined the light up the rows and across the pew to each praying parishioner row by row.

It brings to the forefront of my mind this chilly morning in northern Maine about the scripture in John 8. He states, "I am the light of the world. He who follows me shall not walk in darkness, but have the light of life." I remember living in the darkness and would never trade it for walking in the light. John 12 states, "That Jesus has come into the world as a light, so that no one who believes in him should stay in darkness." In Psalms, it says that "the Lord is a lamp unto my feet, and a lamp unto my path." Oh, how I love the scriptures. Hard to put into words how they nourish the soul.

Someday my grandchildren will come to the road of decision in the path they will walk. I pray they will choose to live a life of faith in the Lord Jesus Christ. I pray every day for that. We all have our own will, and he won't force his upon us. Sometimes we don't want to accept him in fear we won't have our own way. Just to find we believed a lie and walking in the light is a much richer life.

Father, all across this globe today, we pray you warm the hearts of your people. Light a fire in the hearts of those who the enemy of their soul has snuffed out, once again, we pray. Draw all man unto yourself and let revival fires fall. From the north to the south to the west to the east, we say blaze, spirit, blaze. Turn darkness into light.

Thank you, God, for your Word. "The vision is for an appointed time, but at the end it shall speak, and not lie; though it tarry, wait for it; because it will surely come, it will not tarry" (Habakkuk 2:3). What time is it? Awakening time. Thank you, God, for turning darkness into light all across this globe for your glory alone. Amen.

Have a blessed day, beautiful people. Let the sparks fly.

Somebody shout fire! Revival fires.

Remember Grace, Love, and Justice

Good morning, beautiful people, good morning. Isn't God good? As I look out my window this morning, and I see the daisies growing on my front lawn, the daisies that were never there before. It reminds me that his love springs up everywhere. I feel his love. Every petal saying to me, *I love you.* It instills in me the depth of his grace extended to me every day. A grace I never want to take advantage of. His grace is enough for me. Is it enough for you?

His promises to us are forever settled. He is a God of justice. Justice is his; he will repay. "'*Beloved, do not avenge yourselves, but rather give place to wrath; for it is written, Vengeance is Mine, I will repay,*' says the Lord" (Romans 12:19). Don't you cherish how he calls us beloved? He is the God who sees it all.

I am thankful that he keeps his Word to us as we believe. The key word is believe. Sometimes we need to fast to get the unbelief out. Sometimes we need to meditate on the same scripture over and over again until we can get it set in our heart, mind, and soul. Let's pray.

Father, thank you that you, O God, are a God full of love, grace, and mercy. Thank you that you love justice. Thank you for the daisies. We continue to put our trust in you. No matter who has done us wrong, we never have to seek revenge or try to get even. Your Word tells us you will vindicate (Psalm 26:1).

You are the God of payback according to Hebrews 10:30. We thank you for payback in our nation. We thank you for payback in every area of our individual lives. Thank you for being a God of justice and the God of payback. We receive it according to your Word. Amen.

Have a beautiful day, beautiful people. Remember you are loved, and his grace is enough for you!

Speak Lord, We Will Listen Up!

Good morning, beautiful people, good morning. Let's ask the Holy Spirit to speak to us and let's listen closely.

Father, thank you that you speak to your children. As we surrender our lives, our hearts to you, you make every crooked path straight. You said in John 10:27, *"My sheep hear My voice, and I know them, and they follow Me."*

Father, thank you for the Holy Spirit who teaches, leads, and instructs us. Show us things, Lord, that we need for our daily lives. O God, our heart's desire is to be obedient to you. Give us visions and dreams bigger than ourselves that we can accomplish for your kingdom.

Today let our eyes see you working all around us, and our ears hear what the spirit of the Lord is saying. May many believe on the name of the Lord Jesus and be saved according to Acts 16:31.

Father, may people all across this globe pray and believe. May you fill our hearts, and may we hear you speak what is true. Amen.

Have a blessed day, God's beautiful people, for this is the day the Lord has made, and we will rejoice and be glad in it. Now listen up!

Speak to Your Dream

Good morning, beautiful people. I was thinking this morning about a time I traveled to Los Angeles, California, to the Dream Center for a two-week mission trip. At one of the airports on the journey there, a man walked up to me and spoke some words that has stayed etched in my mind. At first, I told him I felt he had me mixed up with someone else. He replied that he did not and repeated the same words to me. After he spoke them the second and third time, I began to believe his words. He really was speaking to the desires of my heart and a future I had dreamed of. He was a pastor from the other side of the country.

Today let's speak to the dream each of us is carrying. Let's speak words to someone else's dreams as well.

Father, thank you for the power of words. Ephesians 4:29 tells us to speak what is helpful for building others up according to their needs, that it may benefit those who listen. Father, may our words be uplifting, edifying, and may we awaken dreams that have died in others today.

Father, thank you for putting the right people in our lives to help us fulfill the dream. You tell us we have not because we don't ask God (James 4:2). Today we ask you and receive the next step in completing the assignment toward fulfillment of our dreams. Remove every barrier, wrong and negative influences, and bring the right people alongside of us to bring the dream to fruition, we pray. Amen.

Have a blessed day, God's beautiful people. Speak to your dream and speak encouragement to the dream in someone else today.

Speak What Is True

Good morning, beautiful people. Let's pray about truth.

Father, this morning, we come to you with praise and worship in our hearts. We once were so far away from you; we were blind to truth. Thank you for removing the veil from our eyes that we see truth. Oh, such joy journeying every day walking in the light.

This morning, we open our heart to you once again and ask you to speak truth from your Word. May we hide this Word in our hearts. Holy Spirit, lead us today in these Holy Scriptures. We want to know the heart of our Father. We surrender our hearts, our lives, to you, O Father. Thank you for making us fit for the master's use. We will never forget our brokenness and how you turned our mourning into joy.

As we read John 17 this morning, righteous Father sanctify us by your truth. Jesus spoke these words with his eyes to Heaven, and said: Father, the hour has come. Glorify your Son, that your Son also may glorify You. Together before the world was (John 17:1–3).

May the world see truth clearly today. May we experience the love that was given from God himself before the foundation of the world (verse 24). You, O God, have given us your Word that we may have joy fulfilled in us (verse 13).

Fill our hearts full of love today once again that your love will be in us as it is in Christ Jesus (verse 26). Amen.

Have a blessed day, beautiful people. Show the world the love of Jesus in you.

Speed Right On Through Your Roadblock

Good morning, beautiful people, good morning. Isn't God good? Every time I feel I have come to a roadblock, and I can't see how to get past it, God himself shows up and gets me to the other side. I laugh at some of the roadblocks that I have sped right through lately. There isn't anything Jesus won't do for his people that is according to his will. It makes me just laugh right out loud this morning.

Faithful Father, thank you that you take us right through every circumstance, every obstacle. When we can't see how to get to the other side, you have the plan. Every bump, every roadblock in the natural is just a means for you to show your glory that you are unstoppable. We are unstoppable too with the power of the living God dwelling inside of us.

Romans 8:31–39 tell us we are more than conquerors. What then shall we say in response to these things? If God is for us, who can be against us? He who did not spare his own Son, but gave him up for us all. How will he not also, along with him, graciously give us all things? Who will bring any charge against those whom God has chosen? It is God who justifies. Who then is the one who condemns? No one. Christ Jesus who died—more than that, who was raised to life—is at the right hand of God and is also interceding for us. Who shall separate us from the love of Christ? Shall trouble or hardship or persecution or famine or nakedness or danger or sword? As it is written, for your sake, we face death all day long. We are considered as sheep to be slaughtered. No, in all these things, we are more than conquerors through him who loved us. For I am convinced that neither death nor life, neither angels nor demons, neither the present nor the future, nor any powers, neither height nor depth, and nor anything else in all creation will be able to separate us from the love of God that is in Christ Jesus our Lord.

Father, because of your great love, no matter what is trying to stop us up, we speed right on through. Up and over, Jesus speed. Our God is unstoppable. Thank you, thank you, thank you. All across this globe today, may the love of God override your circumstances. Seek him, declare his

Word, and go right on through your roadblock. Amen? Amen!

Have a blessed day, God's beautiful people. You are unstoppable because of who lives in you. Believe!

Spring Forth with the New

Good morning, beautiful people, good morning. Soon it will be spring. The newness, the freshness of this season will soon be upon us. Today I wanted to pray into this beautiful season. Many will be birthing new ministries. Many will be seeking God for new assignments and direction in their businesses, ministries, and daily lives. This is such a beautiful season as it is out with the old and in with the new. Let's pray.

Father, thank you for the birth of Jesus, our Savior and King. Because of his life, everything has changed for this world, everything. Just as the flowers will soon once again be in bloom, we join our faith for every person beginning over again, every ministry springing up in power and might, every place of business or ministry that has been seeking a new direction and assignment; it's almost time.

We thank you that your people don't need to be anxious about anything but by prayer and petition, with thanksgiving, present our requests to You, O God (Philippians 4:6). For everyone who has stepped out of the boat to walk on the water, you say good job. You say thanks for stepping out. You say keep looking up to where your help cometh (Psalm 121:1). You say, "I have not given you a spirit of fear but of power, and of love, and of a sound mind (2 Timothy 1:7). You say, "Keep believing, I am the one who has given you favor. I am the God who brings the increase." Amen.

Have a blessed day, beautiful people. Thank God today a baby has changed everything for this world.

Stay Focused

Good morning, beautiful people. Recently I have had some amazing over-the-top experiences journeying with Jesus. I would share them with my prayer partner. She would say, "Angel, stay focused." Isn't this an amazing journey?

I will lift up mine eyes unto the hills, from whence cometh my help. My help cometh from the Lord, which made heaven and earth. He will not suffer thy foot to be moved: he that keepeth thee will not slumber. Behold, he that keepeth Israel shall neither slumber nor sleep. The Lord is thy keeper: The Lord is thy shade upon thy right hand. The sun shall not smite thee by day, nor the moon by night. The Lord shall preserve thee from all evil: he shall preserve thy soul. The Lord shall preserve thy going out and thy coming in from this time forth, and even for evermore. (Psalm 121)

Father, our eyes are fixed on you. No matter what is happening around us, we keep looking to the hills from whence our help cometh. Today no matter what any reader is going through, you are and have the answer. You have all the answers to life's many complex issues. Journeying with you is just downright amazing.

Nothing skips your eye—nothing. You never sleep nor slumber (Psalm 121:4). We can talk to you about anything (pray) anytime. Thank you for being a good Father who listens and answers. You do beyond what we could ever think or imagine. Sometimes it is hard to stay focused because you are so good to us. Thanks for journeying life with mankind. Amen.

Have a blessed day, beautiful people. Where are your eyes looking today? Keep them focused on the one who created you.

Stay in the Fight

Good morning, beautiful people. Let's pray about never giving up.

Father, thank you that we are overcomers. As we mediate on and believe your Word and stay in communion with you (pray), we will overcome. No matter what someone is going through today, they can have victory. Romans 15:13 says, "May the God of hope fill you with all joy and peace as you trust in him, so that you may overflow with hope by the power of the Holy Spirit."

Together all across this globe, we join our faith for people losing hope. Father, draw them to yourself. You are the best father. We stand against depression, anxiety, fear, torment, and every kind of sickness and disease. There is nothing that a person can't overcome with you living inside of them. You are saying to every reader today, don't give up. "For his anger lasts only a moment, but his favor lasts a lifetime, weeping may stay for the night, but rejoicing comes in the morning" (Psalm 30:5).

Father, send hope to someone today who may have lost it yesterday. We say yes, we will go. (Will you?) Go wherever he tells you to go or make that phone call. Just listen for his small still voice to whisper a name or a face and be obedient. You'll be the one to bring the good news to them; they will overcome.

Have a blessed day, God's beautiful people. If you don't know him as Jesus, lover of your soul, talk to him today. He created you, and he has the plan for your life. Never give up. Joy is just around the corner. You have the victory.

Step, Leap, Jump, and Take Off

Good morning, beautiful people, good morning.

Today let's declare this is the year for explosion of the Gospel of Jesus Christ to go all across this globe. We declare through every means possible, invented now, or will be invented this year for creative ways for the gospel to be shared. Time is short, and the harvest is ripe. Today we declare that the airwaves will be full of hope, faith, new beginnings, and the Word of the Lord. People will have encounters with the Lord Jesus Christ himself. We declare that visions and dreams will be fulfilled.

Awaken, oh ye people, awaken and step into the destiny God has called you. It is no time for anyone to neither be slack nor slumber, for time is short, and the need is great.

We declare open doors for God's people in positions of government. We declare the gospel message will spread like wildfire all across this nation and to the nation/s. To the whole world, seven continents, the light of Christ is coming; it is already on its way.

Every morning is a new day, and the spirit of the Lord is drawing you to himself. If you already walk with him, press in and walk closer. If you don't know him, today is your day. He is no respecter of persons, and he has no favorites. You are the apple of his eye (Psalm 17:8).

We declare we will take off in ministry. If we are not quite ready, we will support those who are. We will press in until we are ready and taking off. It's time to enlarge the territory. Together we will expand the kingdom of God.

All across this globe today, we declare it is our year. It is our year for takeoff. We give God all the glory, for great things he is doing, going to do, and will continue to do. He is Lord.

Today we thank him for showing his glory all across this land. Amen. Have a blessed day, God's beautiful people.

Stepping into Destiny

Good morning, beautiful people. Let's pray today about destiny.

Father, thank you for the dreams and visions you have given your people. Today all across this globe, we pray for fulfillment of those dreams. We join our faith and believe for every believer's vision or dream. We will join together with others and help fulfill the purpose you have for each of your people on this earth. If this is true in your heart, tell him so.

"The earth is the Lord's and everything in it, the world, and all who live in it" (Psalm 24:1).

Today we believe you have asked each of us to step out into deeper waters. You desire us to do bigger things than we can comprehend with our limited minds. You have written the vision on our hearts, and we have written it down (Habakkuk 2:2–3). Now it's action time. With you, all things are possible.

We pray for every dream and every vision that you have placed in the hearts of your people. Give them courage to step out, provide for them, Lord, in ways only you can. We will be kingdom-minded people and help others fulfill their dreams and visions. Together we declare fulfillment in the all-powerful name of Jesus.

All across this globe today, step out. You can do it. He wouldn't give you a dream or a vision, unless he was going to show you the way. It requires a step of faith. One step, then another, and another. It is beyond you, it really is. That is why step by step on the journey, you will grow in your faith. Before you know it, the dream or vision is now reality.

Have a blessed day, God's beautiful people. Keep stepping toward your destiny.

Happy Thanksgiving

Good morning, beautiful people, let's all declare the goodness of our God today. As you know from my many writings, I am full of stories. True stories of God's hand working on behalf of his people. I get so excited about it that I like to share it with the whole world. Recently I traveled with a friend to Washington, DC. She had a conference to go to, and I had planned on doing some radio interviews. I met so many wonderful people and had some divine appointments.

On Friday morning, after a telephone conversation with Author Brian Lake on his newest book, Open Doors You Never Knew Existed, I was going to go for a walk and pray. That little still voice said, "Go back and pick up your hotel room. My room wasn't disastrous or anything but just an inkling to return to the room. I strolled on up to the ninth floor, and there I met the young lady that would be cleaning my room. She was seven months pregnant. We talked about life and names she had picked out. I almost came unglued when she said she planned on naming her son Jeremiah. I inquired a little more…why Jeremiah? She said Jeremiah from the Bible.

Jeremiah is the name I felt the Lord gave me for my aborted son. I prayed for her that morning, her pregnancy, and the many doors open to her, for her son, for her family, and for her future. I was overjoyed to have met her. It made me think of a writing I penned: God says everyone is worthy of a name.

I had scheduled an interview with Pastor Dottie Schmitt from Immanuel's Church for that Friday morning. A pastor from Maryland I had met a few years ago at WOW (Women of the Word) Conference in Portland, Maine. Something came up, and she wasn't going to return to Maryland from her speaking engagement until Monday. I chuckled as I thought about how we make our plans, but God orders our footsteps. I wondered who else I would meet on this day. Dottie had a radio broadcast in Maryland and now has a podcast. I need to find this podcast and listen as I enjoyed her CDs I purchased on leadership at WOW.

I decided to journey on and find the right elevator that would take me to the ballroom for dinner. I met a FedEx man, and he showed me in which direction to go. His name tag read Joshua. I thanked him for his guidance and inquired about his name. "Joshua, how did you get that name?" I asked. His reply made me chuckle again.

"My mother got it from the Bible."

I said, "Joshua, do you know who Joshua is in the Bible?"

He laughed and said yes.

I can't remember what I said to him, but I felt it was a powerful word meant just for him.

Meeting Joshua made me think of the books I read by Cathy Lechner. She used to pray FedEx cometh. I had the privilege to meet Cathy at Celebration Center years ago in Fort Fairfield, Maine. She spoke some of those powerful words to me that I am sure she doesn't remember.

We should all be thankful for life, for our journey, and for the amazing people we have the privilege to meet every day. We need to be thankful for the Word spoken to us through the Holy Scriptures and through people we meet who God ordains. Life is a beautiful gift to be treasured.

Today around our thanksgiving table, let's ask God to fill our mouths with his Words and speak words that exhort, empower and words full of grace and peace.

Happy Thanksgiving, beautiful people...Be happy and be thankful.

"Grace and peace to you from God our Father and the Lord Jesus Christ" (1 Corinthians 1:3).

Strength and Compassion

Good morning, beautiful people, good morning. Last week, as I was looking through some of my writings in preparation for the upcoming Healing Waters Women's Conference, this particular writing on compassion brought me to my knees and on my face once again. Then right behind this writing, I had the words to a song, "Not Too Far from Here" (Ty Lacy/Steve Siler).

I wanted to ask you today to pray the words of both of these with me. I wanted to ask you to pray for these very important conferences. Thanks so much.

Compassion (Angel L. Murchison)

My sister, your countenance looks downcast. Your face does reflect.
Your burden looks heavy. Your load, is it too much to carry alone?
For you, my friend, God sent his Son, and he also sent me your way.
I'm his love extended to you. How can I help you today?
If you want to share your burden, I know Jesus will give you the strength to overcome.
You will have the victory. As we journey the path of life together, we have many of trial.
Jesus gave you to me, my sister, to love you and to be his love vial. I want to help you bandage your wounds until Jesus heals you where you hurt. You see, my sister, my friend, we all walk through pain, and the storms, they do blow. But together with Jesus, in him, we both will grow.

"Not Too Far from Here" (Ty Lacy/Steve Siler)
Somebody's down to their last dime
Somebody's running out of time
Not too far from here
Somebody's got nowhere else to go
Somebody needs a little hope
Not too far from here
And I may not know their name
But I'm praying just the same
That you'll use me Lord to wipe away a tear
Cause somebody's crying
Not too far from here

Somebody's troubled and confused
Somebody's got nothing left to lose
Not too far from here
Somebody's forgotten how to trust
Somebody's dying for love
Not too far from here
It may be a stranger's face
But I'm praying for your grace
To move in me and take away the fear
Cause somebody's hurting
Not too far from here
Help me, Lord, not to turn away from pain
Help me not to rest while those around me weep
Give me your strength and compassion
When somebody finds the road of life too steep.
Now, I'm letting down my guard
And I'm opening my heart
Help me speak your love to every needful ear
Jesus is waiting
Not too far from here
Jesus is waiting
Not too far from here

"But you will receive power when the Holy Spirit comes on you; and you will be my witnesses in Jerusalem, and in all Judea and Samaria, and to the ends of the earth" (Acts 1:8).

Let it be so, O God, let it be so. For your glory and your glory alone. Amen.

Have a blessed day, beautiful people. He loves you!

Supernatural to Those Who Will Believe

Good morning, beautiful people, good morning. Last evening, I had the opportunity to pray with a new friend who had pain in her knee. This morning, I'm asking my Heavenly Father to allow me the opportunity to see her again today. I knew it was a supernatural God encounter when I prayed for her. You know when you know when you know something? It is a set up by God himself, and that it is a done deal.

We both laughed as she shared a few other issues that needed God's intervention. I have been thanking God for the same answers in my own life. It brings me such joy to see Jesus working all around the world every day. Was this a coincidence I would meet her yesterday? A lady who was growing weary believing for the same things I had prayed for in my own life. I just know that within seven days, her answer will have arrived. It will be beyond what she could ever think or imagine. Why? Because God is supernatural. He wants to bless her. He loves her. He is no respecter of persons, to all who will believe.

What do need this morning? Talk with Jesus, believe his Word, and watch the supernatural take place right before your very eyes.

Father, thank you for Jesus. More than anything this world could give us, we desire to journey every day with Jesus. He holds the answers to our life journey. Order our footsteps, God, according to your plan. Father, thank for the supernatural. We don't live by what we see or what we feel, we live by every Word that comes from the mouth of God (Matthew 4:4).

Thank you for supernatural intervention in the lives of your people today. Thank you for divine appointments, God encounters, and may today be full of joy as we believe you are watching over your Word to perform it (Jeremiah 1:12). Amen.

Have a blessed day, beautiful people. Believe in the supernatural, walk in the supernatural, and receive the supernatural.

Another Serving of Blueberry Pancakes

Good morning, beautiful people. Isn't it interesting how we continually need to forgive and ask for forgiveness? This is a lifelong journey. It's time to serve up another plate of blueberry pancakes.

This morning, I went to my daughter's home to visit and make blueberry pancakes for my two grandsons, Mason and Evan. Of course, Grandma loves blueberry pancakes too. I sat Evan in his high chair, and he ate almost two pancakes himself along with some fruit. That's a bit for a fifteen-month-old. He picked the blueberries out and rolled them and squeezed them before putting them in his mouth. I laughed at the tip of his fingers as they are now stained blue. I washed them diligently with soap and water, but the stain remains.

I couldn't help but think of the stain sin has on our lives. Some people think that sin doesn't cost them anything, but oh, how I wish they knew the truth. Sin is costly; it ruins lives, families, and leaves its stain on the journey. Even when the sin isn't your own, someone else's sin can cost you dearly.

There is, however, the good news of Jesus Christ, the good news that is almost too good to be true, but it really is. Jesus paid the price, his very life that we may have the victory. Simply by coming to him and confessing our sin and asking him to forgive us, he will grant a new beginning. Isn't that a loving Heavenly Father? You don't have to stay trapped in the sin that has a grip on you. Today, Jesus will show you a way of escape; he will show you the road to victory; or he himself will bring you the victory. No stain left on your hands, for he has taken it all upon himself.

The consequences of sin are different. Relationships may not be restored; the memory of the day doesn't quickly fade; and the wounds that were inflicted may need time to heal. The words that were spoken, the lies that were told, may take a journey that requires grace, strength, and healing from the Creator. Whether the sin was yours or someone else's sin has affected you, there is hope for full recovery. Oh, the wonderful cross. Oh, his love for mankind.

After our blueberry pancakes, Mason inquired if we could watch a movie. He picked a movie from his box of movies, and the three of us sat down to watch it. Somehow I only remember the part of Christmas and forgiveness. It was a movie his parents purchased on a family vacation to Santa's Village in New Hampshire this past summer. In my mind, I still can see the tree, the bright star, and the little boy singing, "Christmas is About Forgiveness." Funny the Bible says a child shall lead them. I found myself checking my own heart and inquiring of the Lord if I had any unforgiveness lurking in my heart. Every time it showed that scene, I found myself letting go of a hurt that was recently inflicted. I chose to forgive.

Today choose to confess your sin and find your victory or journey to victory. Today choose to forgive. Today choose to ask Christ the Healer to make you whole again. It doesn't make what's happened right, it just makes you free.

Today choose to accept his grace, his strength, and his healing. Today let the Lord touch your heart and let your face shine like the star. Forgiveness has been given, and forgiveness now extended. Can you still hear it? Christmas is about forgiveness.

Have blessed day, God's beautiful people... He loves you.

"For if you forgive others their trespasses, your Heavenly Father will also forgive you" (Matthew 6:14).

The Bottom Line, Our Final Answer

Good morning, beautiful people, what's your final answer today? Let's pray.

Father, thank you for your Word. Thank you that we can believe all things are possible because the Word says so. You bring the impossible into the possible when we believe. Forgive any doubts, any unbelief today that has crept in. We declare and decree we will receive our miracle because the Word of God says so.

Thank you that because Jesus has gone to the Father and because we believe, we will do greater things in your name so that our Father may be glorified in the Son. You said to ask anything in your name, and you would do it (John 14:12). (Tell him what you are believing for and thank him for forgiving your unbelief.) We believe.

Today we decree because we walk in the ways of God, we seek his kingdom, his will. We are positioned to receive whatever we ask in his name. Thank you for the open heaven. Thank you for the moving of your spirit across this land. Thank you for meeting every need according to your riches in glory. We believe, and we, therefore, receive (Mark 11:24). Amen.

Have a blessed day, beautiful people. Make sure your receiver is open and continue to speak his Word and believe his Word.

The Cup That Won't Run Dry

Good morning, beautiful people, good morning. Let's ask Jesus to fill our cups today.

Father, thank you for the cup that doesn't run dry. Holy Spirit, thank you that you lead us each and every day if we allow you. O God, thank you for your presence. There is nothing like your presence, O God, no nothing.

Touch hearts today, Lord, as only you can. Strengthen your people, and may they bask in your presence as they journey with you.

Have a blessed day, beautiful people, and spend some time in his presence today.

Lord, you alone are my portion and my cup; you make my lot secure. The boundary lines have fallen for me in pleasant places; surely, I have a delightful inheritance. I will praise the Lord, who counsels me; even at night my heart instructs me. I keep my eyes always on the Lord. With him at my right hand, I will not be shaken. Therefore, my heart is glad and my tongue rejoices; my body also will rest secure, because you will not abandon me to the realm of the dead, nor will you let your faithful one see decay. You make known to me the path of life; you will fill me with joy in your presence, with eternal pleasures at your right hand. (Psalm 16:5–11)

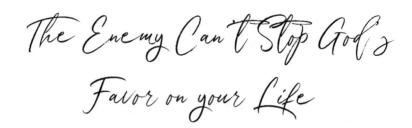

The Enemy Can't Stop God's Favor on your Life

Good morning, beautiful people. No matter how hard the enemy of your soul tries to convince you that you don't have favor on your life, don't believe it. If you are a Christian you have been bought with a price and it was a costly one my friend. He favors you.

"For the Lord God is a sun and shield; the Lord bestows favor and honor; no good thing does he withhold from those whose walk is blameless" (Psalm 84:11).

Father, thank you for favor on our lives. We receive it. There is no good thing you will withhold from us as we walk in your ways. We receive the full inheritance of being a joint heir with Jesus Christ (Romans 8:17).

To all the beautiful Christian people of the world, declare, believe, and receive the favor of God over your life today. Stand strong in the truth of his Word. When the enemy of your soul tells you that this Word is not for you, that this couldn't possibly be you, you tell the enemy that you walk in God's favor and honor because his Word says so. Then the enemy will flee as you believe. Somebody shout truth!

Have a blessed day, God's beautiful people. Believe you walk in his favor today. Enjoy the life God has given you.

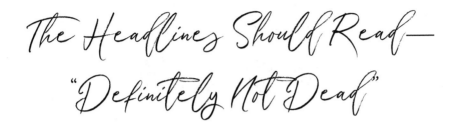

The Headlines Should Read—"Definitely Not Dead"

Good morning, beautiful people. Let's thank God that today he is alive, and he is working on our behalf.

Father, thank you for being a God who is alive. We see the Holy Spirit moving every day. No matter how the world tries to make people believe you are a myth, you reveal the truth. All any person has to do is just ask, and you will reveal who the Great I Am really is.

Thank you for the Holy Spirit. He leads, guides, and illuminates the Word of God to us. Thank you for the abundant life according to John 10:10. Take us deeper in you and less in the things of this world. Amen.

Have a blessed day, beautiful people. Ask God to help you see him working today. He is definitely not dead.

"But because of his great love for us, God, who is rich in mercy, made us alive with Christ even when we were dead in transgressions-it is by grace you have been saved. And God raised us up with Christ and seated us with him in the heavenly realms in Christ Jesus" (Ephesians 2:4–6).

Anxiety, Worry, Stress Are Not Our Portion

Good morning, beautiful people. I was up early this morning, thinking about some transitions I am going through in my personal journey. I have deadlines I must meet, paperwork I need to complete, and sometimes I admit I get a little worked up when things aren't moving like I think they should. Then as I spend time in prayer and worship, my anxious thoughts dissipate. God tells us not to worry. He has our lives covered. He will take care of us and to keep our lives in Father. Thank you that you are the God who sees it all. Thank you that you tell us not to worry, not to be anxious about anything, but by prayer and supplication with thanksgiving make our requests known to you. And the peace of God, which transcends all understanding, will guard our hearts and our minds in Christ Jesus (Philippians 4:6–7).

Father, thank you that you tell us not to worry about tomorrow, for tomorrow will worry about itself. Each day has enough trouble of its own (Matthew 6:34).

Thank you for divine appointments today, God encounters, and directing every step we take. We believe in the providential plan of our God. Amen.

Have a blessed day, beautiful people. No worrying, no stressing, and cast off all anxiety and have a peaceful day.

Anything? All Things?
Believe

Good morning, beautiful people. We all face impossibilities in our lives. There are some things that we think we could never accomplish or a circumstance we just can't get through. God's Word tells us differently. He says, "We can do all things through Christ that strengthens us" (Philippians 4:13). Through Christ, nothing is impossible.

Today if you are struggling with a situation that seems like you have no way out, you can't make it through, tell the enemy of your soul that you are putting your faith in what Jesus has to say. He always has the final say. Do you believe this? Can you do this?

Father, thank you for your Word. Thank you for strength for today. Every impossible situation we can walk right on through as we journey life with Jesus. There is no force, no enemy that can keep what God has ordained. We must keep our eyes focused on his Word and believe he will accomplish the work he has started. Let's pray.

Father, thank you that you tell us in James 1:2–4, "Consider it pure joy, my brothers and sisters, whenever you face trials of many kinds, because you know that the testing of your faith produces perseverance. Let perseverance finish its work so that you may be mature and complete, not lacking anything."

Father, thank you for your strength as we journey the day with you. Thank you for joy, for the joy of the Lord is our strength (Nehemiah 8:10). Amen.

Have a blessed day, God's beautiful people. You got this. With Jesus, you will overcome.

Apply This to Your Life and See What Happens

Good morning, beautiful people. Today let's apply the blood of Christ to our lives. It was his great price for everything we would need in this life and the life to come (eternal life).

In the same way he took the cup also after supper, saying, this cup is the new covenant in My blood; do this, as often as you drink it, in remembrance of Me. (1 Corinthians 11:25)

And when he had taken a cup and given thanks, he gave it to them, saying, "Drink from it, all of you; for this is My blood of the covenant, which is poured out for many for forgiveness of sins. (Matthew 26:27–28)

Well then, should we keep on sinning so that God can show us more and more of his wonderful grace? Of course not! Since we have died to sin, how can we continue to live in it? Or have you forgotten that when we were joined with Christ Jesus in baptism, we joined him in his death? For we died and were buried with Christ by baptism. And just as Christ was raised from the dead by the glorious power of the Father, now we also may live new lives. Since we have been united with him in his death, we will also be raised to life as he was. We know that our old sinful selves were crucified with Christ so that sin might lose its power in our lives. We are no longer slaves to sin. For when we died with Christ, we were set free from the power of sin. And since we died with Christ, we know we will also live with him. We are sure of this because Christ was raised from the dead, and he will never die again. Death no longer has any power over him. When he died, he died once to break the power of sin. But now that he lives, he lives for the glory of God. So you also should consider yourselves to be dead to the power of sin and alive to God through Christ Jesus. (Romans 6:1–11)

Father, thank you for your blood. Thank you for the power that is in the blood. Today we are free because of the working power in our lives of your precious blood.

We declare today, we have victory over every addiction, every sin, feelings of hopelessness and despair, and every other thing that sets itself up against the knowledge of God. Why? Because of your blood. Thank you for teaching us what is our inheritance because of the blood that you shed.

Together all across this globe, we declare victory in every area of our lives because of the blood. Yesterday's failures are under the blood. Every day is a new beginning. We apply the blood of Christ to our lives daily. We win. We have victory because of your blood. Amen.

Have a blessed day, beautiful people. Thank him for his blood that has been applied to your life so you can walk in freedom. If yesterday you weren't successful, apply the blood again and thank him for a new day. You soon will have complete victory. You win because of Jesus.

Take Delight in His Victory

Good morning, beautiful people, good morning. As we reflect back on previous months, and the victory God has given us over our circumstances and trials, let's praise him today. Even though at times we can't see the victory, it is ours because his Word says so. We just need to remember to take him at his Word and believe. This morning take a few moments and reflect on what you have overcome in the last few months. Some have overcome depression, suicidal tendencies, loneliness, heartaches, and many other things all because Jesus gave us the victory. I am sure you will want to praise him too. Let's pray.

Father, thank you for the victory in our lives. No matter what we face, we never face it alone. You have given us the promise that you will never leave us nor forsake us. You always bring us to the other side of whatever circumstances we face with great victory.

Father, we just want to praise your name today and pray for strength for people who are still going through the trial. They are on their way to victory. Our God reigns, and we take delight in him and believe the Holy Scriptures. Amen.

Have a blessed day, God's beautiful people. Take delight in your victory. Jesus overcame the world.

"For everyone born of God overcomes the world. This is the victory that has overcome the world, even our faith. Who is it that overcomes the world? Only the one who believes that Jesus is the Son of God" (1 John 5:4–5).

Are You a Friend of God's?

Good morning, beautiful people, good morning. Today let's pray scriptures from Ecclesiastes 4:9–12.

Two are better than one, because they have a good return for their work: If one falls down, his friend can help him up. But pity the man who falls and has no one to help him up! Also, if two lie down together, they will keep warm. But how can one keep warm alone? Though one may be overpowered, two can defend themselves. A cord of three strands is not quickly broken.

Father, today help us to be a friend and show ourselves friendly. You designed us to help one another. Thank you for all the family and friends you have placed in our lives.

Today, O God, give us assignments larger than ourselves to bring glory to your name. Enlarge our territories and teach us your ways that we may be an instrument used to rebuild broken people's lives. Show us how we can be a part of building strong workplaces, communities, and churches across this globe, we pray.

Today use us to help other people feel important so they may know they matter in this world. Thank you, God, for being a friend to this world and a friend to me personally and a friend to every reader today. (If you don't know him, ask him in your life today. He is waiting to be your friend.) Amen.

Have a blessed day, God's beautiful people. Isn't God a great friend?

Go, Tell, Believe

Good morning, beautiful people. Yesterday I assisted a friend with wrapping and taking their Christmas gifts to an organization that they assist for Christmas. As I prayed over the gifts and the lives of these precious people, my heart petitioned God to draw them, protect them, and bless them beyond whatever they could ever think or imagine. That this Christmas, they truly would see Christ in Christmas.

Today let's thank God for giving us a Christmas assignment. Then let's go, tell, and believe him for the results.

Father, thank you for the birth of Christ. Our lives are forever changed. Today we join our faith across this globe for the less fortunate, the hurting, the people who live among us, carrying life issues beyond what we will ever know.

Father, today we petition you to heal your people from the inside out. God of miracles, thank you for pouring out your love through your people like never before. May the love of Christ flow from heart to heart this Christmas. Give us, God, assignments so much bigger than what we could ever accomplish on our own, we pray. Thank you that signs, wonders, and miracles follow us.

Father, trust us today with much. May we always be willing to go, to tell, and may many believe on the name Jesus Christ this Christmas. May our actions tell, even if we cannot use words.

Have a blessed day, God's beautiful people. Go, tell, and may many believe.

"Then the disciples went out and preached everywhere, and the Lord worked with them and confirmed his word by the signs that accompanied it" (Mark 16:20).

Another Amazing Day

Good morning, beautiful people. Wow! Do we have some snow here in Maine and western New Brunswick. Yesterday I went to help a friend across the border and got snowed in. I waited for several hours before making the decision to go as nothing seemed to be happening. When the snow started, it came fast and furious. There was nothing we could ever do to stop the snow from coming.

It brings my mind this morning to the love of God and his cleansing power. There is no one beyond his reach. There is nothing you could ever do to separate you from the love of God. He will bring you out of a pit. He will clean you up (make you as white as snow), make a way for you in the wilderness, and open doors for you that no man could ever open. (He goes above and beyond.) He loves to journey every day with us. Let's pray.

Father, thank you for the fresh white snow, the cleansing of the land. Cleanse our lives to reflect your glory as we surrender all to you. May we never take for granted the grace that was extended to us and the price you paid.

Father, give us the compassion in our hearts to extend the same mercy and grace to people all around us. Tear down religious mind-sets so we can embrace the fullness of the Godhead. Holy Spirit, lead us today and every day, we pray. Amen.

Have a blessed day, God's beautiful people. Have another amazing day in him.

"Remember ye not the former things, neither consider the things of old. Behold, I will do a new thing; now it shall spring forth; shall ye not know it? I will even make a way in the wilderness, and rivers in the desert" (Isaiah 43:18–19).

Are You a Back-Seat Driver?

Good morning, beautiful people, good morning. Yesterday I facilitated a meeting for a group of diverse people who were on their journey with Jesus Christ. Number 1 bestselling international author, Karen Bode, who penned the book, Clean Heart, came to visit for a few days. Together we once again came before the Lord, seeking a clean heart so we can be of service to him. As everyone in the room did the same and laid down their burdens and opened their heart before the Lord, the atmosphere shifted, and the presence of the Lord was heavy. Prayers erupted, shouts of victory, healings, and deliverance all were in the house.

Karen shared some of her story and how she must take the back seat and allow Jesus to take the wheel and trust him in every aspect of her life. Today let's ask Jesus to do the same for us. Let's allow him to take control in every area of our lives and steer us on our journey as we open our hearts to him. Amen? Amen! Let's pray.

Father, thank you for the grace to trust you more. You said God to trust in the Lord with all thine heart and lean not on our own understanding (Proverbs 3:5). You are a God of love, and you meet us right where we are at. There is not one perfect person, and we all need to come before you and ask you to give us clean hands and a pure heart (Psalm 24:4). This is a work that is continual as we get in the back seat and allow you to steer the direction of our lives.

Father, you said man makes their plans, but God orders our footsteps, and the footsteps of the righteous are ordered of the Lord (Psalm 37:23). Thank you that we are only righteous because of the blood of Jesus Christ. Amen.

Have a blessed day, God's beautiful people. Allow Jesus to steer your life. No more back seat driving.

Flip your Hat and Always Choose Love

Good morning, beautiful people, good morning. This morning, I was thinking about the hat I will flip for Thanksgiving this year for people that I love. Although the day may be different, every day is thanksgiving to me. It doesn't matter how many people are sitting around your table, how elegant the dinner table may be, if there is no love, God's beautiful people, always choose love.

My precious treasure bought on an island here in Maine will be a dish I will use often. I love to hand place each ingredient inside the beautiful crystal bowl to make it look so special. I have used it several times in the last few weeks, and I am excited to use it this Thanksgiving. What a find on the island that day. The moving sale, the five-dollar cost delights my heart every time I carefully remove it from its well-protected box.

No matter how little you have, or who is around your table, be thankful for what you have, God's beautiful people. Always choose love. Let's pray.

"Now these things remain, faith, hope and love. But the greatest of these is love" (1 Corinthians 13:13).

Father, give us eyes to see the hurting soul, the one who doesn't have the crystal bowl. Use us, Lord, to mend the broken heart and prepare a meal for a lonely heart.

Father, everything we do, let us do it out of a heart of love. Not for monetary gain, recognition, or fame, but everything we do, may we do it well in Jesus's name. Amen.

Happy Thanksgiving, God's beautiful people. Flip your hat and always choose love.

Blessed and Thankful

Good morning, beautiful people. This morning, I was counting the blessings of yesterday. We have so much to be thankful for, every breath we take, every step we make, and all the blessings God himself has bestowed upon us. Let's tell him once again that everything we are and everything we will become, including all our shortcomings, we belong to him. We were all created in the image of God, and he guides us every day, shows us the way, and fills our lives with joy and happiness.

It is only the enemy of our soul who wants to rob, kill, and steal from us. Make your decision strong every morning that you will believe the promises of God and journey the day with confidence. Let's pray.

Father, thank you for your promises to us. Thank you that you defeated our enemy at the cross. As we put on the mind of Christ and our spiritual armor every morning and take every thought captive, we will be assured our day will be victorious. Our enemy has no authority, none. He is a defeated foe.

Father, thank you for the many blessings you have bestowed upon us. We are blessed in the city and we are blessed in the country (Deuteronomy 28). Thank you for mercy and grace. Thank you for everything we are and everything we are not. Continue to change us from glory to glory. Amen.

Have a blessed day, God's beautiful people. Stay thankful and blessed.

"All this is for your benefit, so that the grace that is reaching more and more people may cause thanksgiving to overflow to the glory of God" (2 Corinthians 4:15).

Are You Feeding the Wrong People?

Good morning, beautiful people. I was preparing for a meeting several years ago now. It has been on my mind a lot lately. As our team prepared the events of that morning, and I was praying, I heard God say, "You are feeding the wrong people." It was the same people we had been feeding for years. These people were Christians and had been for many years. There was no new life to the group. Somehow that morning, and the message I received has never left me. It was a morning that stayed with me and probably will forever. I have never been a person who belonged to clicks or liked to see people left out. Maybe because I have lived that.

Jesus hung out with people who had not been fed. They didn't even know who he was, and they certainly were rough around the edges so to speak. Jesus fed them, and they didn't even know they were hungry. We better pray.

Father, thank you that your heart is that none would perish (2 Peter 3:9). Your heart should be our heart. Father, forgive us for feeding the wrong people. Father, we should be feeding the ones who doesn't have the peace, the joy, and the happiness of journeying life with you.

Father, break up the clicks, tear down the walls of religion, and open up all our hearts to be obedient to the great commission. Father, thank you for pouring out your spirit for such a time as this. Amen.

Have a blessed day, God's beautiful people. Who will you feed today?

"While Jesus was having dinner at Matthew's house, many tax collectors and sinners came and ate with him and his disciples" (Matthew 9:10).

The Best Author Ever

Good morning, beautiful people, good morning. Let's pray together to the best author ever.

Father, thank you that you are the best author ever known to mankind. You are the author and finisher of our faith. (Hebrews 12:2) These Holy Scriptures are life to our very being. You save us, baptize us with your Holy Spirit and call us unto yourself. Your Word is truly a lamp unto our feet, as we believe.

The most amazing love story from the creator of the universe and a people that was in need of a Savior. You are the author of salvation, and you can, and you will move mountains for your people. Your love is amazing.

Thank you for letting the whole world know that you are the one true God who man can be saved. Thank you for pouring out your spirit on our land. Amen.

Have a blessed day, beautiful people. Believe the Word of the Lord.

In the last days, God says, I will pour out my Spirit on all people. Your sons and daughters will prophesy, your young men will see visions, your old men will dream dreams. Even on my servants, both men and women, I will pour out my Spirit in those days, and they will prophesy. I will show wonders in the heavens above and signs on the earth below, blood and fire and billows of smoke. The sun will be turned to darkness and the moon to blood before the coming of the great and glorious day of the Lord. And everyone who calls on the name of the Lord will be saved. (Acts 2:17–21)

Thankful Days and Peaceful Nights

Good morning, beautiful people, good morning. This morning, I was thinking on how quickly life can change. Yesterday my daughter called to let me know that someone had passed away. We are here today but no promise of tomorrow. Every day we need to be thankful people. Life passes by quickly, and our time here on earth goes by before we know it.

No matter what we are facing today, let's choose to be thankful. Our day will soon turn into night, and our thankful hearts will rest well.

Today let's ask God to forgive us for our sins, our shortcomings, and the Holy Spirit to remind us to be thankful as we journey our day. Let's pray.

Father, thank you for journeying life with us. We are wealthy beyond any wealth this world could ever know. Our wealth is not measured by gold or silver but by the love of our God. His love (Agape) surpasses it all.

Father, thank you for life. May we never measure our worth or our value on what we own or possess. Every day the life you blessed us with turns into night, and our tomorrows depend on the life you have predestined for us. Every day you bless us. We will choose to be thankful and embrace the sweet peace of the night. Trusting that our master knows our future and the way we should take. Amen.

Have a blessed day, God's beautiful people. Be thankful today and rest well tonight.

"You will keep in perfect peace those whose minds are steadfast, because they trust in you" (Isaiah 26:3).

Thankfulness or Greed, You Get to Choose

Good morning, beautiful people, good morning. It is almost time for thanksgiving. We have so much to be thankful for. Even through some of our hardest times, we have much. Of all the wealth we could ever obtain, nothing compares to walking with Jesus.

Jesus allows us to make our own choices. We can become greedy people and never have enough, or we can be content with what we have. When we are content children of God, we are willing to share what we have with others.

Someday everything we own will be passed down or sold. The years we had to enjoy our lives, we realize have now flown by like a vapor. The selfishness of obtaining things really was meaningless. At the end of it all, what will we be remembered for? What have we taught to the ones we love the most?

God's Word tells us to "give thanks to the Lord, for he is good; his love endures forever" (Psalm 107:1).

"I have learned to be content whatever the circumstances" (Philippians 4:11). Let's pray.

Father, thank you for life. Thank you for all the things you have allowed us to obtain. There is no good thing you withhold from your people. Everything we are, everything we own, everything we will ever receive, we give back to you. Help us not to hold on tightly to things that have no eternal value.

You tell us "in everything give thanks, for this is the will of God in Christ Jesus concerning you" (1 Thessalonians 5:18). We give you thanks, for you have blessed our lives richly with the greatest gift we could ever have. Your Son, Jesus, Emmanuel, he is with us. Amen.

Have a blessed day, God's beautiful people...choose to be thankful.

A Rough Patch

Good morning, beautiful people. Yesterday I heard two different people share with me their quilt stories. As I lay in my bed this morning, asking God what to pray for the readers, I felt inspired to share my own quilt story. Feel his love today, readers. You truly are the apple of his eye (Psalm 17:8).

At a local outreach, a raffle was being drawn for a homemade quilt. I glanced at it, setting on the bench by the tree, wondering why it was there. You must be present to win what was announced. Some people had left or went outside to smoke. A man's name was called, not there. Another name drawn, not there. Then a woman's name was called. She began to jump up and down and cry. She ran up and received the quilt. She loved it and was so blessed. Everyone around her was blessed as they shared in her excitement.

I was leaving the outreach to go home that day, and there she sat in the lobby with a gentleman who had accompanied her. A man, passing by, said, "God loves you, and he wanted you to know how special you are." She hugged her quilt, and with tears in her eyes, she replied, "I feel loved today. I have never had anything this nice before." She held the quilt up against her tattered blue coat with a smile and a glow that would make your heart leap for joy. It made me think of the scripture, "Rejoice with those who rejoice and weep with those who weep" (Romans 12:15). I so rejoiced with her. I couldn't help but say, "Thank you, God."

Father, how much we take for granted, a warm blanket, a quilt, to someone who is a priceless gift. I pray, Lord, as she wraps herself in that patchwork quilt, she will remember how much you love her. Wherever life may take this lady in the tattered blue coat, may she remember the day you handpicked her to receive that special gift. Most of all, Lord, may she know the greatest gift given, your Son, Jesus. May she feel the warmth of your love each and every day, I pray.

Father, I pray for the readers today, O God, that your love would saturate their being. That they would wrap themselves up in the love of Christ and lay all their burdens at your feet. I pray no matter what they need, Father, whether a warm blanket, a cold drink, or a warm embrace, you would provide.

I pray for faith for your people to pray, to believe, and to receive according to the Word of God. For your Word is "yes and amen" (1 Corinthians 1:20). Today may your people receive. Amen.

Have a blessed day, beautiful people.

"You are loved" (John 3:16).

The Miracle Basket

Good morning, beautiful people, good morning. This morning, I ran across this picture of the miracle basket from a trip I was on. I had prayed for the woman who would go on this trip to accompany a team from Aglow International. I didn't think for one minute it was me. I didn't have the resources, and I believed I would give a donation to assist her. Well, to make a long story short, it was me. On this trip, there was a basket they asked people to give to replenish the cost of the communion expenses. I called it the miracle basket. The blood he shed was enough for everything we have need of. I love communion; it alone is our miracle. Let's pray.

Father, thank you that your blood is enough for mankind's sins. The miracle of Christ's birth, death, and resurrection is available to everyone. Thank you for the abundant life according to the Holy Scriptures in John 10:10. When we accept Jesus in our lives, you look at us through the blood of Jesus. You see us as perfect. Jesus is the sacrifice because we could never reach this on our own. Thank you that we are righteous only because of the blood of Jesus Christ. It is the cross that makes us flawless; the blood of Jesus Christ was enough. Amen.

Have a blessed day, God's beautiful people. His blood is enough. Sow into your miracle basket today.

"This is my blood of the covenant, which is poured out for many for the forgiveness of sins" (Matthew 26:28).

He Holds Your Miracle

Good morning, beautiful people, good morning. This morning, I am up early praying for people who are about to give up. Please, beautiful people, don't give up, don't give in, hold on, have faith and believe. Jesus holds your life in his hands. Pray and thank him today for your miracle. He is a miracle-working God, and nothing can stop it. Did I say nothing? You are not stuck, and you're not alone. Jesus holds your miracle, and his eye is on you. Let's pray.

Father, thank you for being our God and we your people. Thank you for watching over your Word to perform it. We speak to the enemy of man's soul and declare him defeated once again

Father, thank you for this miracle season. Because of your great love for us, we can believe you hold our every tomorrow. Yes, yes, we can! Amen.

Have a blessed day, God's beautiful people. He holds your miracle. Believe and receive.

No matter what you are believing God for, beautiful people, be confident. He hears your prayers. His heart is toward you, and he will answer. Yes, God is in the waiting. Just begin to thank him that the answer is on the way. Let's pray.

Father, thank you for hearing our many prayers. Sometimes you say, "Wait, wait on me. My timing is perfect." Forgive us, God, for our impatience, for when we try to put you in our time zone. You are omnipotent. You know what's best and the right timing for every person created. You answer our prayers in your perfect timing, stamped with love.

Father, thank you for being in the wait. Thank you for always having the final say. Thank you we can rest assured as children of the Most High God. Our lives are in your hands. We can trust and rest in you. We are never alone, and thank you, God, for bringing beauty from ashes.

Have a blessed day, God's beautiful people.

The Best Consultant Ever

Good morning, beautiful people. I was reading this morning in Deuteronomy. I love the covenant God has made with his people. I love to read from the Old Testament, as well as the New Testament. I love that he is a jealous God (Deuteronomy 6:15). Today let's ask him to forgive us when we put other things ahead of him. Sometimes we make our plans and don't even consult with him. Not good.

Father, thank you that you are a jealous God. You want to be our first love. You want us to seek you first about everything. Forgive us when we put things ahead of you. Every detail of our daily lives needs to be submitted to you. This removes the frustrations of the day. Knowing you, O God, you order our footsteps. We need not worry about where we will live, what we will eat, and which way to go. You are right there, saying this is the way, walk ye in it. You lead us right to the promise land. Thank you for delivering us out of Egypt. Never to return, no never.

Thank you for growing our faith from mustard seed faith to where we are today. For without faith, it is impossible to please you (Hebrews 11:6). Take us higher, mature our faith, we pray. We want to soar with the eagles and fulfill the purpose we were created for. Amen.

Have a blessed day, beautiful people. Declare today, "I will fulfill my destiny! I am headed to the promise land. Goodbye, Egypt!"

Taste and See

Good morning, beautiful people, good morning. Yesterday my granddaughter and I made some Christmas cookies and fudge. She was so excited as we packaged some for her to take home for her family. She ran to the bows and wanted to put them on the top. We talked a lot about Christmas and what it means. Although not quite three years of age, she loved to stir and kept wanting to taste as soon as she could. I would ask her where does Jesus live while we put the ingredients in the bowl. She would reply, "In my heart." I would tease her and say, "In your liver," and she would smile and reply, "No, in my heart."

While waiting for one batch of cookies to bake, she went in the living room and got my prayer box and took it down from the shelf. She opened the drawer to the small but heavy chest and pulled out a prayer card and brought to me. I inquired if she wanted to put a prayer request in the box. Ironically enough, the card had my Christmas prayer on it from a few years ago. I gave her a new card, and she made some scribbles on it as she said a few names. Kids are so innocent and pure.

Every once in a while, I would notice she would taste one of the Hershey kisses waiting to be placed on top of the cookies. She was anxiously waiting to taste after each batch as the cookies came out of the oven. I kept thinking about the scripture: "Taste and see that the Lord is good; blessed is the one who takes refuge in him" (Psalm 34:8).

Oh, so thankful that Christ journeys life with us and lives in our heart. Let's pray.

Father, thank you for the innocence of children. We come to you today with childlike faith and believe you will lead and guide us every day by the power of your Holy Spirit. In Matthew 18,

Jesus tells us when asked who is the greatest in the kingdom of heaven? And Jesus called a little child unto him and set him in the midst of them and said, "Verily I say unto you, except ye be converted, and become as little children, ye shall not enter into the kingdom of heaven. Whosoever therefore shall humble himself as this little child, the same is greatest in the kingdom of heaven. And whoso shall receive one such little child in my name receiveth me."

Father, thank you that you hear and answer the prayers of your children. Amen.

Have a blessed day, God's beautiful people. Taste and see!

He Is in the Waiting

Good morning, beautiful people. Yesterday I finished a big writing project. It has taken me much longer than I anticipated to complete it, but it sure feels good to have it finished. Now I must wait. This morning, as I begin to pray and probably will begin the next writing project, I am confident God is in the wait.

Father, thank you for being in the wait. Thank you for always having the final say. Thank you we can rest assured as children of the Most High God, our lives are in your hands. We can trust and rest in you. We are never alone, and thank you, God, for bringing beauty from ashes.

Father, we join faith across this globe for your beautiful people, created in your image, that they will hold on. They will thank you for the answer while they are waiting. You are the God in the wait. Amen.

Have a blessed day, beautiful people. God is in your wait. Timing is everything.

"Come to me, all you who are weary and burdened, and I will give you rest. Take my yoke upon you and learn from me, for I am gentle and humble in heart, and you will find rest for your souls" (Matthew 11:28–30).

Everyone Has Something to Give

Good morning, beautiful people, good morning. Everyone has something to give this Christmas. It doesn't need to cost money, but it can if you so desire. Sitting with a lonely person to bring hope is a priceless gift. In giving of our time, ourselves, our resources, we find the joy in giving. From the abundance of our hearts that should be full of the love of Jesus Christ, we give.

Today let's ask the Holy Spirit once again to reveal where he would have us sow our time, resources, etc.

Father, thank you for a heart of abundance in which we can freely give. You have blessed our lives in so many ways, and we want every person in the world to experience the love of Christ for themselves. May people all across this globe ask their Creator for an avenue to give of themselves today and be faithful to the assignment. God is a God of love, and he poured out his life that we may find it in him. May others discover the love of Christ as we share the good news. Amen. Have a blessed day, God's beautiful people. Give some love away.

Christmas Hope Rises

Good morning, beautiful people, good morning. Christmas is almost here. The gift of all gifts was given to us on that day many years ago. Every day we are thankful that the greatest gift and the giver of the gift choose to journey our lives with us. Because he does, we can walk in hope, peace, and joy. Let it arise in each of us today. Let's pray.

Father, thank you for Christmas. Thank you for hope. Romans 15:13 tells us that "the God of hope will fill us with all joy and peace as we trust in Him, so that we may overflow with hope by the power of the Holy Spirit." Thank you for the overflow. "Hope deferred makes the heart sick, but a longing fulfilled is a tree of life" (Proverbs 13:12). Thank you for filling every longing, every longing of our heart with your presence. You are the God of all hope.

Father, thank you for joy. For the joy of the Lord is our strength. "The Lord is my strength and my shield; my heart trusts in him, and he helps me. My heart leaps for joy, and with my song I praise him" (Psalm 28:7).

Father, thank you for peace today. James 3:18 tells us, "Peacemakers who sow in peace reap a harvest of righteousness."

Father, may hope arise all across this globe today. Because Jesus lives, we can have hope for tomorrow. May the God of hope arise in the lives of people today. Amen.

Have a blessed day, God's beautiful people. Let hope arise!

"And we know that in all things God works for the good of those who love him, who have been called according to his purpose" (Romans 8:28).

Thank Him for This Awakening

Good morning, beautiful people, good morning. I was at an appointment recently, and of course, I was trying to discover if this person knew Jesus. His comment alerted me to a question that people in the world may have. He said, "You Christians need to figure out if you believe Jesus is a mean God or a God of love. Which is it, you folks, should settle that?" Oh, I exclaimed it was settled long ago. He is a God of love. We discussed some different scriptures, and I was soon on my way. However, his words to me have stayed in my mind since they left his lips yesterday afternoon.

Today let's thank God for his presence in our lives. Let's thank him for his grace, his love, his mercy, his peace, and everything needed in our lives for our souls to be set free. He tells us in Hosea 4:6, "My people are destroyed from lack of knowledge." Let's thank him today for the many blessings he has bestowed upon us, our families, our nation, and the world. Settle it today, beautiful people. God loved you enough to die for you. That is the ultimate sacrifice. Thank him every day for wisdom and revelation knowledge as you continue to worship him in spirit and in truth. Let him awaken our soul today for Jesus, the lover of our soul. He truly is Emmanuel, journeying life with us, in us, and through us. Let's pray.

Father, thank you for Jesus. Thank you that he loved us enough to die for us. What more could he give to us? We are so thankful today and every day of the greatest gift ever given to mankind. Thank you today, Father, for answering the many questions and prayers we bring before you.

Father, thank you for this awakening in our spirit. May the love of Christ reach across this nation and around the world to all whom will believe. Amen.

Have a blessed Thanksgiving, God's beautiful people. He loves you!

"For God so loved the world that he gave his one and only Son, that whoever believes in him shall not perish but have eternal life" (John 3:16).

New Eyes for Christmas

Good morning, beautiful people. A few weeks ago, I was texting with a friend, and I made a comment that wasn't very uplifting but sort of in a roundabout way criticizing for this person's lack of responsibility. The person responded, "I did the best I could." In this person's eyes, I bet they thought they did. In my eyes, I thought they did not. Thank God for the Holy Spirit. I immediately felt convicted of my words. I began having thoughts like what if they are telling the truth? What if this is their best? Maybe there is some things in their life you do not know. I began to ask for forgiveness and ask God for his eyes. I prayed, "God, please keep my heart soft and pliable unto your mighty working hand."

Father, today we thank you for your love. Your love changes us from glory to glory. Thank you for not leaving us as we are. Your heart is our heart's desire. Sometimes we think wrong, or we think others should live up to our expectations, and they are giving or doing their very best. Forgive us, God, and sharpen our compassion for others. Do a deeper work in us (in me), we pray. May our eyes see what you see. Thank you for ordering our footsteps today. Every person is valued. If they were important enough for you to die for, empower us to reach them and treat them accordingly. Forgive us (me), when I have failed them and give us new eyes today. May we see as you see.

Have a blessed day, God's beautiful people. Thank him for new eyes for Christmas.

"Blessed are your eyes because they see, and your ears because they hear" (Matthew 13:16).

Go, Tell, Believe

Good morning, beautiful people. Yesterday I assisted a friend with wrapping and taking their gifts to an organization that they assist for Christmas. As I prayed over the gifts and the lives of these precious people, my heart petitioned God to draw them, protect them, and bless them beyond whatever they could ever think or imagine. I prayed that this Christmas, they truly would see Christ in Christmas.

Today let's thank God for giving us a Christmas assignment. Then let's go, tell, and believe him for the results.

Father, thank you for the birth of Christ. Our lives are forever changed. Today we join our faith across this globe for the less fortunate, the hurting, and the people who live among us, carrying life issues beyond what we will ever know.

Father, today we petition you to heal your people from the inside out. God of miracles thank you for pouring out your love through your people like never before. May the love of Christ flow from heart to heart this Christmas. Give us, God, assignments so much bigger than what we could ever accomplish on our own, we pray. Thank you that signs, wonders, and miracles follow us.

Father, trust us today with much. May we always be willing to go, to tell, and may many believe on the name Jesus Christ this Christmas. May our actions tell, even if we cannot use words.

Have a blessed day, God's beautiful people. Go, tell, and may many believe.

"Then the disciples went out and preached everywhere, and the Lord worked with them and confirmed his word by the signs that accompanied it" (Mark 16:20).

The Time Is Now

Good morning, beautiful people, good morning. Let's pray together about the seasons once again.

A Time for Everything

There is a time for everything, and a season for every activity under the heavens: a time to be born and a time to die, a time to plant and a time to uproot, a time to kill and a time to heal, a time to tear down and a time to build, a time to weep and a time to laugh, a time to mourn and a time to dance, a time to scatter stones and a time to gather them, a time to embrace and a time to refrain from embracing, a time to search and a time to give up, a time to keep and a time to throw away, a time to tear and a time to mend, a time to be silent and a time to speak, a time to love and a time to hate, a time for war and a time for peace. (Ecclesiastes 3:1–6)

"You crown the year with your bounty; your wagon tracks overflow with abundance" (Psalm 65:11).

Father, thank you that your Word is yes and amen. Today all across this globe, we declare the time is now. Our appointment with destiny has arrived. Count me in, totally in, O God.

If this is your prayer, and you are totally in, tell him so. Let your yes be yes and your no be no. Whatever you can trust us with, Lord, we will do for your glory alone.

Today we declare we will stand for all that we believe in. Yes, we will… United. The wagons are here.

Have a blessed day, God's beautiful people. The time is now.

This Best Gift under Your Tree

Good morning, beautiful people, good morning. I am hoping to put my Christmas tree up today. I always like to put something under the tree for the man who created me, not a literal gift but something from my heart. Something that is going to cost me. In order to do that, I need to seek him. He wants fellowship with us more than he wants our money and our good deeds. Everything we do should be a result of fellowshipping with the Good Father. Let's give him more of our heart, more of our time, more in study of his Word, and let God himself brighten the light that is shining within us. Let's pray.

Father, thank you for Christmas. As the trees are beautifully decorated, and the lights shine brightly across this globe, may the light of Christ shine through us like never before. There will be packages wrapped and ribbons curled under the tree for friends and family, but let us not forget to give to you our King. As we commit to seek you, to worship you, may our hearts be tenderized by your love. Holy Spirit, teach us each and every day.

Father, may this Christmas be different than all the Christmas before. May your presence saturate our homes, our cities, and our lives as we surrender more of our lives to you. Yes, Lord, we give you our heart. Amen.

Have a blessed day, God's beautiful people. Put the best gift under your tree this year. More of him, living in you.

"See what great love the Father has lavished on us, that we should be called children of God! And that is what we are!" (1 John 3:1).

He Is the Light of the World, Merry Christmas

Good morning, beautiful people, good morning. Today the world changed forever because of the birth of Jesus Christ. His life poured out for you and for me and to all whom will believe in him all across this globe.

Today as you unwrap your presents, my biggest prayer is that his presence saturates your life and your home. His grace, his mercy, and his love are gifts that never wear out, and no man can give them to us, and no man can take them away. He came to us this day as our redeemer, and thirty-three years later, he gave the ultimate sacrifice of dying on the cross so all of our sin's past, present, and future are all washed away. His birth, burial, and resurrection are signs that he lives today in us through the power of the Holy Spirit. John 14:26 tells us, "The Advocate, the Holy Spirit, whom the Father will send in my name, will teach you all things and will remind you of everything I have said to you."

Whatever you have need of today, beautiful people, because he lives, you can have it. Healing, deliverance, provision, and all that is wrapped up in his atonement (our inheritance) is yours to all who will believe. I must tell you once again.

Tell Them
Tell them I love them.
Tell them they are mine.
Tell them I will never leave them nor forsake them.
Tell them they are precious gems.
Tell them I see them as perfect.
Tell them they reflect my image.
Tell them not to look back.
Tell them to look straight ahead.
Tell them I laid out the red carpet for them.
My blood, it was enough.
Tell them, tell them, tell them again!
Merry Christmas, God's beautiful people. Believe in him and be saved.

Bring your Offering Today

Good morning, beautiful people. The weather here in Maine has been quite cold, but the beauty of the season warms our hearts. Christmas is such a beautiful time of year. The decorations are everywhere, and Christ in Christmas makes our heart sing louder than any other time of year. The joy of giving, the joy of loving, and the joy of journeying life with Jesus Christ. The whole reason for the season. Let's pray.

Father, thank you for Jesus, the light of the world. We have so much to worship and sing about. King of Kings, Lord of Lords, Messiah, Prince of Peace, Lamb of God, Immanuel, God is truly with us. You gave us the best gift we would ever receive. Oh, how we celebrate. There is not one detail of our lives that you don't know or see. Our eyes are fixed on you day and night. You work everything out for our good. How good is that? We can truly worship you from the depths of our heart and soul because you are the Good, Good Father. May we pour out our lives as an offering to you.

All across this globe today, sing a little louder, worship a little more, and remember to keep Christ at the forefront of Christmas. May your day be filled with love, joy, and peace as you enjoy the Christmas season. Amen.

Have a blessed and beautiful day, God's people. Bring your offering of praise to him today.

"For to us a child is born, to us a son is given, and the government will be on his shoulders. And he will be called Wonderful Counselor, Mighty God, Everlasting Father, Prince of Peace" (Isaiah 9:6).

Cherish the Moment

Good morning, beautiful people, good morning. Let's cherish every moment. Let's pray.

Father, no matter where people are this Christmas, may they cherish the moment. Some will be with family and friends, and others may be celebrating at home alone. One thing for sure, no believer in Christ is ever alone. Your presence is the best present any person could ever receive. I pray you visit them in a way only a Heavenly Father can.

In Philippian's 4:11–13, it says,

I am not saying this because I am in need, for I have learned to be content whatever the circumstances. I know what it is to be in need, and I know what it is to have plenty. I have learned the secret of being content in any and every situation, whether well fed or hungry, whether living in plenty or in want. I can do all this through him who gives me strength.

Thank you for teaching us to be content in whichever circumstance we are in.

This year may many come back to the heart of Christmas. May we all slow down and remember the whole reason we celebrate Christmas. Let love flow this Christmas across this globe, we pray. Amen.

Have a blessed day, God's beautiful people. Lend a helping hand, cherish the moment, enjoy your life while you can.

Celebrate Every Day This Year and Don't Forget to Pray

Good morning, beautiful people. I was thinking this morning about how my grandchildren when they are excited, they clap their hands. The look on their face is priceless. That's how we should be as Christians. We should be excited for every day. It is always so much fun to see who is in our day, where we will go, and what our God assignments are. It makes every day a celebration. Today let's thank God for life and for ordering our day.

Father, thank you for life. Thank you that this is the day that you have made, and we will rejoice and be glad in it. Thank you for the precious people you will trust us with today. Thank you for joy. The joy of the Lord is our strength (Nehemiah 8:10).

Father, thank you that we can talk to you anytime (pray). You are the way, the truth, and the life (John 14:6). Journeying life with you is downright amazing. Oh, how we love to commune with you. We love to worship you in spirit and in truth (John 4:24). Thank you for the open heavens over us. You hear every prayer. Every day is like Thanksgiving and Christmas journeying with you. Thank you that we can celebrate every day all-year long. Our lives are full because of your amazing love for us. Thank you for ordering our footsteps today. Yes, we believe. You have us etched in the palm of your hand (Isaiah 49:16). Amen.

Enjoy your day, beautiful people. Give some joy away.

"My heart leaps for joy and I will give thanks to him in song" (Psalm 28:7).

Birth, God's Idea

Good morning, beautiful people. Aren't you glad that Jesus was born? Isn't it great to know that life was on God's heart first? Whomever knew that this birth would be the most important birth that this world would ever know. His life changed everything for you and I.

I am sure Mary had many questions as she journeyed the birthing of Jesus. I ponder at times what Mary was thinking as she carried our Savior. Life is so precious, a gift from God himself. His birth, every birth, a life to be fulfilled with destiny.

Today, let's thank God that Jesus was born. Today, let's thank God for life. The birth of Jesus has changed everything. He has come to give us life and life more abundantly (John 10:10). Praise his wonderful name.

Father, thank you for the birth of Jesus, our Savior and King. Thank you for life. It was all your idea. Thank you for getting involved in our daily lives. No matter what the situation, you are greater. You have a plan, and you have given us promises in your Word that you will work it all out for good in our lives.

Today, all across this globe, we join our faith together and stand for life. We stand against the wiles of the enemy, the thief, who comes to rob, kill, and destroy life. Together, we pray the blinders that have veiled the eyes of your people be removed as the god of this world (enemy) has blinded them (2 Corinthians 4:4). May truth reign in the lives of people as they open their hearts to the birth of Jesus. Oh, the importance of choosing life. Today, may the light in your people shine brightly as we stand strong in your Word. Faith comes from hearing the message, and the message is heard through the Word about Christ (Romans 10:17). Amen.

Have a blessed day, beautiful people. Thank God for the baby who changed the world. Thank God for life, and may we always support life.

"For unto you is born this day in the city of David a Savior, which is Christ the Lord" (Luke 2:11).

Are You on Your Way?

Good morning, beautiful people. As I opened my eyes this morning and before my feet even hit the floor, I began to think about a friend in heaven. I met this dear lady many years ago now. I just had to share about her once again.

Alice (not her real name) had long stringy unkempt hair, was very thin, and was an alcoholic. She lived all alone in an almost bare apartment that needed cleaning.

Her refrigerator shelves held the beer she consumed daily but had very little food. Everyone seemed to complain about her life. I've met a lot of people on my journey thus far, but nobody taught me more about the love of Christ than her.

I began to pray for her. I would take bleach and clean her toilet that she never seemed to flush. I'd wipe down her dirty counters on occasion. I tried hard to keep her in an apartment where it seemed everyone was against her.

One day, I had the opportunity to sit down and talk with her about her life. It hadn't been easy. Leaving what she knew as home at the age of twelve in search of a better life must have been frightening. She had been through so much on her journey here. Alcohol was just suppressing the pain. She could not read or write. She had no formal education and was basically a loner. I felt for her. I really did.

That Christmas, I put her name in at a local church for a food box. Some folks from the church Christmas caroled and delivered some food items to her. A dear friend of mine from the church prayed with her.

A neighbor later told me that she had tried to eat the pumpkin pie that was in the box without first baking it. She had knocked on the neighbor's door and inquired why the pie was so runny.

I often pondered where she got the courage to knock on that door one more time as she had been rejected so many times before. It seemed the pie was quite runny, and she was having difficulty eating it. Can you imagine how awful that must have tasted?

My daughter, Alyssa, and I delivered her a few Christmas presents that year. Nothing elaborate, just basics. A clean pillow to rest her head (she had a stained mattress on the floor in her bedroom without any sheets or pillows). We had wrapped a couple of towels and washcloths and basic items in hopes she would use them. Her apartment had no sign of Christmas. No tree, no lights in the window, and barely any life left in herself. I knew even without the thank you, she appreciated it.

I continued to pray for Alice. At times, my heart would ache for her, and my pillow would be filled with tears as I asked God to intervene on her behalf. Alice had endured so much. As she shared a small part of her life story with me, I knew she was burying the pain in her life with alcohol. I continued to pray and to reach out to her in small ways.

One day, I received a phone call that she was quite ill and needed to go to the hospital. She was refusing to go by ambulance. I was unable to take her, so I bowed my head and prayed and asked my Heavenly Father to make a way for her.

After twenty minutes or so, I received a phone call from a relative of Alice's. She told me that she did not own her as a relative but was related to her. She had heard she was sick and would go drive her to the hospital. Thank you, Jesus. You are the best Father.

I asked some folks from the church I was attending to go pray for her and talk to her about Jesus. I was not confident enough at that time and didn't want to mess anything up. I have since learned Jesus looks at the heart, and the Holy Spirit will help you. Just go…

One man from the church took her a small stuffed animal. I am almost certain that was the only stuffed animal that she had ever received. Another man went as well and prayed with her.

When I arrived at the hospital later that evening, the room was empty. Somehow I knew she had died. I came home and filled my pillow with more tears.

I knew she was with Jesus, and that her life was full of joy now, and she was now free from the pain that she endured in this life. I had prayed for her so much. I felt as if I were losing a sister. In essence, I was. I know just as sure as I am writing this post today, she is in heaven. The good Father has given me that assurance.

I know that the Lord did not put her in my path by mistake. He used her to teach me a great deal. There was no funeral, no calling hours, and no flowers. Her belongings all went into the dumpster.

The Lord showed me that the alcohol was keeping the pain down in her life. He told me to look past the alcohol and look to her heart. Her value didn't seem like much in this world. She had no assets, friends, or relatives who owned her. She did have a child, whom I had met once. He told me about her attempt to take her own life when he was young, but he intervened. He smelled of alcohol too. I was told he only came to get money once a month from her. I don't know if that was even true.

Today I just had to thank Jesus once again for salvation. Thank him for saving my friend. Thank him for teaching me through the power of his Holy Spirit. Thank him for the church, the food box, the people he sent, the answered prayers, and the stuffed animal. Thank him how he loves people. Even the people that the world overlooks, he doesn't. Thank you, Jesus.

We are commanded to love one another. Lord, help your church to love each other. Lord, teach us to look beyond our four walls of our own churches and go into the highways and byways and compel them to come in with your love, the love of Jesus Christ. Father, teach us, strengthen us that the petty issues of life doesn't really matter. Today give us people who you can trust us with God. Work though us today for the Alice's of this world. Only give us what you can trust us with. The hurting doesn't need any further hurt. Direct them where to go, direct us where to go.

Forgive us, God, when we messed it up. Today, God, we join our faith across this globe for the Alice's of this world. Your heart is our heart. Show us today where our next Alice is, we pray. Amen.

"And the Lord said unto the servant, go out into the highways and hedges, and compel them to come in, that my house may be filled" (Luke 14:23).

Time with the King

Good morning, beautiful people. This morning, I just wanted to continue to encourage you to persevere in prayer. This is no time to let up in prayer. We serve a covenant-keeping God. His Word is yes and amen, and he is watching over his Word to perform it (Jeremiah 1:12).

So I say to you: Ask and it will be given to you; seek and you will find; knock and the door will be opened to you. For everyone who asks receives; the one who seeks finds; and to the one who knocks, the door will be opened. (Luke 11:9–10)

Another key is that we must have the right motive.

You desire but do not have. You covet but you cannot get what you want, so you quarrel and fight. You do not have because you do not ask God. When you ask, you do not receive, because you ask with wrong motives, that you may spend what you get on your pleasures. (James 4:2–3)

As God's people come together with a time of prayer and repentance, it will release the greatest outpouring of his spirit. It is time to intercede as never before as we stand in the gap on behalf of others, as well as entire nations. Invite others to join you in prayer. The power in the prayer of agreement from Matthew 18:19, "Again I say to you, that if two of you agree on earth about anything that they may ask, it shall be done for them by My Father who is in heaven."

This past Friday evening, I had the privilege to join my faith with others at the Caribou Meeting Place in Caribou, Maine, for the simulcast Cry Out, a three-hour nationwide prayer event for women. It was nice to see people from different denominations coming together, praying for families, marriages, the unborn, etc. Maisie Grace (my granddaughter) and I were blessed to be a part.

Today spend some time with the King. Today get to know him more intimately. Let him speak to you and then obey. It will cost you but only time. Time with the King, there is no better way to start your day.

Lift up your heads, O you gates! And be lifted up you everlasting doors! And the king of Glory shall come in. Who is the King of Glory? The Lord strong and mighty, the Lord mighty in battle. Lift up your heads, O you gates, Lift up you everlasting doors! And the King of glory shall come in. Who is the King of Glory? The Lord of hosts, he is the king of Glory. (Psalm 24:7–10)

Have a blessed day, God's beautiful people. Continue to spend time with the King.

Don't Be Haughty Now, It's Called Grace

Good morning, beautiful people, good morning. This morning, I was thinking about my conversation with a friend recently. We shared stories back and forth of how God was using his people to change the world. The more we talked about what we saw happening, I could sense the more important we were beginning to feel. It didn't take my God long to lead me to some scriptures to bring us back down from the clouds we were puffing on.

It's easy to think more highly of ourselves than we should. We are all the same at the foot of the cross. There is not one of us that could earn, or do we deserve the free gift given to us. No matter how good we are, or think we are, we are undeserving of his grace and mercy. This free gift cost Jesus his very life and us nothing. May we never forget it. Angel Murchison, may you never forget it!

We are blessed that he chooses to use us. He alone could change everything in an instant. May we never be haughty but count our blessings every day. Let's pray.

God, the blessed and only Ruler, the King of kings and Lord of lords, who alone is immortal and who lives in unapproachable light, whom no one has seen or can see. To him be honor and might forever. Command those who are rich in this present world not to be arrogant nor to put their hope in wealth, which is so uncertain, but to put their hope in God, who richly provides us with everything for our enjoyment. Command them to do good, to be rich in good deeds, and to be generous and willing to share. In this way they will lay up treasure for themselves as a firm foundation for the coming age, so that they may take hold of the life that is truly life. Guard what has been entrusted to your care. Turn away from godless chatter and the opposing ideas of what is falsely called knowledge, which some have professed and in so doing have departed from the faith. Grace be with you all. (1 Timothy 6:13–21, NIV)

Father, thank you for mercy and grace. Thank you that everything we are or will ever become is because of the love, mercy, and grace you have for us. May we always remember where you brought us from. Thank you that you, O God, oppose the proud but shows favor to the humble (James 4:6).

Father, you tell us in 1 Peter 5:6 "to humble ourselves under the mighty hand of God so that at the proper time, you may exalt us."

Thank you to the God of our salvation for the abundant life you have given us. Amen.

Have a blessed day, beautiful people. Don't be haughty now, it's called grace.

Lost But Now Found

Today let's pray together scriptures on salvation.

So he told them this parable: "What man of you, having a hundred sheep, if he has lost one of them, does not leave the ninety-nine in the open country, and go after the one that is lost, until he finds it? And when he has found it, he lays it on his shoulders, rejoicing. And when he comes home, he calls together his friends and his neighbors, saying to them, 'Rejoice with me, for I have found my sheep that was lost.' Just so, I tell you, there will be more joy in heaven over one sinner who repents than over ninety-nine righteous persons who need no repentance. (Luke 15:3–7)

For the Son of Man came to seek and to save the lost. (Luke 19:10)

What do you think? If a man has a hundred sheep, and one of them has gone astray, does he not leave the ninety-nine on the mountains and go in search of the one that went astray? And if he finds it, truly, I say to you, he rejoices over it more than over the ninety-nine that never went astray. So it is not the will of my Father who is in heaven that one of these little ones should perish. (Matthew 18:12–14)

I am the good shepherd. The good shepherd lays down his life for the sheep. (John 10:11)

And saying, "The time is fulfilled, and the kingdom of God is at hand; repent and believe in the gospel." (Mark 1:15)

For the wages of sin is death, but the free gift of God is eternal life in Christ Jesus our Lord. (Romans 6:23)

Father, thank you for watching over your people. We join our faith across this globe today and believe you are drawing prodigals back to the fold. We thank you for laying your life down for your sheep. May many hear the gospel this day and believe. Together we rejoice. Hallelujah. Welcome home. Amen.

Have a blessed day, beautiful people. Journey every day with Jesus.

Shape Our Lives, O God

Good morning, beautiful people. I meet the most interesting people every day. I am sure you do too. When you see people through the eyes of Jesus, life changes. His heart is for the best for every person, the best.

Sometimes our hearts get hardened by the hurt, the pain others have caused us. It is hard to believe that he would want the best for the person who hurt us. He does, and his plan is to heal the brokenness in us and them. His mercy is extended to us all. His grace and mercy are sufficient for us all. Let's pray.

Father, thank you for shaping our lives. We thank you for tearing down the walls we build up to protect our hearts. We forgive every person who has done us wrong, brought hurt or pain to us. We release them today. We thank you that your grace is sufficient. May others forgive us when we have brought hurt or pain to them knowingly or unknowingly. We live in less than a perfect world, and we are far from being perfect people. We are in need of you cleansing our hearts and shaping our lives. Thank you for mercy and grace. We totally surrender our life to you. (Tell him.)

Father, we pray the very best for each other. Purify our hearts, O God. We are not more important than the next person. Your heart is that none should perish. May we all desire the very best for each other. Thank you that in our weakness, you make us strong. Amen.

Have a blessed day, beautiful people. He desires the very best for you. Believe.

"Search me, God, and know my heart; test me and know my anxious thoughts. See if there is any offensive way in me, and lead me in the way everlasting" (Psalm 139:23–24).

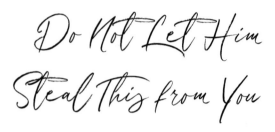

Do Not Let Him Steal This from You

Good morning, beautiful people. The weather was looking a bit like spring, then we had another winter storm. As I glanced out my window, I laughed right out loud. I thought even the weather can't steal our joy. Our fickle feelings, our less than perfect circumstances, don't dictate to us. We are walking with the creator of the universe, and he decides what's best. I turned my radio on and began to enjoy the day the Lord has made.

No matter what you are going through today, don't let the enemy of your soul steal your joy. Put your gospel music on and do your victory dance. Renew your mind with God's promises and have yourself a joyous day. Determine today, nothing, nobody is going to steal my joy. Celebrate every day to the fullest. This day will never come around the same again, so make up your mind to enjoy it to the fullest.

Have yourself a great day, God's beautiful people. Find some time today to spend with the person who knows you best. He created you, and he has the answers to all your life's issues.

Father, thank you for joy. Amen.

The joy of the Lord is my strength (Nehemiah 8:10).

"May the God of hope fill you with all joy and peace as you trust in Him" (Romans 15:13).

"Shout aloud and sing for joy, people of Zion, for great is the Holy One of Israel among you" (Isaiah 12:6).

The Only Way to Go

Good morning, beautiful people, good morning. As I put away my Christmas tree and find the perfect place for each gift I received, I can't help but think back over the days journeyed in prayer. From the very first prayer prayed at the beginning of the year to the very last one I will pray this year, I will still stand strong in my belief: Prayer changes things. I stand strong in my belief of praying the Holy Scriptures and having faith in them.

I have witnessed so many answers to prayer. I have seen the sick healed. I have personally experienced provision from on high. I have experienced open doors, closed doors, and the list is endless of the stories of the faithfulness of our God. I believe the bowl has been tipped, and the answers to the many prayers we prayed together in 2017 are on their way. Not because I say so or believe so, but because Jesus said so. Faith in Jesus is the only way to go. Today if you haven't talked with him (pray), please take time to do so. If you haven't begun the journey with him, today is your day to begin. Your redeemer lives.

Father, thank you for your Word. Romans 10:9 states that if we confess with our mouths the Lord Jesus and believe in our hearts God has raised him from the dead, we will be saved. Romans 10:13 states, "Whoever calls on the name of the Lord shall be saved. Thank you for mercy, thank you for grace." Ephesians 2:8–9 says that we are saved by grace through faith, and not of ourselves; it is the gift of God, not of works, lest anyone should boast. Together we join our faith that many will call on your name today and be saved.

In Matthew 21:21–22, Jesus said, 'Assuredly, I say to you, if you have faith and do not doubt, you will not only do what was done to the fig tree, but also if you will say to this mountain, be removed and be cast into the sea, it will be done. And whatever things you ask in prayer, believing, you will receive." Thank you for answering our prayers as we put our trust in you. Amen.

Have a blessed day, God's beautiful people… Believe in the Lord Jesus Christ and his free gift to you. Journey with him every day in prayer and believe. Stay blessed!

Closing the Book

Good morning, beautiful people, good morning. Today we will wrap up a lot of different things for the year. This is it. It's over, and we will never live this time in our lives again. We are left with only memories whether good or bad. Sometimes we relive the memories of the day as the mind tries to process the choices we made, the events that happened, and the plan God himself has for our lives.

Today let's finish up and wrap up the year strong. Let's close the books so to speak. As we let go of the bad memories, hurts, and disappointments, and embrace the good times, good memories, and all that God has planned for us in our future. Let's thank him for keeping us strong and let's enter into the New Year with great expectation. Let's pray.

Father, thank you for a great year. You have seen us through the good, the bad, and the ugly. Your Word tells us in Isaiah 26:3, "You will keep in perfect peace those whose minds are steadfast, because they trust in you." We have journeyed our days with you in your Word and looked to you, the author and finisher of our faith (Hebrews 12:2). We continue to put our trust in you.

Father, we thank you for the grace to let go of what needs to be let go of and embrace the plan you have predestined for our lives. We give you all the praise, honor, and glory. Thank you for being our God and we your people as we close the book and journey on.

Have a blessed day, God's beautiful people. Enjoy the day well and close your book strong. We made it.

From the Author

Thank you for taking this 365-day journey with me. Thank you for praying with me, believing with me, and most of all, allowing God to use you to make a difference in our world.

You are amazing, and I love that our paths have crossed through prayer. I hope your life is richer, fuller, and blessed because of God's Word.

Journey again with me next year as my next 365-daily devotional will be published soon.

You are beautiful, my special friend.

Much love and many prayers, Angel L. Murchison.